Three Weeks to
eBay®
Profits

Three Weeks to eBay Profits

THIRD EDITION

Go from Beginner to Successful Seller
in Less than a Month

SKIP McGRATH with **LISSA McGRATH**

STERLING

New York

STERLING
New York

An Imprint of Sterling Publishing
387 Park Avenue South
New York, NY 10016

Originally published in 2006 by Sterling Publishing Co., Inc.

ISBN 978-1-4549-0581-3

Library of Congress Cataloging-in-Publication Data

McGrath, Skip.

Three weeks to eBay profits / Skip McGrath. -- Third edition.

pages cm

Includes index.

ISBN 978-1-4549-0581-3

1. eBay (Firm) 2. Internet auctions. 3. Consignment sales. I. Title.

HF5478.M3873 2013

658.8'777--dc23

2013004185

Distributed in Canada by Sterling Publishing
c/o Canadian Manda Group, 165 Dufferin Street
Toronto, Ontario, Canada M6K 3H6
Distributed in the United Kingdom by GMC Distribution Services
Castle Place, 166 High Street, Lewes, East Sussex, England BN7 1XU
Distributed in Australia by Capricorn Link (Australia) Pty. Ltd.
P.O. Box 704, Windsor, NSW 2756, Australia

For information about custom editions, special sales, and premium andcorporate purchases,
please contact Sterling Special Salesat 800-805-5489 or specialsales@sterlingpublishing.com.

Manufactured in the United States of America

2 4 6 8 10 9 7 5 3 1

www.sterlingpublishing.com

Almost anyone's success in life can be traced back to their parents—especially their moms. And mine is no exception. I was raised by a single mother long before there was welfare. She often held two jobs to keep me in private schools where I received a first class education. My mom, June, is a veteran of the Navy Waves in WW2 who worked in the office that broke the Japanese Naval Code. When the war ended she had me and when the Korean Conflict started she joined up again. After that, she came home to raise me and that was her biggest job for the next 20 years. More than the education she provided for, the biggest gift she gave me was a work ethic that she demonstrated every day of her life.

My Mom is still alive today and her work ethic is still intact. At the age of 90 she still works a full time job.

This is for you, Mom.

✦ CONTENTS ✦

GETTING READY TO SELL 5

PUTTING YOUR AUCTIONS TO WORK 147

RUNNING YOUR EBAY BUSINESS TO MAXIMIZE INCOME

✦ INTRODUCTION to the Third Edition ✦

WELCOME TO EBAY, the world's greatest marketplace—electronic or otherwise. More than 100 million people have bought or sold items on eBay during the last twelve months. Millions of items are listed for sale and sold on eBay every day. In 2012, more than $75 billion worth of merchandise changed hands on eBay. That is almost $2,400 every single second. Yet eBay itself sells nothing but access to its platform. eBay does not sell one antique or collectible, one razor blade, even one digital camera—although tens of thousands of digital cameras are sold on eBay each month. It is you and I who do the selling. If every eBay seller were an employee of eBay, it would be the largest private employer in the world—larger than Walmart and Lowe's combined.

When you launch an eBay business, you are opening a store in a city of 104 million people. Except you have no rent, no employees, no costly advertising, and very little overhead. What could be better?

But, eBay is not a static marketplace. Over the years I have seen many changes, including several major changes since the first edition of this book was released in 2006. There have been changes in fees, selling practices, feedback, payment methods and systems, and even in how eBay buyers find your items. The latest trend is that eBay optimized their site in 2012 to adapt to mobile devices, and today over 17 percent of sales come from these devices. These changes have required sellers to change how they list their auctions, how they ship their items, and how they relate to and communicate with their customers. Learning these updated techniques is what will put profits in your pocket on the new and improved eBay.

I have been selling on eBay for over twelve years and writing books and newsletters about selling on eBay for the past eleven. During that time, I have spoken to and answered e-mails from thousands of my readers who were seeking advice. Although the questions always differ in their specifics, a basic theme recurs: "OK, I'm registered on eBay. What do I do next?" That question was what first prompted me to write this book.

At first glance, selling an item on eBay looks simple. But once people become immersed in the process, they are confronted with dozens of choices and decisions related to listing formats, titles, item descriptions, payment, shipping, image placement, eBay promotional options, and more. As they start to list their first two or three items for auction, new sellers begin to wonder if they can really build an eBay business—or is this whole thing just too complicated?

1

It *is* somewhat complicated—but not overly so. Almost anyone can master selling on eBay: You just need to take the time to understand the process and the unique nature of the eBay selling platform. Millions of people worldwide have sold items on eBay. With some guidance and perseverance, you, too, can join the ranks of those professional sellers who make their primary income on eBay.

So what makes this book different from all the others that teach the ins and outs of selling on eBay? Most books on this subject tend to focus on mechanical aspects of the process, answering questions like the following: How do I upload photos? How do I get paid? How do I create a listing? Understanding how all these elements work is certainly important, and we do cover these points clearly. But rather than getting bogged down in details that are soon to become second nature, this book offers answers to one simple yet all-encompassing question: How do I make money on eBay?

Three Weeks to eBay Profits is designed to take you through the process, step by step, in a logical manner, so you understand and master each step. Why three weeks? It won't take you three weeks to sell your first few items—you can do that within a few days of starting. But we are talking about you reaching Top-Rated Seller status (only 15 percent of all sellers reach that level)—not just making a few quick sales. Yes, reaching Top-Rated Seller level does take a little longer (eBay requires that you have been selling on eBay for ninety days), but it is the foundation you build in those first few weeks that will set you on the right track to make Top-Rated Seller as soon as it becomes available to you.

Setting up and organizing your business, researching and finding the right products, and putting in place the automated systems and services to save time will take the average person about three weeks. If you are not currently working a traditional job, but are running an eBay business full-time, you may actually master all these steps even sooner. On the other hand, if you have a full-time job and can devote only a few hours to your eBay business every evening, it may take you four or five weeks before everything is humming along and you are making money consistently, week after week.

How you define success on eBay depends on your personal goals and how eBay fits into your life. If you are a stay-at-home parent or a working person just looking to supplement your income, you might be looking to make an extra $100 to $200 a week. However, if you are trying to replace your income from a job lost to downsizing, then your vision of success might be earning $500 or $1,000 a week—or more. Both scenarios are doable—it's just a matter of time, work, and learning the ropes.

Building a business on eBay is also a lot of fun. If you enjoy selling on eBay, then this is the greatest gig in the world. Not only have I made a lot of money on eBay over the past twelve years, but I have had a fabulous time doing it. I have made dozens of online friends—many of whom I went on to meet in person. My wife, Karen, and I work together in the business and we still get as excited today watching the last few moments of an auction as we did when we entered an item in our very first auction more than twelve years ago.

If you are already registered and have sold things on eBay, you might be tempted to skip through the first few chapters of this book. I suggest that, at the very least, you scan them for new information. I frequently see items being auctioned on eBay by veteran sellers who are still making rookie mistakes. Clearly, they didn't set up their business for success right from the start.

To get the most out of this book, take the time to set up and organize your business correctly (chapter 1) before you start launching your first auctions. Work through the first few chapters to do the research and to select the products you will sell. This is one of the most important decisions you will make, and one you will be continually working on if you want to get the most out of your eBay business. Then set your goals and write your success plan (chapter 12). Benjamin Franklin once said, "An investment in knowledge pays the best interest." Make the investment now to maximize your interest and dividends later.

BIZ BUILDER

As you read this book, you will come across Web sites for various companies and products. To save you the trouble of typing each link into your browser, I have set up a special Web page just for the readers of this book at www.skipmcgrath.com/3_weeks.

Below is a quick outline of how this book is organized.

WEEK 1: GETTING READY TO SELL

In the first week, we concentrate on setting up your business correctly, learning the keys to operating on eBay, researching and settling on the products you will sell, and learning how and where to find sources for those products.

WEEK 2: PUTTING YOUR LISTINGS TO WORK

Almost anyone can use the eBay interface to launch a listing, but the devil is in the details. Learning how to make your listings stand out from the millions of others, how to maximize your bids and final values, when to choose Fixed Price over Auction Style formats, how to promote your listings, choosing the right shipping prices and strategies, and how to build a strong Feedback Profile are the keys to long-term success.

WEEK 3: RUNNING YOUR EBAY BUSINESS TO MAXIMIZE INCOME

There's no great trick to selling on eBay, but only a professional can make money doing it week after week. In the third week, we show you how to control your costs, save time with automation, deliver superior customer service, drive repeat business to your listings, and open an eBay Store, and we also show you steps you can take to expand your business beyond eBay to the rest of the Internet.

Here's to your success!

GETTING READY TO SELL

You are probably ready to jump right into selling on eBay, and I promise to get you there very soon. But first, you need to take a few crucial steps in order to set up your business for the long term. If you have been buying on eBay or have sold a few items, you already may know some of this information, or you may have done some of the important tasks spelled out in the Week 1 chapters. Still, I would advise you to read through each chapter, looking for something you may have missed or for changes you may want to make to improve your current practices.

Strategies to help you conduct product research (chapter 4), select the right products (chapter 5), and figure out how to buy those products at the best price (chapter 6) are critical to your long-term success. Forgoing these strategies makes most new eBay sellers wonder what is going wrong; many give up before they ever really get started. Doing the research and going through the processes outlined here will help you avoid costly mistakes, so your first selling experience will be much more enjoyable—and profitable.

In Week 1, we will cover setting up and organizing your business, finding your way around eBay, and researching, choosing, and sourcing products to sell. In addition, we will explore the different listing format types, and which may be right for your specific product. Then we will walk step-by-step through the process of launching your first listings on eBay. Finally, we'll examine listing and pricing strategies, ways to quickly build positive feedback, and then tie together everything you've learned in a targeted business plan that will ensure your success.

At the end of each chapter is a short checklist of actions for you to take. Some of these actions can be done within a few hours; others might span a few days. You may opt to carry out each task right away, or you may want to keep reading and come back to certain ones later on. If you choose to return to some of them later on, make a list of the tasks you're setting aside, be sure to do each one at some point, and check it off as you complete it. Don't be intimidated if your list looks long. None of the tasks is that difficult or time-consuming, and many are actually fun. Just take them one at a time and you will see progress every day.

I also find it helpful to keep a three-ring binder near my computer so I can print out information as I come across it, punch three holes in the sheets, and file them for easy reference. It is worth making a bookmark folder in your browser for links you visit frequently. This can save you a lot of time. Some people prefer to do this in a Word document. Either way is fine; just make sure you have easy access to the links you use a lot.

CHAPTER 1

✦ SETTING UP AND ✦ ORGANIZING YOUR BUSINESS

TO START SELLING ON EBAY, there's only one step that's absolutely required: registering an eBay selling account, which also requires you to set up a PayPal account if you don't already have one. However, following a number of other steps will make your path to success much smoother.

This chapter will walk you through how to register and set up your eBay and PayPal accounts, as well as how to create your About Me page, so that prospective bidders can learn about you and your business. Keep in mind that before learning how to sell on eBay, you need to understand the entire eBay process—both buying and selling. So we will first take a look at *buying* on eBay—how to gain experience, earn your first feedback ratings, and use your My eBay page to track your activity. Finally, we will address the issue of business licenses and explain how to get a state sales tax number so you can buy inventory for resale (without paying sales tax on the purchase) from wholesalers and other distributors.

SETTING UP YOUR EBAY ACCOUNT

If you do not yet have an eBay account, the first thing you need to do is register as a buyer on eBay. You can do this by clicking on the link that says Register on the eBay homepage at www.eBay.com.

eBay will ask for your name, address, telephone number, and e-mail address; then you will set up a user ID (username), password, and secret question, and then enter your birth date to confirm you are over eighteen years old. Next, eBay will send you an e-mail with a link to click on and a confirmation code to enter. Once you do this, you are eligible to bid and buy on eBay. Note that when you create your eBay user ID, you cannot use any spaces. So, for example, *BidMoreOften* works, but *Bid More Often* will not be accepted. (However, you may use the underscore as a separator, as in *Bid_More_Often*.) You can click the *Check your user ID* button to see if your chosen user ID is available before continuing with the registration process.

Give some thought to your user ID. Don't pick a name that will limit your business unless you will be concentrating on a specific niche. Something like *TheCameraDude* will work fine if all you plan to sell are cameras and photo equipment. A more generic name such as *HillsAndDales* or *SamsGreatStuff* will allow you to sell almost anything.

Next you need to register as a seller. Simply click on the *Sell* tab at the top of any eBay page (see Figure 1.1).

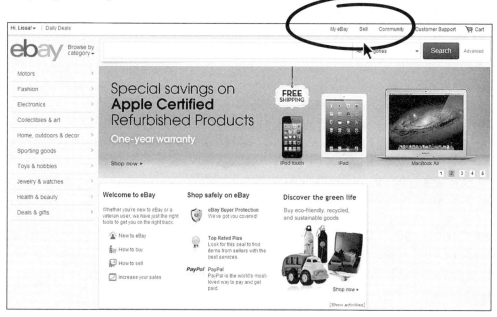

Figure 1.1 eBay Main Navigation Links

eBay will recognize that you are not yet registered to sell and will direct you to register. To register as a seller, you need to verify your identity by providing a credit card or debit card number and your checking account information. Both sets of information must match your registered name and address. Note that eBay will *not* charge your credit card or access your checking account unless you authorize them to charge your eBay selling fees. You also have the option of paying your eBay selling fees by check or by PayPal. (We'll discuss eBay selling fees in chapter 21.)

OPENING YOUR PAYPAL ACCOUNT

The next step, if you haven't already done so, is to open a PayPal account. PayPal is the payment service owned by eBay. PayPal has a long record of reliability and service to eBay sellers. As a new seller, you are required to have a PayPal account. This is actually okay, because over 90 percent of eBay users also are registered with PayPal. Buyers like the payment protection they get from using PayPal and the convenience of paying with the same service for almost all sellers. There are a few other options you can use (ProPay, Paymate, Skrill, Escrow.com, an Internet merchant credit card processor), but to be honest, most buyers aren't familiar with them and they're not worth bothering with (with the exception of Escrow.com if you sell very, very expensive items). I offer buyers the choice of both PayPal and credit/debit card processing through an Internet merchant account I pay a monthly fee for through my bank. I don't bother with the other services.

Your PayPal account is free, but if you are going to receive funds on a regular basis (or are registered on eBay as a business seller), PayPal requires you to have a Premier or Business account. This is also free, so if you haven't signed up for PayPal yet, go ahead and get one of these from the start. The only difference is that the Business account is in a company name, whereas the Premier one is for an individual who sells online. To register, simply go to www.paypal.com and click *Sign Up*. After you initially sign up, you may be offered a "line of credit" through Bill Me Later. This is not a requirement and you can skip it by clicking *Go to My Account* at the bottom of the page.

Once you are registered, you will notice a link on the account overview that says *Get Verified*. When you click on this link, PayPal will ask you to enter your bank name, bank routing number, and your account number. PayPal will then make two small deposits to your bank account—both in pennies—such as $0.08 and $0.17. After that, PayPal will send you an e-mail instructing you to contact your bank and determine the amount of the two deposits. The e-mail will have a link to click on where you enter the information. If the information you supplied was accurate, you will now be PayPal Verified.

To link your PayPal and eBay accounts together, click on *Profile* from your PayPal account overview and select *My Selling Tools* (see Figure 1.2). Now, click *Update* next to the eBay ID line. Now you can add your eBay account. You will need to provide your eBay user ID and your eBay password to link the accounts. Now you can easily buy directly from eBay with your PayPal account, and any payments made to you through eBay will come to this PayPal account.

When you buy something on eBay using your PayPal account, PayPal gives you several payment options. You can elect to use the credit or debit card you have on file, or you can write an e-check from your bank account. An e-check is essentially the same as a regular check. The funds are not immediately debited from your account, so it takes time to clear. Sellers really dislike e-checks because they add a few days to the processing and buyers don't typically like waiting that extra time before their item is mailed. If you have cash in your PayPal account—which you will as soon as you become a seller and people start paying you—PayPal will first access that balance whenever you authorize a payment. If you have both a credit card and bank account on file with PayPal, you qualify for *instant transfers*. This basically works like an e-check, except there is no waiting period for the transfer to clear from your bank account. PayPal sends the money to the seller instantly (as if you had the funds already in your PayPal account) and then debits it from your bank account. If the funds are not available in your bank account, PayPal then charges the purchase to your credit card. This gives you the convenience of e-checks without the long wait for them to clear. PayPal will *never* debit your credit card or your bank account without your authorization. There is no fee to purchase something using PayPal; however, there is a fee for sellers. Every time you as a seller receive a payment from PayPal, typically 2.9 percent of the transaction

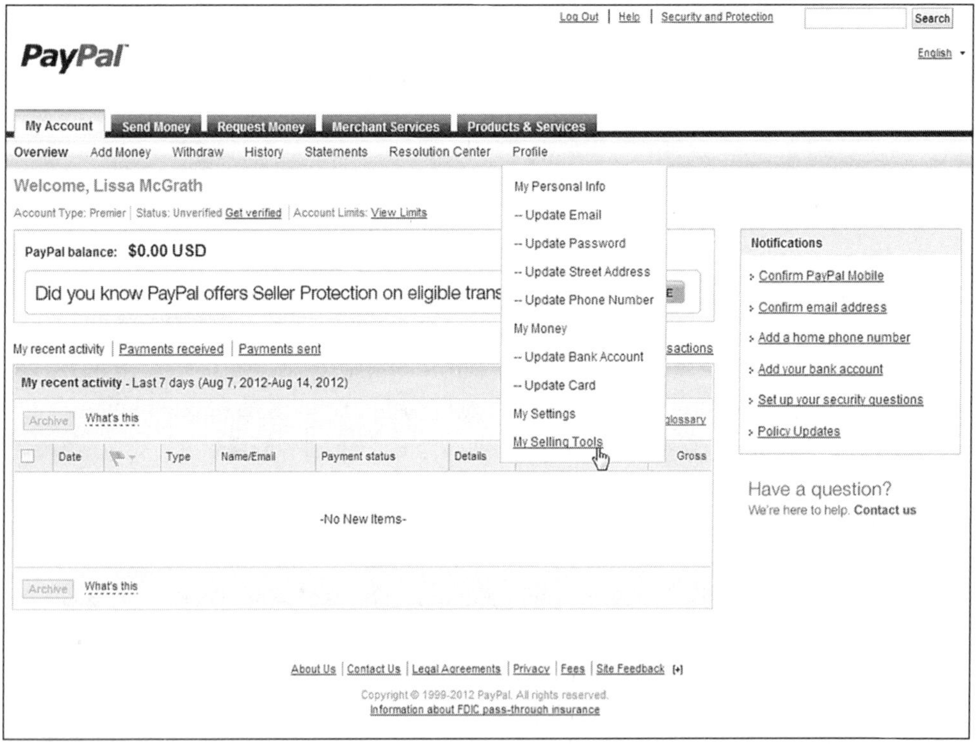

Figure 1.2 Linking Your PayPal and eBay Accounts

amount is deducted, plus $0.30 per transaction (the fee is a little higher if your buyer is from another country, and a little lower if your monthly transaction volume is very high). This may sound like a lot, but it is actually cheaper than the rates and fees charged by merchant credit card companies like Visa and MasterCard. Depending on the bank where you open a merchant account, rates may vary from 2.5 percent to as high as 4 percent of the amount paid, plus transaction fees that can run as high as $0.40 per transaction. In addition to that, most merchant credit card companies have high setup fees and recurring monthly charges.

Not only is PayPal cheaper than merchant credit card companies, but it is the payment system eBay buyers prefer. Don't worry if one of your buyers doesn't have a PayPal account. You can still send him an electronic invoice via PayPal that allows him to enter his credit/debit card information.

PAYPAL FUNDS HOLD

This is very important. When you first start selling on eBay and you receive a payment via PayPal, you will be subject to a funds hold (i.e., you cannot withdraw the money to your own bank account or spend it) until you establish your seller track record. The length of time of the hold can be as much as twenty-one days from when the buyer paid. You may think this is outrageous, many people do, but it is eBay's way of making sure you really are going to ship the items and are not just a fly-by-night scam artist who lists a few items and skips off with the cash.

To establish your seller track record, all three of the following must happen:

1. It must be over ninety days since your first sale.
2. You must have made twenty-five sales.
3. You must have sold more than $250 worth of items.

In addition, your seller performance should be *Standard* or *Above Standard*. This won't mean much to you right now, but essentially it means that you follow all of eBay's policies and that the feedback from your buyers on how well you describe your items, ship them, etc. is mostly good. We will cover this later, but for the purposes of the PayPal funds hold, just know that you cannot be Below Standard, even if the other requirements are met, if you want to establish your seller track record.

There are things you can do to get the hold period down to three days, which is a lot better than twenty-one days. The following are the options available to you and the impact they will have on when you will receive your funds.

Using eBay Labels

If you use eBay Labels or otherwise print your shipping label at home through PayPal, (which doesn't have any additional fees over the standard online postage rates) the funds are automatically released to you three days after confirmed delivery of your item to your buyer. Since your tracking information is automatically uploaded, this is the easiest option and the one most likely to work as it should. In addition, if you use United States Postal Service (USPS) domestic or first-class international for the shipping service to your buyer, you will receive some of the funds immediately to cover the cost of shipping. If the transaction was under $50, you can get up to $15 immediately to cover the shipping. If it is over $50, you can receive up to 30 percent. Note, though, that this is not available for United Parcel Service (UPS) or Canada Post shipments, only for USPS.

Not Using eBay Labels

If you choose not to use eBay Labels or not to pay for your shipping label through PayPal (e.g., if you go to the post office yourself), there are a few scenarios that can play out. If you use USPS tracking (the delivery confirmation number is acceptable for this) and upload the tracking number to eBay through My eBay, then your funds will be released three days after confirmed delivery, just as if you had used eBay Labels. The only differences are that you don't get the shipping funds available immediately to cover the cost of shipping and you have to upload the tracking number manually. Personally, if you're going to go to all that effort, you may as well use eBay Labels and save yourself time and effort, and not be out of pocket on the shipping cost for a few days.

If you do not upload the tracking number but you do mark it as "shipped" in My eBay, you will receive the funds seven days after the latest estimated delivery date for your parcel. This is based on your handling time and the carrier's published delivery estimations for the service you used.

The third option is not to upload anything, and not mark the item as "shipped" in My eBay. If this is the route you take, you will wait twenty-one days from when the buyer paid you until any of the funds are released to you.

Clearly the best option while you're a new seller is to use eBay Labels. It's quicker, easy to use, uploads the tracking information for you, and you are going to get the funds released more rapidly than by any other method. The sooner you get the parcel into the mail, the quicker you get the funds released, so you should always aim for a one-business-day turnaround (eBay defines this as by the end of the next business day after the buyer pays you).

Remember: The PayPal funds hold is temporary until you establish yourself. Once you build a seller track record, it will go away and you will receive 100 percent of the funds immediately. It is simply an extra way to protect the buyer from new sellers who may not describe their items correctly, or who may be complete scams. This way there is less risk for the buyer (and PayPal through their protection policies, which we cover in chapter 20).

GAINING EXPERIENCE

Now that you have a PayPal account, you are ready to buy and sell on eBay. Before you start selling on eBay, however, you should first bid on and win several auctions. *Don't skip this important step.* You can't really understand the selling process on eBay unless you become a buyer first. This way you will learn how other sellers deal with winning bidders. For example:

- How do they communicate with you after the auction?
- How do they ask you for payment and what are their policies?
- How did they ship your goods, what did shipping cost, and how were the items packaged?
- Did the seller attempt an upsell—offering you a discount if you bought a related product?
- How quickly did the seller post feedback for you, if at all?
- Just how smooth and comfortable was the process? Did you feel pleased with the transaction? If not, what could the seller have done better? If so, what aspect of the transaction really pleased you?

Bidding on (and winning) items from several different sellers is a valuable part of your education as a seller. If you forgo this step, you will certainly make mistakes later that you could easily avoid. Hundreds of ordinary products are for sale on eBay, things that you use every day, such as shampoo, razor blades, diapers, and beauty products. Many of them are less expensive on eBay than at your local drugstore or supermarket, so bidding on them and buying them to gain experience in working through the process doesn't cost you much—and may even save you some money. The other advantage of buying on eBay is that you can start building your feedback rating, which we turn to next. Make sure to try out different listing formats too. Bid on an auction, but also purchase a Fixed Price item. If you can find one that has drop-down menus to select the options you want, even better! (This is called a Multiple Variations Listing and we will look at that in detail later, but it's good to see it from the buyer's perspective too!)

FEEDBACK

We will discuss feedback in detail in chapter 11, but we need to introduce the concept here because it is related to several of the initial steps you should take as a seller. When Pierre Omidyar started eBay in 1995, most observers thought it was an insane idea. *People are just not going to buy products over the Internet from strangers* was the recurring critique from the Silicon Valley know-it-alls. However, Pierre embedded in eBay two major concepts that no one at the time understood: eBay would become a community of users and the community would become self-policing. Indeed, eBay became a community because of the intimacy and the direct contact the platform provided—and, yes, because the idea was just quirky enough to attract the same kind of people who were attracted to chat rooms and playing games online. Self-policing came about through the concept of *feedback*.

Here is how feedback works: Every time an item is sold, each party—both buyer and seller—is encouraged to post a short comment about the other party. Those comments become a *permanent* part of the buyer's and seller's reputations on eBay. If you open any eBay auction, you will see the user ID of the seller followed by a number in parentheses—for example, BidMoreOften (74). The number 74 is the Feedback Score. Each transaction is calculated by assigning either a positive comment left for BidMoreOften as +1 or a negative comment as -1. The score is the sum total of these positives and negatives. Before you bid on an item from a seller, you get to look at his feedback—what other actual customers have to say about their experience with that seller. Figure 1.3 shows an example of feedback comments left for a seller.

Feedback is an enormously powerful tool and has now been copied in various formats by many other auction sites and Web shopping portals. Imagine if you walked into your local shopping mall and outside each store was a board where you could post comments about the quality of the products sold there and the customer service you received—and *the store was not allowed to remove those comments!* Don't you think the stores would work harder to provide good service? This is the power of feedback.

You can view a member's Feedback Profile by clicking the number in parentheses next to their user ID. In addition to listing the comments from other eBay users (both buyers and sellers), eBay also keeps track of the percentage of comments that are positive, called the Feedback Rating. Very few sellers have perfect feedback (100 percent positive feedback), but over time, eBay users have set the bar fairly high. A rating of less than 98 percent (two negatives out of one hundred transactions) is considered a yellow caution flag. Less than 95 or 96 percent, and you will find your bids dropping off substantially. So if you want to build a long-term business on eBay, protecting your feedback rating is critical to your success.

	1 month	6 months	12 months		Criteria	Average rating	Number of ratings	
Positive	15	94	191		Item as described	★★★★	154	eBay Buyer Protection
Neutral	0	0	1		Communication	★★★★	156	Covers your purchase price +
Negative	0	0	0		Shipping time	★★★★	158	original shipping
					Shipping and handling charges	★★★★	175	Learn more

Feedback as a seller	Feedback as a buyer	**All Feedback**	Feedback left for others

9,859 Feedback received (viewing 1-25)   Revised Feedback: 0   ?

Period: All ▼

Feedback	From/price	Date/time
Fast shipping, Makes perfect coffee, I love it.. Excellent Ebayer A+++++	Buyer: usedteleman (166 ☆)	Aug-13-12 07:07
Sowden Oskar SoftBrew Coffee Maker with Scoop - 8 Cup, New in Box (#120950390092)	US $67.95	View Item
Awesome!! Great buy!	Buyer: leaalmy518 (100 ☆)	Aug-11-12 17:11
Make Money on eBay Complete eBay Business System Manual (#370615533076)	US $97.00	View Item
Received quickly; can't wait to start using it; thank you!	Buyer: arabianhorsefan (1424 ★)	Aug-10-12 03:50
THE COMPLETE eBay MARKETING SYSTEM BOOK BY SKIP MCGRATH (#370615452294)	US $97.00	View Item
AWESOME transaction & seller. Best customer service on ebay. Thank you!	Buyer: bmt54 (856 ☆)	Aug-06-12 19:21
Trader Jacques, French Liquid Hand & Body Soap Orange Blossom Honey & Vitamin E (#370631048610)	US $27.99	View Item
A + transaction! Love the firepit! Can't wait to use it!	Buyer: blflower11 (61 ★)	Aug-04-12 20:20
~ TEXAS COWBOY OUTDOOR PATIO FIREPIT GRILL Fire pit New (#120666866060)	US $239.00	View Item
Thanks you for the smooth transaction! Great seller!!!!	Buyer: greenxabl (234 ☆)	Jul-29-12 13:20
~ HANDMADE OUTDOOR PATIO FIREPIT GRILL MOON STARS DESIGN - Free Shipping (#120881955194)	US $239.00	View Item
Sorry 4 late feedback! Best co. on ebay Best firepit EVER Love the mcgrrrrrs'	Buyer: kevinruhr (106 ☆)	Jul-25-12 20:38

Figure 1.3 eBay Feedback Comments

When you start to sell on eBay, you need to have a feedback rating of at least ten to fifteen to attract bids. Personally, I rarely buy from any seller with a rating lower than fifty, and at that low rating, her feedback had better be 98 or 100 percent if she wants me to bid.

Another aspect of feedback you will see in the Feedback Profile is the Detailed Seller Ratings (DSRs). The DSRs are a score from one to five stars on each of four critical aspects of the transaction (*item as described, communication, shipping time,* and *shipping and handling charges*). Five stars is a very good rating and one star is a low rating. Buyers can choose to leave these anonymous ratings in addition to a feedback comment. Your Seller Performance Standings are affected by your DSRs. If you receive too great a percentage of one- or two-star ratings, your listings may not show up as well in the *Best Match* default search results, and you may even have your selling account suspended. DSRs are on file for twelve months, so this can have a big impact. Now, most buyers will only give a one- or two-star rating if you really really messed up in your transaction with them, but it does happen. We will talk about how to minimize the impact of DSRs later. There are some very easy strategies that can really take the anxiety out of DSRs.

This brings us back to the importance of buying on eBay before you start selling. You can only know how a buyer feels about each of those DSR points by becoming a buyer yourself. You also earn feedback comments (but not DSRs) when you buy; remember, both parties to a transaction get to leave feedback, but only buyers can leave neutral or negative comments.

ABOUT ME PAGE

You can set up an About Me page to describe your business (see Figure 1.4). You can link to it in your listing description, and there is also an icon link next to your user ID on your Feedback Profile.

You can personalize the page any way you want. Some sellers use it to talk about themselves and where they live, often including photos. Others explain their policies and experience on eBay on their About Me page. Still others create an About Me page to help brand their business.

Figure 1.4 About Me Page

MY EBAY PAGE

A link to your My eBay page appears at the top of every eBay page you access; it's located in the navigation links. When you click on this, you will be prompted to sign in with your user ID and password, because your My eBay page contains your account and personal information.

The My eBay page has four tabs: Activity, Messages, Account, and Applications (as shown in Figure 1.5). The Activity tab is the default and here you will find, as you would expect, all your eBay transaction activities.

As you can see in Figure 1.5, the left sidebar shows drop-down sections for Buy, Lists, Purchase History, and Sell. These are all pretty self-explanatory. As a seller you may want to change the default view to start on *All Selling* (the option is at the top of the *Sell* list), since you are most likely to be looking at this section.

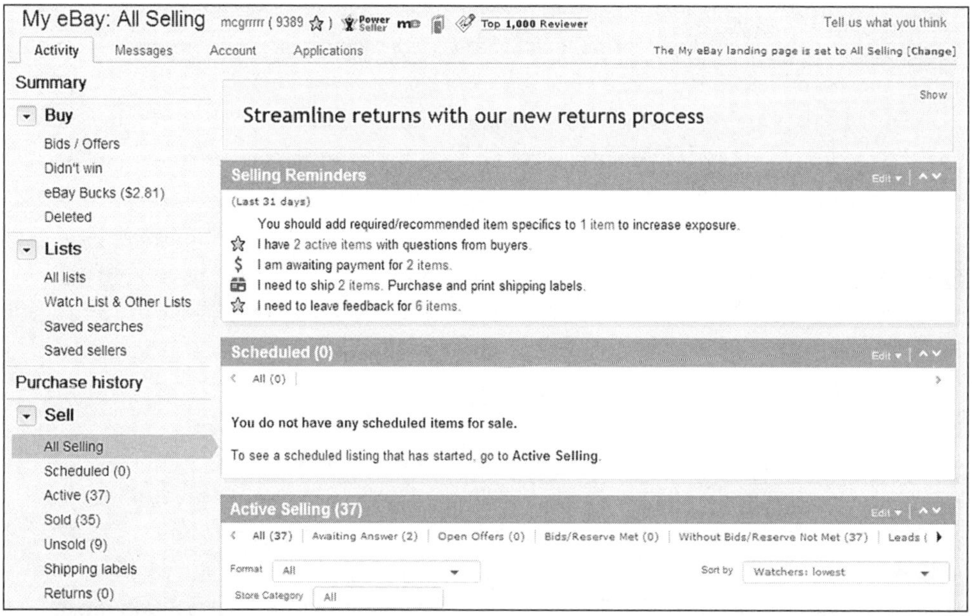

Figure 1.5 My eBay Page

Under the All Selling heading, the first things you will see are a list of all the items you are selling, the current price and number of bids, whether or not your reserve has been met (if you have one), and the number of people who are watching your auction. If you click on the *Sold* link, you will see a list of the items you have sold and their status, as well as actions you can take just by clicking on the button next to each item.

These actions include *Send Invoice, Print Shipping Label, Add Tracking Number,* and *Leave Feedback.* Later, we address the issue of automation as it relates to selling on eBay. eBay sells a program called eBay Selling Manager, which, once it's integrated into your My eBay page, enables you to automate a lot of sales-related functions, such as sending out invoices and shipping notices and posting feedback. Back at the top of the My eBay page, under the *Account* tab, there is a link to your *Seller Dashboard,* where you can see your DSR scores and other info for sellers. This is where you see your seller performance and how well you are doing per eBay requirements. You won't see the Seller Dashboard until you have received ten DSRs, so don't go looking for it yet, but when you do reach that point, the Seller Dashboard will be an important part of My eBay for you to continue to check regularly.

For the moment, just spend some time clicking on the various links on your My eBay page to become familiar with all the information that is available to you. Once you have some listings launched and items sold, this page will become a useful tool for tracking your sold and unsold items, customer communications, payment and shipping status, and feedback.

Your My eBay page also includes an important link to *Messages* (which has its own tab under My eBay). Whenever eBay or a potential eBay bidder sends you an e-mail, you will receive the message in your personal eBay account, accessible via your Messages page. These e-mails are also forwarded to the e-mail address you registered with. You will also see a red bar next to any item in your Active Selling section (under the *Sell* menu) that has an unanswered question related to it, so you can't easily miss it.

BUSINESS LICENSES

If you are running your business out of your home, you will most likely *not* need to obtain a local business license from your town or county. Typically, local business licenses are for businesses that have customers visiting the business location. If, however, you open an office or rent space in a commercial location, you may need to get a local business license. This license is usually inexpensive—under $100 in most towns and cities. You can apply for it at the city clerk's office.

STATE SALES TAX NUMBER

If you live in a state that charges sales tax, you need a *state sales tax number.* Other states that do not charge sales tax, such as Oregon and Idaho, typically issue a business-use tax number that serves the same purpose.

AVOIDING
SPOOF E-MAILS

Be wary of spoof e-mails. These are messages that arrive in your e-mail inbox and **appear** to be from one of your bidders or buyers, often claiming that the buyer has not received an item he bought from you. The message will contain a link to sign into your eBay account. **Never click on one of these links in an e-mail.** The link is bogus: It will bring up a page that looks just like the eBay sign-in page—however, it is really a fraudulent Web site designed to capture your user ID and password. We delve into the topic of spoof e-mails and other types of fraud in chapter 20, but since you may receive one of these messages shortly after signing up with eBay, you need to be aware of this scam right off the bat, as a lot of new eBay users fall for this.

If you receive an e-mail relating to an eBay auction or transaction that purports to be from eBay itself—or you receive any message whose origin you are unsure of—just go to your Messages tab under My eBay. If the message is authentic, it will also appear there. Remember: Neither eBay nor PayPal will ever send you an e-mail asking for your account details.

A sales tax number allows you to purchase merchandise for resale without paying sales tax to the vendor. Whenever you sell something in your state that is delivered to an address *in your state,* you must collect sales tax from the customer, and you must remit the sales tax to your state's tax department. Most states require you to file and pay your sales taxes quarterly, although some states do it monthly, often depending on the volume of sales generated by your business.

You *do not* have to collect, or pay, sales tax on orders that you ship *out of state.* However, if you live in a state with a large population, such as New York, Illinois, or California, most likely you will sell a lot of items on eBay to buyers within your state.

You should always collect and pay sales tax, because state tax authorities are aware that many Internet sellers are skirting this requirement, and they are cracking down. Sometimes a state compliance officer, masquerading as a legitimate eBay bidder, will purchase something low cost from you, or just send you an e-mail pretending to be a bidder and ask if you charge sales tax. If you don't collect the tax, you will be subject to some serious fines. In some states, you're liable for criminal penalties as well.

················ BEST PRACTICES ················

INTERNET SALES TAX

Several bills are floating around the US Congress designed to change the federal law and allow states to collect sales tax on out-of-state Internet transactions (including eBay sales). One bill that several states have adopted does require Internet-based sales taxes to be collected and paid on out-of-state shipments; however, it exempts businesses that do less than $4 million in annual sales. eBay has been at the forefront in the fight against this kind of legislation. Each year, eBay selects fifty top sellers—one from each state—and they go to Washington, where they roam the halls of Congress, meeting with legislators and lobbying against any form of Internet tax. So far nothing has been passed, but it's something to watch for the future.

Most states require you to fill out a simple form once a quarter that lists all your taxable sales and ask you to mail it into the state with a check for the sales tax you collected. Later on, we'll look at a simple way to maintain these records and automate the process so that it takes only a few minutes a week to keep track of sales tax collection and handle the payments.

Besides collecting and paying taxes, the other reason you need a state sales tax number is to purchase merchandise. Most legitimate wholesale companies simply will not sell to you unless you have a sales tax number.

It is very simple to get a state sales tax number. In most states the fee is low, typically ranging from $25 to $100, although some states require new businesses to put up a deposit, which may be as high as $500. This is usually returned after one year of paying your taxes on time.

To get the lowdown on state sales tax, visit the Web site for this book, www. skipmcgrath.com/3_weeks, and click on the navigation link *State Sales Tax*. This takes you to a page where you can link directly to the Web sites of the tax departments in all fifty states. There you can get all the information you need and download the required forms. In most cases you can apply for a state sales tax number online.

BIZ BUILDER

Luckily, eBay makes it simple to collect sales taxes on in-state transactions. When you list your item, you have an option to enter the name of your state and the percentage of sales tax to collect. When a listing ends, if the buyer is located in your state, eBay automatically adds the sales tax to the final selling price and the shipping amount if needed. It also displays the rate charged and what state it applies to on the listing page. This alone can prevent you from being targeted by a state compliance officer.

COMMERCIAL CHECKING ACCOUNT

Since you are probably going to buy from wholesale companies, you will want to open a commercial checking account in the name of your business. Most legitimate wholesale companies and distributors prefer to deal with businesses rather than with individuals. They require you to have both a state sales tax number and a business checking account to purchase from them. Later on, we give you tips on how to get into wholesale trade shows and merchandise marts, which also require this proof of business status. When you apply for a state sales tax number, you can register a business name at the same time. Simply take your certificate with the business name to your local bank and ask to open a commercial (or business) checking account. Most banks will do this for a minimum deposit of $100. At this time you should also apply for a credit or debit card for the account. You will be making wholesale purchases on the Web and paying online for different services, including your eBay fees. This way all your business expenses are handled through one account—and you will simplify both your record keeping and your taxes at the end of the year.

POWER MOVES

❏ Register your eBay account and sign up for a PayPal premier or business account.

❏ If you haven't ever purchased anything on eBay, gain some experience by bidding on and winning a few items so you can learn about the process and get a good grasp of it.

❏ As you are bidding and buying, be sure to look at each seller's feedback rating. When you win an auction, post feedback for the seller and make sure the seller posts feedback for you. E-mail the seller a polite request if she forgets to do this.

❏ Set up your About Me page.

❏ Explore the resources on your My eBay page.

❏ Apply for a state sales tax number for your state.

❏ Open a commercial checking account and sign up for a business debit card.

CHAPTER 2

✦ FINDING YOUR WAY AROUND EBAY ✦

BESIDES THE MY EBAY and About Me pages, there are many more resource pages on eBay. As a seller, you need to become familiar with pages that allow you to manage your items for sale, revise your auctions, end a listing early, and handle disputes from nonpaying bidders. You may not need to access these pages for your first few listings, but if you do, it is imperative to know what actions eBay allows you to take and how to quickly find the tools you need.

SITE MAP

eBay's site map is the best place to start investigating the tools available to you. The link is on the bottom of the eBay home page under the Tools heading. Table 2.1 shows the most important links for sellers.

The middle column of the site map, *Selling Activities* (see Figure 2.1) contains several links you, as a seller, will be using often. Some of these links are quite valuable and you will refer to them often, so you will want to bookmark them (add them to

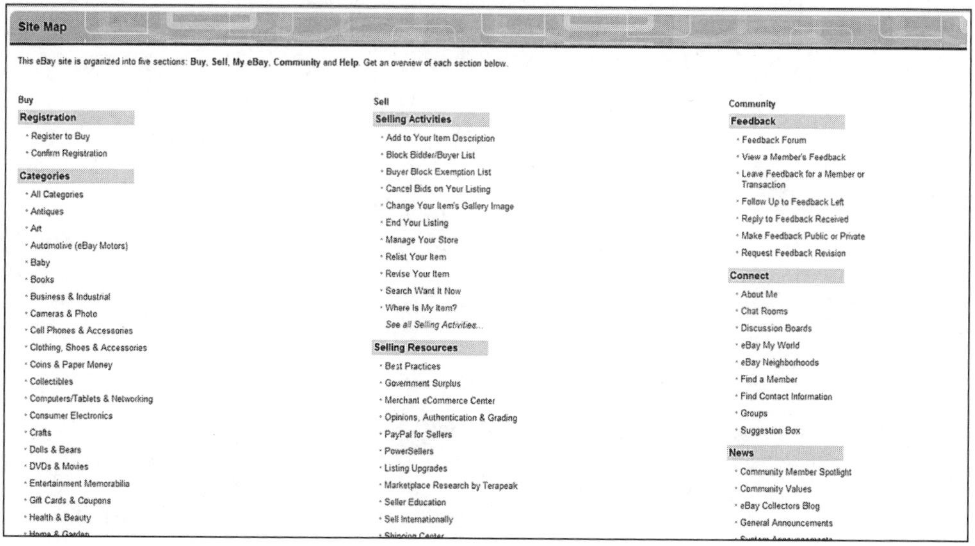

Figure 2.1 The Selling Activities List on the Site Map

your Favorites in your Internet browser). To access the others, you can just refer to the site map as you need them.

TABLE 2.1 Useful eBay Links

REVISE YOUR ITEM	Like all of us, you will occasionally make a mistake in one of your listings. This link allows you to fix any mistakes you made or add new information.
CANCEL BIDS ON YOUR LISTING	If you need to end an auction, you will first have to cancel any bids on your item. This is a page where you can do that.
END YOUR LISTING	You can end your listing at any time, but if there are bids, you must cancel them first (see above), and you will pay a cancellation fee.
RESOLUTION CENTER	This is where you can report buyers to eBay who have not paid for an item, or sellers who failed to ship an item that you purchased. You can also link to the Resolution Center from your My eBay page.
BLOCK BIDDER/ BUYER LIST	This is where you can block certain bidders from bidding on your auctions. If a bidder leaves me negative feedback, I always block him from bidding on my future auctions.
POWERSELLERS	Once you are a PowerSeller or Top-Rated Seller, bookmark this page, because this is where you can access special tools for PowerSellers and communicate with PowerSeller support.

SELLING RESOURCES

Farther down the middle column of the site map is a heading titled *Selling Resources*. Selling Resources contains many valuable resources for eBay sellers, including:

* **BEST PRACTICES:** These are listings of strategies and techniques developed by eBay PowerSellers to help you increase sales. I strongly recommend that you read them after you have read this book, although some of them might not make a lot of sense until you understand the context.

* **MARKETPLACE RESEARCH BY TERAPEAK:** Here you can link your eBay account to Terapeak and perform market research to see the best times and days to list. There are proven pricing strategies and sale prices for items you are interested in selling. We will look into research in a lot more detail, but this is where you can set up the link to Terapeak (note, however, that this is not a free service).

* **SELLER EDUCATION:** This is a great page to bookmark, because it takes you to a site map of all the resources available to the seller, conveniently listed in one place. It is sort of a "sellers only" site map.

Other headings farther down on the site map include My Account (which you can access through your My eBay page more easily) and My Selling Account. The latter has some useful links you may want to bookmark, such as *Request Final Value Fee Credit*. We will talk about this later, but this is where you access the form to get a fee credit if a buyer doesn't pay for an item he or she purchases from you. This is definitely a link you will want to keep at hand.

I recommend you also look at the *Help Topics* heading of the site map and bookmark the link to Selling & Seller fees. I will extensively discuss eBay fees, but they are complicated and it is worth having a quick reference link available. Currently, the direct link is http://pages.ebay.com/help/sell/fees.html.

EBAY COMMUNITY PAGE

eBay is a unique community. Its members have a long history (*long*, that is, in terms of the Internet Age) of helping each other out. You can connect to other members in several ways. On the eBay Community Page (see Figure 2.2) you will find three links to places to connect with other eBay users: Discussion boards, Groups, and Answer center. There are other links on the Community page, but these are the ones that connect you to other eBay users.

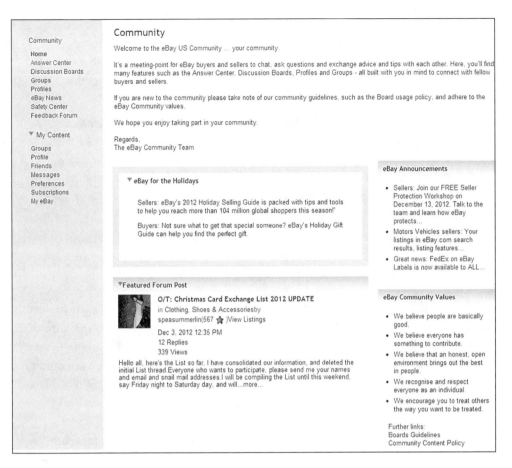

Community

Welcome to the eBay US Community ... your community.

It's a meeting-point for eBay buyers and sellers to chat, ask questions and exchange advice and tips with each other. Here, you'll find many features such as the Answer Center, Discussion Boards, Profiles and Groups - all built with you in mind to connect with fellow buyers and sellers.

If you are new to the community please take note of our community guidelines, such as the Board usage policy, and adhere to the eBay Community values.

We hope you enjoy taking part in your community.

Regards,
The eBay Community Team

eBay Announcements

- Sellers: Join our FREE Seller Protection Workshop on December 13, 2012. Talk to the team and learn how eBay protects...
- Motors Vehicles sellers: Your listings in eBay.com search results, listing features...
- Great news! FedEx on eBay Labels is now available to ALL...

▼ **eBay for the Holidays**

Sellers: eBay's 2012 Holiday Selling Guide is packed with tips and tools to help you reach more than 104 million global shoppers this season!"

Buyers: Not sure what to get that special someone? eBay's Holiday Gift Guide can help you find the perfect gift.

▼ **Featured Forum Post**

O/T: Christmas Card Exchange List 2012 UPDATE
in Clothing, Shoes & Accessoriesby
speasummerlin(567 ☆)View Listings

Dec 3, 2012 12:35 PM
12 Replies
339 Views

Hello all, here's the List so far, I have consolidated our information, and deleted the initial List thread.Everyone who wants to participate, please send me your names and email and snail mail addresses.I will be compiling the List until this weekend, say Friday night to Saturday day, and will....more...

eBay Community Values

- We believe people are basically good.
- We believe everyone has something to contribute.
- We believe that an honest, open environment brings out the best in people.
- We recognise and respect everyone as an individual.
- We encourage you to treat others the way you want to be treated.

Further links:
Boards Guidelines
Community Content Policy

Community
Home
Answer Center
Discussion Boards
Groups
Profiles
eBay News
Safety Center
Feedback Forum

▼ My Content
Groups
Profile
Friends
Messages
Preferences
Subscriptions
My eBay

Figure 2.2 eBay Community Page

✳ **DISCUSSION BOARDS:** Here you can post and reply to messages on thousands of topics—category-specific, help-topic specific, general discussion, news and information, and more. Almost any eBay subject you can think of is covered here. And, if it's not, you can start a new board to discuss it.

✳ **GROUPS:** These are message boards arranged by type (seller groups, special interest, mentoring, collectors clubs, and so on), so you can kibbitz with people with the same interests. Regional groups, by city and state, can be found here as well, so you can meet up online with folks in your local area.

✳ **ANSWER CENTER:** This is the place to ask any questions you may have, such as "How do I insert a photo into my auction?" or "How do I pack and ship a six-foot-long didgeridoo?" Other sellers and eBay employees will answer almost any question you pose. You can identify employees by the color of their user IDs—employee user IDs are always pink. If you see someone refer to a "pink," she is talking about an eBay employee.

One thing to note about the discussion boards: There are unhappy or unsuccessful people in every community. While most posts are positive and helpful, there are always some posts from these unsuccessful sellers or people who just love to complain. I take all of these with a grain of salt and rarely let them influence my decisions.

To reach the Community page, click on the *Community* heading on the navigation bar at the top right of every eBay page. There are also links to the specific pages at the bottom of the eBay homepage.

POWER MOVES

❑ Familiarize yourself with the eBay site map, especially the links under *Selling Activities* and *Selling Resources*.

❑ Bookmark important pages in a special eBay Pages folder so that you can readily access important tools without searching through the site map every time.

❑ Visit *Seller Education* and familiarize yourself with the resources and tools available to eBay sellers.

CHAPTER 3

✦ WHAT SELLS ON EBAY? ✦

WITH TENS OF THOUSANDS of categories and subcategories, you can sell virtually anything on eBay. But choosing what to sell can often be overwhelming. You should first examine your own professional experience, hobbies, and interests. If you currently own a small retail store, gallery, or antiques shop, experiment to figure out which of your products will sell well on eBay.

If you want to start an eBay business from scratch, then you have to decide what business you are going to be in and what kind of products to sell. The biggest mistake new sellers make is jumping from product to product trying to find the latest, hottest-selling gadget. If you are going to launch a sustainable business, you will have to specialize in something—preferably something where the competition is minimal or where you have a distinct competitive edge.

In this chapter, we'll explore which products sell consistently well on eBay and what categories might be right for you. We'll also focus on several product areas that are fairly easy for any eBay seller to enter. I am not suggesting that you choose one of these areas. Instead, I am trying to show you that there are plenty of categories where people can make money, even *with* competition. Perhaps reading about some of the possibilities in this chapter will inspire some ideas of your own.

CONSIDER YOUR INTERESTS

If you worked as an audiovisual technician, then you have the knowledge to sell audiovisual equipment. Do you love cooking? Then get into cookware, restaurant equipment, or gourmet food items. Do you collect sports memorabilia? If so, start there. Perhaps you love to read and you always wanted to own a small bookstore but you could never afford the overhead. On eBay, you can start with only a few dozen books and build your business from there. The same goes for art. You can buy art posters or prints wholesale, just a few at a time. Thousands of art prints and posters sell every day on eBay.

If you are a computer or software whiz, look to the computer area for items to sell. Better still, write your own software or build a computer-related product or accessory and sell it on eBay.

YOU CAN'T SELL *THAT* ON EBAY!

Although you can sell anything from your kitchen sink to your pet rock collection on eBay, certain items are prohibited. Items you can't sell on eBay include human body parts; merchandise that has been recalled by the manufacturer; counterfeit brand-name goods, such as knock-off Rolex watches or Gucci handbags; live pets; any tobacco product; electronic surveillance equipment; animals and wildlife products; drugs and drug paraphernalia; firearms; bootleg recordings; and satellite or cable TV descramblers.

The complete list is quite long. In addition to prohibiting the sale of certain merchandise outright, eBay also places restrictions on other items, such as travel, real estate, paintball and air soft guns, and others. To find out more about prohibited and restricted items, click on the Customer Support tab at the top of any eBay Page and type *prohibited items* into the search box.

Your business and product ideas are limited only by your imagination, *but make sure there is a market for the products and/or services you love and plan to sell.* (In the next chapter, we'll discuss researching a product to determine if there is a market for it on eBay, and what kind of prices you can realistically charge.)

Whatever you decide to sell, work to become an expert at it. Go to the library and read up on your products, talk to other merchants and collectors, research your competition, learn something about the history of your product, and study the manufacturers. Knowing your product category in depth will pay many dividends down the road.

If you don't believe in what you're selling, and you aren't willing to stand behind your product, your online business will most certainly fail. You should never sell a product you aren't enthusiastic about. If you wouldn't buy the product for yourself, or strongly recommend it to a friend or family member, then do not sell it to unwary consumers. See chapter 11 on feedback to understand how important this logic is.

Certain items definitely outsell others. Information and software products are particularly hot sellers. Why? Because everyone buying on eBay already owns and uses a computer. And using a computer means they need hardware and/or software. Therefore, almost anyone buying on eBay is a potential customer for computer hardware, software, or accessories.

Software is a huge seller on eBay. Here's why: If you wrote a highly specialized application, you would have a difficult time selling it to a software company. Such companies are not interested in a product unless it can generate millions of dollars in sales. But *you* could probably make a lot of money selling a few hundred or a few thousand copies on eBay and the other auction sites. Trading-card collection software has become very popular (although there is so much of it around now that the price has fallen drastically). Or perhaps you have figured out a way to automate an eBay function. You can apply to work with the eBay application program interface (API) and write (and sell) a software program for eBay users.

Computer games are also big with eBay buyers. Just make sure you are selling a popular game and not one that is considered passé. Yesterday's hot game that sold for $69.95 in the stores can be bought from the closeout dealers for $5.00 each. You could still make this situation work, because there are people willing to buy old games for up to $15.00 each. Just don't expect to sell them for much more.

A certified public accountant with a large accounting firm here in Seattle collects sports memorabilia. He spent hundreds of hours scouring eBay for bargains. He realized right away that the market for common sports memorabilia was saturated and profit margins were too small for him to make much of a profit. So he decided to specialize in oddball and unusual items. He purchased a lot of 500 unused tickets from the third Ali–Frazier fight (the "Thrilla in Manila") and began auctioning them off on eBay, one ticket at a time. The last time I saw him, he was still selling them, at up to $40 each. I believe he bought the whole lot for under $200.

My wife and I used to sell antiques. We worked through one of the largest antiques malls in upstate New York. The mall had a common Web site shared by all the vendors, and I ran auctions for the dealers. This gave us the image of being one large dealer with a high feedback rating. Whenever customers purchased from us, we would then introduce them to our Web site. Customers would link to our Web site over and over again because of the large variety of items available there.

At first I tried to use eBay to unload our slow-moving items. It didn't work! Slow-moving merchandise moves slowly for a reason; there isn't much interest in it on eBay or in the store. After a few tries, I switched to selling our higher-quality, more expensive items. Our sales took off and we were getting bids 10 to 30 percent higher than we were selling the items for in the store.

Whatever your interest—clothing and fashion, sports, cars, cooking, high finance, antiques, art, books, education, children's items, collectibles—there are products you can sell on eBay and other auction sites. And, yes, eBay fortunes have been made on Furby toys, Pokémon cards, and Beanie Babies! The "hot" Christmas item of 2011 was the Leapfrog LeapPad; in 2012 Monster High dolls were incredibly popular. Next year it will be something else—guaranteed.

TARGET EBAY SELLERS

Another excellent sales strategy is to sell supplies to other eBay sellers. Bubble mailer envelopes, printer ink cartridges, and packing tape are big sellers on eBay. You can also sell supplies to collectors. Card collectors buy card holders and software to catalog their cards; doll collectors buy display cases; coin collectors buy coin holders; and so on. Look at a current fad and try to find some way to supply every collector with something he can use to give his collectibles extra value—instead of selling the collectible itself.

.... BEST PRACTICES ....

A WORD ABOUT HOT OR POPULAR CONSUMER GOODS

I always get e-mails from eBay sellers who want to sell the latest digital cameras, Blu-ray players, home theater equipment, cell phones, tablets and computers, games, or hot apparel items. Beware: *This is a very difficult business to enter.* First of all, the wholesale distributors for these products will not even talk to you unless you have a minimum $250,000 line of credit and can place orders of at least $50,000. I once spoke to Apple's distributor about selling iPods online. The distributor's representatives were happy to sell the product to me at a wholesale cost of $122 for the $199 retail unit. However, I had to prove that I had a $200,000 line of credit and I had to purchase one hundred units at a time.

If you have the kind of money it takes to place large wholesale orders and you want to find these goods, the best strategy is to contact the manufacturer of the product you wish to sell and simply ask for the name and contact information of the company's wholesale distributor in your area. As long as you can meet the distributor's buying criteria, you can place an order.

The other issue is competition. If you are selling any hot or high-demand product, then so are hundreds of other sellers, and the profit margin on these products tends to be very low—sometimes so low that a small seller just can't compete.

USED GOODS

Hundreds of eBay sellers (many of them PowerSellers) sell used goods they pick up at flea markets, garage sales, and thrift shops. Almost any product you can think of has been sold used on eBay. Some of the best-selling products are children's clothing, women's plus-sized clothing, cowboy boots, ice skates, used athletic equipment, old cameras and any type of photo or darkroom equipment, old computers (i.e., pre-1990), small appliances (such as Juiceman juicers, pasta machines, food processors, and mixers), and, of course, used watches and jewelry.

Used electronics, including vintage hi-fi equipment (pre-1980s), early computers, reel-to-reel tape decks, and 8-track players and cartridges, are excellent products—always in high demand on eBay. Because many eBay users consider themselves at the cutting edge of technology, used electronics often have a quaint appeal. So do old film cameras and darkroom equipment. I recently learned there is a good market on eBay for old flashlights—even those are now collected.

If you decide to sell used goods, you must first research what is selling. So before you buy that Juiceman at your local thrift store, check out the ones selling on eBay to make sure it's a desirable model and is selling for a price that allows you to make a profit.

Only buy items that are in good to excellent condition. Don't attempt to sell anything defective or broken unless you are selling it for parts—and be sure to say this in your item description. If you sell anything used, it is critical that you completely and accurately describe its condition. In addition, you should take good photos and be sure to point out any defects. People will buy used goods with minor defects or blemishes as long as they understand the product's condition upfront.

USED BOOKS

Used books are big sellers on eBay, and this is a very easy business to start. There are hundreds of eBay sellers making over $1,000 a week selling used books.

Unless you are an expert bookseller, forget about novels, literature, or rare expensive books. Any used bookstore owner will tell you that her daily bread and butter are nonfiction books on art, photography, crafts, cooking, history, sports, cars, trains, motorcycles, and music, as well as children's books and even textbooks. The same is true on eBay. You can buy plenty of these books at garage sales, flea markets, and thrift stores and resell them on eBay for markups as high as 100 to 500 percent.

The easiest books to sell are the large "coffee table" editions about art, photography, transportation (trains, boats, cars, etc.), and sports. I recently purchased a beautiful history of Porsche motor cars at a local thrift shop for $1.00. It sold on eBay for $29.00. I was browsing the closeout table at Barnes & Noble just after Christmas and bought a brand-new, marked-down *History of the Superbowl* for $5.99. The cover price was $29.95, and it sold on eBay for $17.50. I once purchased a set of Ansel Adams photography books at a garage sale for $15.00. I sold them individually on eBay for a total of more than $90.00.

Cookbooks can be excellent sellers. Look for cookbooks by big-name authors such as Julia Child, Rachael Ray, Emeril Lagasse, and Bobby Flay, as well as classics like *The Joy of Cooking* and *The Saucier's Apprentice*.

Children's books are great sellers, if they are in very good condition. Any pop-up book is highly sought after. Children's pop-up books can be found for a buck or so at garage sales and will sell on eBay for prices up to $50 if they are in excellent condition and collectible. If you are selling low-cost books, such as cookbooks or children's books, group them into sets of three to five books each, so you are not running a lot of small, individual auctions and so you save on listing fees.

Another great category is old law and medical books, especially anything pre-1950s. It is amazing how many of these turn up at garage sales. Some of them, such as an early edition of *Black's Law Dictionary*, can go for huge amounts of money on eBay.

Finally, look for books on fine woodworking, as well as woodworking magazines. And while I recommend that you stay away from general "how-to-fix-anything" books, books that contain plans for building objects tend to sell readily.

Stay away from book club editions and series books, such as the Time-Life books, unless you have a complete set in perfect condition. I once found the complete Time-Life Photography series at a used bookstore for $65. I sold it on eBay for $122—less than I hoped to get, but still a nice profit.

Only buy books in good condition, preferably with intact dust jackets. Never pay more than 30 percent of what you think the item will sell for, and no more than 25 percent of the cover price. You can find plenty of books at garage sales for less than $2 that will sell on eBay for $10 or more. Stay away from books that would sell for less than $10; otherwise, you will have to sell dozens of books every week to make a decent income.

A great way to find books to sell is to place a small classified ad in your local paper like the following:

> Local dealer will pay top dollar
> for nonfiction books in good
> condition. Call Kathy, 666-555-1111

CLOSEOUT MERCHANDISE

Closeout merchandise is new merchandise that a retailer couldn't sell, or surplus goods left over at the end of a season. You can make good money selling closeout goods, but beware of some pitfalls in this area. We will cover buying closeout merchandise in great detail in chapter 6. In the meantime, the following surplus items sell well on eBay and are worth considering if you want to go this route.

Clothing

Name-brand surplus clothing is readily available from a number of wholesale dealers. The key words in the last sentence are *name-brand*. Non-name-brand clothing may sell on eBay, but it will not bring the prices you need to make a profit. We will show you how to find unlimited supplies of name-brand clothing in chapter 6.

Surplus Electronics

As noted earlier, it is both difficult and expensive to source *new* consumer electronics to sell. However, you can find tons of *surplus* electronics—goods that stores couldn't sell and must now unload to clear shelf space for new models—and these are strong sellers on eBay. Make sure you are buying surplus goods and not *returns*—products customers brought back because they didn't work or there was some other problem with them. For ideas on how to acquire this merchandise, see chapter 6.

Remanufactured Electronics and Consumer Goods

Manufacturers of almost all types of expensive electronic and mechanical merchandise offer "remanufactured" or "refurbished" goods. These run the gamut from computers and digital cameras to stereo and television equipment and home appliances.

Remanufactured equipment and merchandise are typically goods that were returned by consumers and, although not used, could not be sold as new because the package had been opened or some of the items had been assembled. In some cases, refurbished items are warranty returns. Typically, the manufacturers run these items through their normal quality-control process and repackage them. These goods are almost always offered with a full warranty. In the case of subsequent warranty returns, the items are repaired and once again run through the quality-control process.

Some large manufacturers, such as Sony, actually have outlet stores where they sell this merchandise directly to the public. For example, I once bought a Sony digital camera at the company's outlet store in Dallas at one-third the cost of retail. I used it for almost a year and then sold it on eBay for almost double what I had paid for it. You can shop Sony's outlet online at www.sonystyle.com (click *Sony Outlet Store* from the homepage). You can also find a list of Sony's bricks-and-mortar outlet stores on the same Web site.

These remanufactured goods can be great items to sell on eBay. How do you find them? The best way is to visit the manufacturer's Web site and see if there is a link to an outlet for these goods. If not, then e-mail the manufacturer and ask how and where the company sells its refurbished items. As a last resort, you can call the company and ask for the purchasing department; a representative will usually tell you how you can access these products. In chapter 6, we will discuss specific Web-based closeout dealers offering remanufactured goods.

COLLECTIBLES

There are all kinds of collectibles you can sell on eBay. Almost anything you can think of is collected by someone. Did you know, for example, that people collect and pay big money for old eyeglasses? "Great—where do I find old eyeglasses?" you may ask. You will probably never see them at a garage sale. However, if the people putting on the sale are over age fifty or are wearing eyeglasses, try asking them if they have any old eyeglasses, or even old sunglasses, lying around the house. You will be amazed how many people will come up with them. Antique or vintage eyeglasses, both prescription and nonprescription, sell on eBay in the $25 to $200 range.

The same is true of many more collectibles. Everyone knows that The Beatles and Elvis memorabilia are highly collectible. The trick is to find the lesser-known items that most people don't think of. I have a friend who sells nothing but old fishing equipment and lures on eBay. He brings in more than $2,000 a month. That doesn't sound like much money, but he usually gets a 500 percent to 1,500 percent markup. He can buy an old fishing reel at a garage sale for $5 and sell it on eBay for $75. Other sellers do the same thing with vintage stereo equipment, old computers and cameras, old golf clubs and tennis rackets, and so on. You just need to do the research to see what is selling.

EBAY MOTORS

eBay Motors is a huge marketplace. More vehicles are sold on eBay Motors than on all the other automobile-sale Web sites combined. For example, according to eBay, a Ford Mustang sells every seventeen minutes. Selling cars may be problematic, because most states have regulations that prohibit you from selling more than three or four cars a year unless you have a dealer's license. But most states exempt vehicles under 3,000 or 4,000 pounds from that requirement. This covers motorcycles, motor scooters, Airstream trailers, pop-up camper trailers, boat trailers, car engines and parts, and all types of automotive accessories and after-market products.

The husband of the manager at my local Starbucks has developed a great business buying old cars, breaking them up, and selling the parts on eBay. For a few hundred dollars, he can buy an old Plymouth from the 1950s or 1960s that's in such bad shape it can't be profitably restored, and make several thousand dollars by selling everything from the brake pads to the window winders on eBay. A single piece of interior hardware can be worth $50 to $100 to someone who is trying to restore an original car. A friend of mine had a British Triumph TR7, one of the worst British cars ever made. He fully restored it and drove it for about a year and then tried to sell it. He had over $3,000 invested in the car and couldn't even get an offer of $2,000 for it. He ended up selling it for parts on eBay and made over $4,500.

Another prolific eBay seller scours the countryside for old Airstream trailers. If he finds one in good condition, he does some simple cosmetic repairs and can usually make 50 to 100 percent on his investment. If the trailer is in poor condition, he breaks it up and sells the parts, again always doubling his money.

One of the largest PowerSellers on eBay is a young man who started his business while he was a junior in high school using his dad's eBay account. He started selling race car seats that he got at a good discount from his local auto parts store. By the time he was a senior in high school, he was importing after-market car seats and performance parts from Asia and grossing over $20,000 a month on eBay. Today, he is a Platinum PowerSeller, someone who averages minimum sales of $25,000 to $150,000 a month on eBay.

CONSIGNMENT SELLING

When you sell something on consignment, you are selling an item for someone else as a service. This is the perfect eBay business. You do not need to purchase any inventory, so there is no risk involved (except for the small amount you must pay in eBay listing fees). Someone gives you something to sell. You photograph the item, write a description of the piece, and put it up for sale on eBay. If it sells, you earn a commission—sometimes as high as 40 percent. Since the buyer pays for the shipping, whatever commission you collect is pure profit. If it doesn't sell, you simply return it to the consignor and you are out only a couple of dollars for eBay listing fees. In fact, many consignment sellers charge the fees to the buyer so they are not out anything except the time it took to research the price and list the item.

eBay actually has program for consignment sellers called Trading Assistant. If you become a registered Trading Assistant, eBay will list you in its directory and will help you promote your business in your local community with flyers, letters, business cards, and a co-op advertising program. These materials are available from eBay as Microsoft

Word downloads. Simply enter your personal information (name, phone number, and so forth) and have them printed at a local print store. To attract customers (consignors), distribute your business cards to appropriate contacts and post the flyers on any free community bulletin board.

How much can you make as a Trading Assistant? When I was working on the manuscript for the first edition of this book, I got a call from someone who saw my name in the eBay Trading Assistant directory. He was trying to sell a vintage Indian motorcycle. I went to his house and took the photos, launched an auction that night, and within two days a buyer in San José, California, hit the *Buy It Now* button and bought the motorcycle for $13,500. My commission was 10 percent for about one hour's work.

We are going to cover eBay consignment selling in chapter 27 in great detail. But before you get too excited, this is a skill that takes some experience. You will want to have successfully completed at least a couple hundred listings before embarking on consignment selling. (Don't worry, I am going to show you how to do that within a month or two.) Although getting a consignment business up and running may take longer than three weeks, it's important to understand how this technique works from the outset. If you decide that you're interested in consignment selling, you'll want to work this strategy into the overall business plan you will develop as you read this book.

The Business & Industrial Category

Take a look at the Business & Industrial category on eBay. Some of the subcategories are construction equipment, farm equipment, medical equipment and supplies, and restaurant equipment. This is a great area for consignment selling. For example, you can contact doctors and hospitals looking to sell their used equipment, building contractors who are replacing tools and gear, and farmers looking to sell their farm equipment for top dollar rather than trading it in to a dealer for rock-bottom value. We will cover more of this in chapter 27 on consignment selling.

Children's Clothes and Toys

One certainty of life is that a child will grow out of clothes, shoes, and age-specific toys very quickly. Parents are always searching for ways to save some money, and buying these items on eBay does exactly that. This is a huge market, but it also provides a never-ending supply of items for you as a consignment seller too. Many parents simply do not have the time to list the clothes their children have grown out of. You will always see tons of kids' clothes at garage sales for this reason. Look on Craigslist and other local classified sites too. If someone posts about having hundreds of pieces of clothes, it might well be worth a look. Only buy name-brand clothes in excellent condition and check very carefully for stains and damage. You can take four shirts and a couple of pair of pants and put them together in a "lot" listing for sale. Now you've taken items you paid maybe 50 cents each for and you've created a lot that can sell for $15 to $20 or more, depending on the brand. There are small and large lots of children's clothes selling on eBay for very good money.

I know one lady who shops at Gymboree in their clearance section. She always uses Gymbucks that she has saved up from items she bought for her own daughter and buys these brand-new items for a fraction of retail. Gymboree is a very hot seller on eBay, but other brands are popular too. A word to the wise though—never include shoes in a lot with clothes. Every child is different; you may lose a potential buyer if the outfit is the right size but the shoes won't fit. A better option is to run two listings and make a note in the item description about the companion item that is also for sale and that shipping can be combined for both (or even better, that you will ship the second item for free).

Children's toys are hot sellers too. You'd be amazed at how well older items sell. Sometimes a parent remembers a toy that an older child adored but it is no longer being manufactured. Or a friend has it and their child played with it during a visit. You can buy used toys on Craigslist or at yard sales, and resell them for good money. You will often need to wipe the toy down before photographing, but that takes only a couple of minutes. A word to the wise—always take C and AA batteries with you when you go to check out toys so you can confirm that any electronics work correctly before buying. You should also stay informed about current recall items. The last thing you want is to buy something from a yard sale that you cannot resell on eBay because it is recalled. You can see the recalls list at http://cpsc.gov/en/Recalls/. This includes all products, but you can select a specific product category if you specialize.

I've mentioned children's books already, but another thought is to sell a "lot" of a particular series or character. Dora the Explorer, Clifford the Big Red Dog, Tinkerbell and Pixie Hollow Fairies, Thomas the Tank Engine, superhero characters, and so on are hugely popular. Look to see what characters are currently popular and sell a set of books about the same character together. Parents like convenience. If they can get a set of six or ten books from one listing they will take that over bidding or purchasing from individual listings.

In this chapter, I have touched on only a few of the categories of items that sell on eBay. As part of your research, I suggest that you spend a couple of hours surfing the various eBay categories and the many subcategories of products available on the site. Then look at the auctions in those subcategories to become familiar with all the items and services that sell on eBay. As you do this, you will see myriad possibilities and opportunities for areas to specialize in. In chapter 4, we are going to show you how to use eBay's powerful search engine to conduct product research.

POWER MOVES

❏ In your notebook, make a list of your hobbies and interests.

❏ Next, brainstorm all possible products that fall into those categories. Don't rule anything out at this point.

❏ After reading the next chapter on product research, search on eBay to determine if there is a market for these products.

CHAPTER 4

✦ PRODUCT RESEARCH ✦

I AM OFTEN ASKED, "What is the secret to making lots of money on eBay?" It's not exactly a secret, but the answer to that question is simple: *selecting the right product to sell*. What makes something the right product? First of all, there must be a market for the product. You have to have something that other people want to buy. Second, you must find a product that you can buy for a price that allows you to make a profit reselling it. Last, the market for the product you're selling cannot be overly saturated. A moderate amount of competition is fine; you can always best your competition. Also, competition usually shows that there is a market for the product—otherwise, other sellers would not be selling it.

In chapter 3, we covered some of the popular selling categories on eBay. Here we'll explore how to dig into these and other categories to find products that are marketable on eBay and can earn you consistent profits as an eBay seller.

TYPES OF SEARCH TOOLS

There are three tools for searching out products on eBay:

* eBay Advanced Search feature
* Terapeak Marketplace Research
* HammerTap research tool

The eBay search engine is very powerful and, best of all, it's free to eBay members. Terapeak sells their service for $29.95 a month (or $275.40 a year, which translates to $22.95 a month) through their Web site, which offers ninety days of trend data and a full year of ended listings data. HammerTap is not integrated on eBay's site, but you can still access ninety days of data through their service. The biggest difference between Terapeak and HammerTap is that Terapeak is Internet-based while HammerTap is a program that you download onto your computer.

Both services give you access to important statistical data, such as a product's average selling price, popular keywords on successful listings, the most profitable listing format, and the best day and time to list a specific item.

THE EBAY SEARCH ENGINE

If you want to know what something is consistently selling for on eBay, you need to search completed listings. Looking at an ongoing auction will only reveal what the current bid is—you want to know what an item actually sold for.

To the right of the search box on the eBay homepage you will see a linked word that says *Advanced*. If you click on this link, you will go to eBay's advanced search page. Here you will be presented with a list of search options, including *Completed listings* (see Figure 4.1). Check this box before beginning your search.

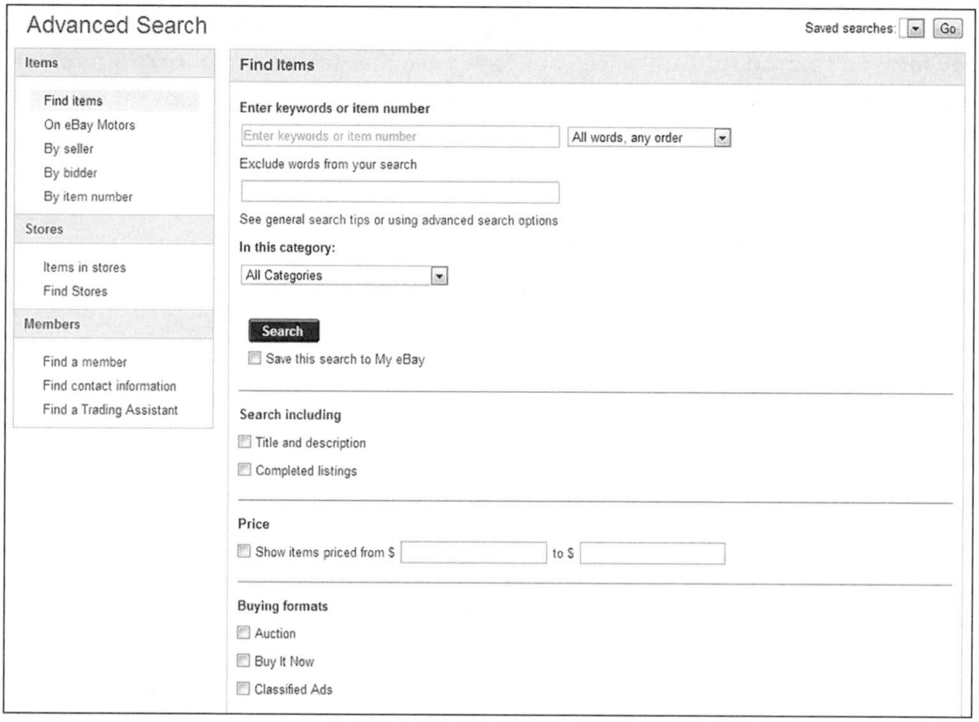

Figure 4.1 eBay Advanced Search Page

Another search check box is *Title and description*. Do not check this box: It will bring up every auction that includes any of your keywords in the description, which could be thousands, depending on your keyword. For example, if you searched for *old fountain pen*, selecting this option would bring up every auction with the word *old* or *fountain* or *pen* anywhere in the title or the description.

At the very bottom of the Advanced Search page you will find a *Sort by* menu (the default will be Best Match). This allows you to sort by *Best Match; Time: ending soonest; Time: newly listed; Price + Shipping: highest first;* and *Price + Shipping: lowest first; Price: highest first;* and *Distance: nearest first.* When I am searching for a product I want to sell on eBay, I usually sort by *Price: highest first.* This identifies the listings that I want to be similar to, so I can look at the time and day the successful high-priced listings started and ended, and other listing details such as keywords used in the title, listing options such as Buy It Now, Best Offer, and so on. Just be aware that any price in red *did not* sell. You want to look at only the listings with green prices on the *Completed listings* results page. If you end up with search results that show active listings, you forgot to check the *Completed listings* box at the top of the advanced search page. Just click back and make sure that it is checked and then perform the search again.

Narrowing Your Search

Since using a single word for your search can return hundreds of thousands of listings, you may want to narrow the search. For example, suppose you are looking specifically for Omega watches, as opposed to just any brand of watch. You can find exactly what you're looking for by simply entering *Omega watch* in the search box. This will return a list of all results with both the words *Omega* and *watch* in them (in any order and with any other words between them), and exclude all that do not contain both words.

To narrow your search even further, look for items that include certain phrases or words that go together in a specific order. For instance, if you are searching for teddy bears, you can use quotation marks: *"teddy bear."* This will return all listings with the words *teddy bear* in them in that order. The word *bear* must immediately follow the word *teddy* with no other words in between or the listing will not come up.

Finding Auctions with Multiple Search Terms

If you wanted to find all listings with one of a selection of words in the title (e.g., *cat* or *kitten*), then you would enter *(cat,kitten)* in the search field. This returns all listings that have either the word *cat* or the word *kitten* in their title. Make sure you type the parentheses and *do not* insert a space between the comma and the two search terms—for example, *(cat,kitten)* not *(cat, kitten)*. You can also include other keyword functions. For example, *(cat,kitten) crystal* will return all items that have *crystal* and either *cat* or *kitten* in the title, thereby narrowing your search to crystal figures of cats or kittens. Note: There is a space between the closed parentheses and the search term outside the parentheses.

Eliminating Words from Your Search

eBay's search engine also locates auctions that include one word in the title but not another. For example, if you are looking for watches, but are not interested in Casio watches, you can use a minus sign in the search field: *watch -Casio*. This will return all results whose listing titles include the word *watch* but exclude the word *Casio*. Note: There is no space between the minus sign and the excluded word.

Spend some time playing with eBay's search feature until you are an accomplished searcher. This talent will put money in your pocket.

If this is a little much for you, immediately to the right of the search box near the top of the Advanced Search page you will see a drop-down menu with options that match each of these examples: *All words, any order; Any words, any order; Exact words, exact order;* and *Exact words, any order.* Use whichever method works easiest for you.

Learning from Listings

Besides discovering what a given product is selling for on eBay, there is much more you can learn from the eBay search feature. If you are about to sell a product you haven't sold before, look at all the listings for that product and related products and analyze them. What could you have done better? Could you improve on their listing titles? How do the descriptions read—could you write a better one? What about the photographs? Did successful auctions have low or high starting prices? Compare two listings for the same or similar products. Which one got the most bids? A little research at this point will pay huge dividends down the road.

TERAPEAK

Terapeak is the most powerful and sophisticated research tool available today. All this power comes at a price: Terapeak charges $24.95 a month. Terapeak breaks its research reporting into four categories:

* Product overview
* Listings
* Trends
* Top Sellers
* International Metrics

Let's use a name-brand item that has been popular over the last few years to look at each report that Terapeak offers: *Pandora Charm.*

Basic Reports

Figure 4.2 shows a seven-day sales report for the keyword phrase *Pandora Charm*. The first page you see is the Product Overview and here you can get a great snapshot of the popularity of the item and the listing options most commonly (and effectively) used by sellers. The most critical information (the average selling price, the starting price, and the sell-through rate) is shown at the top of the page along with the number of listings and the average shipping price. This is a good place to start because you want to know how well the item is selling. The sell-through rate of 64.97 percent is quite good.

Looking farther down the page, you can see more specific details about the listings, sales prices, what day and time of day to list, the most effective duration for the listing, the most commonly used category, the listing type, and even the most commonly used keywords (in this case "authentic" was the number one because this product is a name brand and there are a lot of compatible but not authentic Pandora charms on the market). You will want to make note of the keywords and use as many of the ones that apply to your item as possible.

Look at the Listing Types box. Interestingly, more items were listed as auctions, but the sell-through rate and the average end price were significantly higher for the Fixed Price format. So make sure when you're looking at these details you don't just look at which has the highest number. You need to look at what was most effective. In this case, the average price was over $5 per item higher (which is significant when the price is around $35) and the sell-through rate is over 7 percent higher for Fixed Price over the auction format.

Filters You have the option to apply filters to the results to narrow them down. For example, if you've decided you want to look at only Fixed Price listings, you can click the Show Product Filters button above the Views bar and it will expand this section (see Figure 4.3).

Now you can select Fixed Price. Maybe you want to see how successful Multiple Item Fixed Price listings were, so you could check Multiple Item. You can select international or domestic sites, specific price ranges, etc. For example, if you're selling a charm that retails for $30, you don't want to be including $300 gold beads. They will just skew your results. So you might select an end price range from $15 to $50. One very important filter is the Item Condition filter. You cannot compare the selling price of a new item with a used one. So you should certainly select the condition of your item so you are looking at results comparable with your item.

Figure 4.2 Terapeak Research Report for Pandora Charm

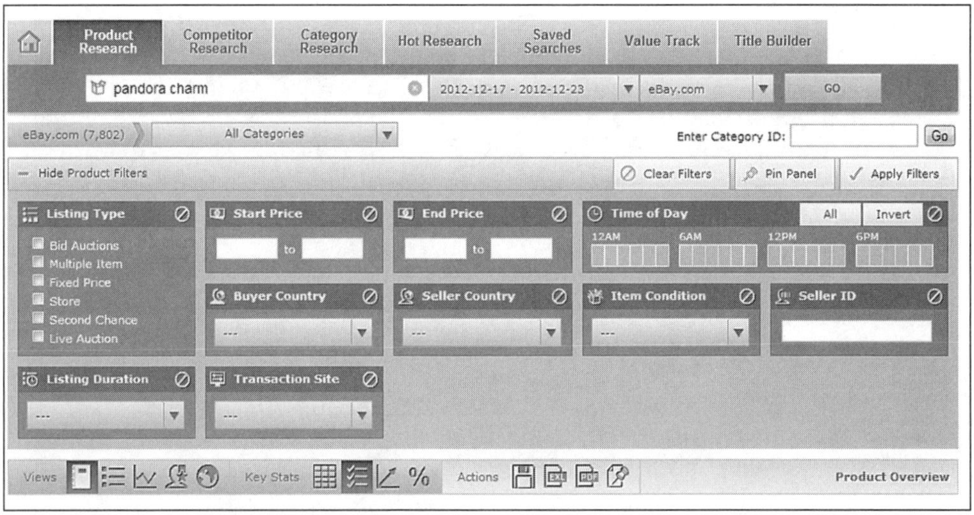

Figure 4.3 Terapeak Report Product Filters

Figure 4.4 shows the results using these filters. As you can see, these are much more specific results. Instead of nearly eight thousand listings, there are just 383. And the sell-through rate is much higher at 80.68 percent, which shows that there is certainly a market for this type and price of item.

I should note here that I am using the generic "Pandora charm" keywords for this search, which could help me see which particular charms by that brand I might want to carry. But if I had a particular charm to sell I would include more specific keywords to make sure my research report matched my item as closely as possible. For example, *silver, dog, anchor, lampwork, murano, purple,* or whatever keywords specifically match your item.

Other Page Views So far we have talked only about the Overview page, but if you look at the bar across the page titled Views you will see multiple icons for different pages. The second one is Product Listings.

Product Listings If you click on the second icon next to View (looks like a three-point bulleted list) you will see actual listings that match your results (it automatically keeps your filter settings) as shown in Figure 4.5. This is a great way to see exactly what the successful listings did within the titles and descriptions. Each listing is a clickable link.

Figure 4.4 Terapeak Results with Filters

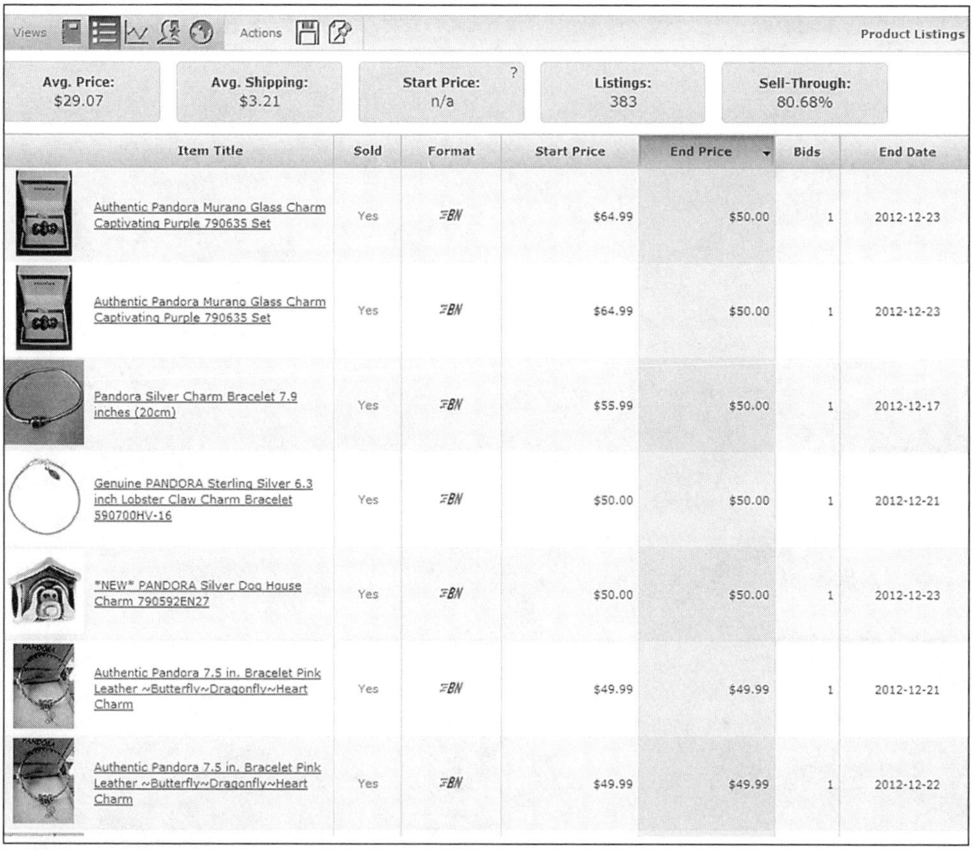

	Item Title	Sold	Format	Start Price	End Price ▾	Bids	End Date
	Authentic Pandora Murano Glass Charm Captivating Purple 790635 Set	Yes	⩵BN	$64.99	$50.00	1	2012-12-23
	Authentic Pandora Murano Glass Charm Captivating Purple 790635 Set	Yes	⩵BN	$64.99	$50.00	1	2012-12-23
	Pandora Silver Charm Bracelet 7.9 inches (20cm)	Yes	⩵BN	$55.99	$50.00	1	2012-12-17
	Genuine PANDORA Sterling Silver 6.3 inch Lobster Claw Charm Bracelet 590700HV-16	Yes	⩵BN	$50.00	$50.00	1	2012-12-21
	"NEW" PANDORA Silver Dog House Charm 790592EN27	Yes	⩵BN	$50.00	$50.00	1	2012-12-23
	Authentic Pandora 7.5 in. Bracelet Pink Leather ~Butterfly~Dragonfly~Heart Charm	Yes	⩵BN	$49.99	$49.99	1	2012-12-21
	Authentic Pandora 7.5 in. Bracelet Pink Leather ~Butterfly~Dragonfly~Heart Charm	Yes	⩵BN	$49.99	$49.99	1	2012-12-22

Avg. Price: $29.07 — Avg. Shipping: $3.21 — Start Price: n/a — Listings: 383 — Sell-Through: 80.68%

Figure 4.5 Terapeak Product Listings Page

The default is shown by the end price with the highest price first. This is a good way to see the successful listings and learn from them, but you can change the sort order by any of the column titles.

Product Trend The third icon (it looks like a graph) takes you to the Product Trend page. This is a graphical representation of the results shown to you on the first page. You can use the Compare drop-down menus to look at various different options. For example, you could look at the trend of Total Sold Listings to Average Price. This is one place where a seven-day report really doesn't help you much. You need to select thirty, forty-five, sixty, or even ninety days to see any kind of trend. Take a look at Figure 4.6 and Figure 4.7. The first graph shows Total Sold Listings to Average Price over seven days. Figure 4.7 shows the same information over a sixty-day period.

Figure 4.6 Seven-Day Product Trend

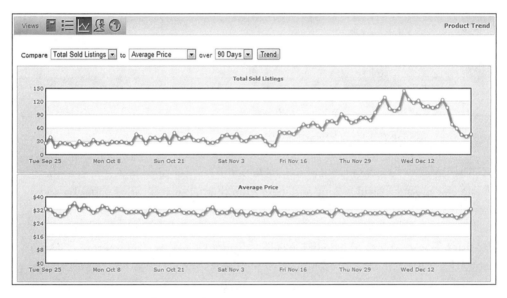

Figure 4.7 Ninety-Day Product Trend

You can see that the price is hovering between $28 and $35 consistently. But the more interesting trend is the total sales. This is the ninety-day period before Christmas so you expect a surge in sales between mid-November and about December 20th.

And that is exactly what is shown on the graph. If we looked at only the seven day sales graph it would look like the market for these charms was on a downturn. But in fact, it is just going back to nonpeak sales. If we looked at the graph for Total Listings it shows the same trend with a spike for the holidays and beginning to regulate back to normal.

Product Top Sellers The next icon on the View bar is the Top Sellers (it looks like a silhouette of a person with a star ribbon next to it). This page shows you your competition. The default (as shown in Figure 4.8) is by Total Sales, but you can select any of the columns to change this. Maybe you want to see who has the best sell-through rate or the highest average price.

Clicking on the seller's ID (in the second column) filters the results to that specific seller and shows you the overview page but all the information relates to sales that make your keywords *and* are also only from this seller. This way you can see what the most successful sellers are doing with their listings.

Rank	Seller ID	Total Sales ▾	Total Listings	Successful Listings	Bids	Items Sold	Average Price	Sell-Through
#1	profiseller-321	$6,191	69	65	208	208	$29.77	94.20%
#2	perfect_city11	$2,482	21	18	75	75	$33.09	85.71%
#3	trak-shuhnstar	$1,393	3	3	74	74	$18.82	100.00%
#4	yueyuelove21	$1,208	17	17	40	40	$30.19	100.00%
#5	plainpaperbox	$1,160	56	33	33	33	$35.15	58.93%
#6	lilyflower921.11	$938	11	11	27	27	$34.74	100.00%
#7	protechtrader	$787	2	2	21	21	$37.47	100.00%
#8	charmingcharlies	$724	10	10	37	37	$19.56	100.00%
#9	marryk25	$703	11	11	19	19	$37.00	100.00%
#10	dollarbabydoll	$691	17	12	20	20	$34.55	70.59%
#11	tazbrown84	$633	4	4	22	22	$28.79	100.00%
#12	fastbuyandwin	$545	8	8	16	16	$34.06	100.00%
#13	beadman8	$432	4	3	11	11	$39.30	75.00%
#14	kyledownes	$406	2	2	25	25	$16.23	100.00%
#15	hotbabe2008	$302	4	4	9	9	$33.56	100.00%
#16	bestdealer4ever	$290	5	5	10	10	$28.97	100.00%
#17	gal	$250	3	3	8	8	$31.19	100.00%
#18	andzela81	$238	6	6	8	8	$29.74	100.00%
#19	chickencooptreasures	$222	5	5	6	6	$37.04	100.00%
#20	gmartin352	$219	6	5	5	5	$43.79	83.33%

Figure 4.8 Top Sellers

Product International If you are interested in selling to buyers overseas (or interested to see how many sellers are outside the United States) this last icon on the Views bar (it looks like a globe) is for you. Figure 4.9 shows the information you can find on this page. Essentially, it breaks down all the metrics for you based on each eBay international site so you can see which are most effective and which you might want to market to specifically (using International Site Visibility, attractive international shipping policies, etc.).

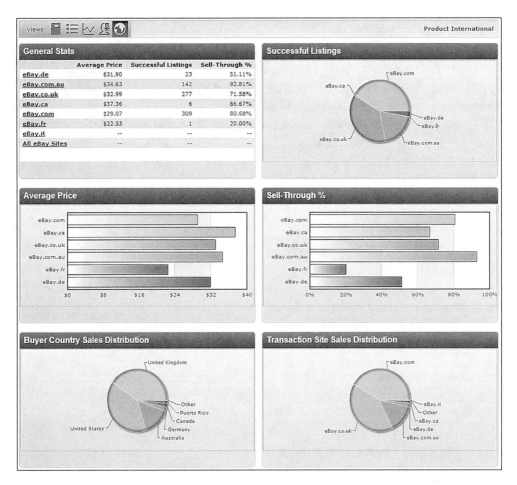

Figure 4.9 International Metrics

The key to using Terapeak effectively is to narrow down the results to as close to identical to your item as possible. Use the same search options as you use in the eBay search engine. The most common one you will use is the minus sign immediately preceding a word. For example, if I were selling a Pandora dog charm I might use the search term *authentic Pandora dog charm -bracelet -gold*. That will exclude any listings that are also selling the bracelet (which would skew the price higher) or in a different material. Not every seller is going to put "silver" in the title, but they will put "gold" if it is a gold charm, so this is a more effective way of seeing the actual competition.

Everything I said about using the Completed Listings search on eBay applies to the Terapeak search engine too (after all, Terapeak is pulling its information directly from the same database as eBay; they just analyze it more in depth and give you more than two weeks' worth of results).

As you narrow down the list of products you want to sell—and discover new products as your business grows—continually return to and verify your research. Here is a quick way to do this: Open a Word document and list the items you want to sell. Now open the Terapeak research page in another window. Copy and paste products from your list of items one at a time into the Terapeak research box and perform a search on each one. Print out the basic report for each item and study it offline.

Once you have your printouts for each product, ask yourself the questions discussed in the next chapter. This research and analysis should help you to make an informed decision about which items would be best for you to sell.

HAMMERTAP

Earlier we also mentioned HammerTap. HammerTap is very similar to Terapeak. They do offer a ten-day free trial, which Terapeak does not, so you may want to try them first to see if you like them.

POWER MOVES

❏ Go to Terapeak (www.terapeak.com) and read the features and benefits. Determine if you would like to sign up and then go through the necessary registration processes.

❏ Review your list of potential products to sell from chapter 3. For each product you are considering, use the eBay advanced search tool—as well as Terapeak, if you have signed up—to determine:

- Marketability

- Average selling price

- Effective promotional features

- The best days and times to list the product for sale

❏ Be sure to keep detailed notes on your research so that you can use this information when you begin listing items for sale.

❏ Based on your research, begin eliminating products from your list that do not appear to have a market, or whose average selling prices are lower than you are looking to charge per item. (You will narrow this list down further in chapter 5.)

✦ WHAT SHOULD YOU SELL? ✦

YOU HAVE NOW GIVEN SOME THOUGHT to products you would like to sell, and you've learned how to research whether a specific product has a market on eBay. The key words in the last sentence are "on eBay." There are plenty of products that might sell well in a specialty store or at your local mall but that cannot get any traction on eBay. This is why it is so important to take the time to research a product thoroughly before committing to purchasing a large quantity of merchandise.

We're about to move on to one of the most important topics in eBay selling: product acquisition (chapter 6). However, in this chapter let's review some final factors to consider before deciding which products and categories are right for you as a seller.

MARKET SIZE

First consider this: *Does the product you are thinking of selling have a viable market on eBay?* This question can best be answered by using the research tools we covered in chapter 4. If you searched for an item and found that only three items of its kind sold in the past month, then it doesn't have a large enough market to sustain a business.

COMPETITION

How much competition is there for the product you want to sell? Competition is a relative term. If thousands of items are selling in a given category, but there are only a handful of sellers, then the competition is low. On the other hand, when we were looking at Pandora charms, we saw that only a few hundred of these items matched our criteria sold each week. It's crucial to examine the number of competitors very closely. A large number of sellers indicates a high level of competition. One clue as to the level of competition is the average price the product is going for. If you are looking to sell an item and you see that the average price for the item is ridiculously low, either there is probably too much supply or there are too many sellers.

PROFIT MARGIN

Can you source (buy) the product at a price where you can make money? We are going to cover how and where to buy products to sell on eBay in chapter 6.

However, in evaluating which products to sell, you need to understand basic pricing and margin strategies. Your *margin* is how much you make before you deduct fees and overheads.

For example, if you are buying a product for $9.00 and selling it for $13.00, it would seem that you are making $4.00 "profit" on each product you sell. But profit is what you have left *after* you deduct all your other costs. Four dollars works out to a 31 percent margin ($4 divided by $13). That may seem fine at first, but remember, eBay listing and selling fees will eat up around $1.50 to $2.00 and PayPal fees will be $0.80 of your margin. That brings your profit down to $1.70 per item (at best), because $4 − ($1.50 + $0.80) = $1.70. At $1.70 per item sold, you have to sell one hundred items a week to make $170.00 profit. That is an awful lot of work for $170.00. If you are selling a $75 item and making a 33 percent profit ($75 x .33), then you are grossing $24.75 on each auction before fees (which run approximately $7 to $7.50 for eBay and $2.60 for PayPal). In the case of the item that sells for $75, you don't have to sell as many to make a decent amount of money. You are clearing around $15 per item profit after fees, because $24.75 − ($7 +$2.60) = $15.15. While there is no set rule for how much of a margin you should be aiming for, always keep in mind the following indisputable fact: The lower your selling price, the greater your margin must be to make a profit. If I am selling an item for less than $25.00, I want my margins to be much higher—closer to the 50 to 75 percent range; therefore, I have to be able to initially buy the item for less.

SELLING USED VERSUS NEW ITEMS

Used or vintage products often have higher profit margins. But the drawback to selling any used or individually purchased product is that you have to photograph and write a description on every item you sell. Whereas if you are selling a brand-new product—for example, you buy a case of identical birdhouses to resell—you can simply create one listing and just keep relaunching it (or have a multiple-quantity listing where you can sell more than one identical item to different buyers from the same listing). Your profit will be lower from selling new items versus used items, but so will your workload. Since time really is money, this is something every seller should consider.

Also, eBay requires you to be very specific about the condition of your item. No longer can you simply specify "new" or "used," so it is more work if your item is not brand new and sourced from the manufacturer, as you have to determine exactly which of the options fits for each item you list. Still, if the margin is right, it can be worth the extra work.

INVENTORY

Do you have a reliable continuing source of supply for your product? If you are selling closeout-type products or buying your products from a range of vendors, your inventory may become depleted and you might not be able to restock. Unless you are selling a broad category of closeout products, such as apparel, where there is always a large supply, you may want to pick a product that you can source from a manufacturer or distributor on a regular basis.

UPSELLING

Does your product lend itself to upselling? An *upsell* (some people call it a *cross-sell*) refers to attaching a second product or a multiple quantity to the first sale. Let's look at bird feeders, for example. When someone buys a bird feeder, he also needs bird food. I could send the winning buyer an e-mail offering free shipping if he also buys a package of bird feed, which I could ship with his order. I would have a fixed-price listing of bird feed with a quantity of a hundred or more, so I would have only one listing fee for the whole thing, then I'm only paying the additional final value fee on the bird feed if he decides to buy it. It is very little extra work to include a bag of feed in the box I'm packaging anyway, and the buyer might come back to me for more feed if he decides he particularly likes that one.

Note: You cannot offer to sell an item to someone outside of an eBay listing. You can get in a lot of trouble with eBay for trying to do that. But upselling complementary items that you have available in other listings is completely acceptable, and is even encouraged by eBay.

Upselling is one of the keys to making huge profits on eBay. Whatever product you decide to sell, make sure there are compatible products that you can upsell to the buyer at the time of sale. We will explain how to do this in detail in chapter 25.

EASE OF SHIPPING

Does this product present any shipping challenges? Shipping costs can be a big turnoff to your buyers. Large or unusually shaped products may require substantial shipping costs. I once had a great source of Australian didgeridoos. They weren't that expensive to ship, but the specialized boxes ended up costing me $11 each. The price I listed on eBay was attractive—until I tried to pass the extra $11 onto the customers.

One way to compete with other sellers of a heavy item, or one that is otherwise expensive to ship, is to offer free shipping and just include the shipping cost in your fixed-price item cost. You will get a boost in the Best Match search results for having free shipping, plus buyers aren't going to be turned off by having a $40 shipping cost. You'd be surprised how many people are willing to pay a higher item price for the promise of free shipping. eBay charges you the final value fee on the total cost of the item including shipping, so there are no fee benefits to breaking the shipping out separately from the item cost.

BIZ BUILDER

Whenever I have a large item to sell, I usually list it on Craigslist (www.craigslist.com), a free classified advertising service partly owned by eBay. My wife recently decided to sell an old electric potting wheel that weighed about a hundred pounds. We put it on Craigslist and the next day there was a woman in my driveway with $400 who took it off our hands.

LONG-TERM VIABILITY

Does your product have legs? The phrase "having legs" refers to staying power. Is this a fad product or does it have either a lasting or an evolving market? Millions of people bought Beanie Babies at the height of the craze and are still stuck with them today. I know one seller who bought the contents of a video rental store that was going out of business. He ended up with thousands of VHS tapes at a time when the rest of the world had moved onto DVDs and Blu-ray.

SIMILARITY TO YOUR OTHER PRODUCTS

Is this a niche product that complements your other products? Does this item fit into your current product niche, or will this represent a new direction for your business? If it's a new category, are there other products you can find to complement it?

If you ask yourself these questions before deciding which products to sell, you will avoid errors that many new sellers make. There is still no foolproof way to select a product. You may find a hot product only to have a competitor come along and undercut you. This is why you should always be looking for new products and product categories. Both eBay and the Internet are highly competitive and fluid. If you are going to run even a small successful business, you must be on the lookout for new products and opportunities all the time.

WEEK 1

POWER MOVES

For each item on your narrowed-down wish list of products, ask yourself the following questions:

- ❏ Is there a sufficient market for this product?
- ❏ How much competition is there for this product?
- ❏ What is the projected profit margin for this product?
- ❏ Is there a continuing, reliable source of supply?
- ❏ Does the product lend itself to upselling?
- ❏ Can this product be packaged and shipped easily?
- ❏ Does the product have a long-term market?

Based on the answers to these questions, eliminate any products from your list that do not appear viable at this time. You should now have a final list of products you would like to sell on eBay. In chapter 6, we will explore ways to source this merchandise quickly and economically.

✦ PRODUCT ACQUISITION ✦

"WHERE CAN I FIND PRODUCTS at wholesale prices to sell on eBay?" is one of the questions most frequently asked by new eBay sellers. Learning how and where to acquire wholesale products can be intimidating. However, it doesn't need to be. Successfully working with wholesalers is mostly a matter of learning their jargon and how the market works, as well as finding wholesale companies that will agree to work with small businesses.

In this chapter, we are going to learn just what *wholesale* means; in addition, we'll discuss the different types of wholesale suppliers, how to locate wholesale sources that will work with you, and how to deal with these suppliers once you are ready to buy. We will also introduce you to specialized terminology of the wholesale world and some of the more common paperwork and forms used by wholesale suppliers.

DEFINITION OF *WHOLESALE*

First of all, you need to understand exactly what *wholesale* means. The term *wholesale* is a very fluid concept that loosely refers to the discounted amount at which you buy an item to resell at a (hopefully) higher price. Unfortunately, there is no such thing as a standard wholesale price or percentage. If I buy a pair of antique silver candlesticks at a local auction for $190 and sell them on eBay for $230, then $190 was my wholesale price. That is not a very large margin, but I did buy for less than I sold it for, so my purchase price could be considered a wholesale price.

To better understand wholesale pricing, it helps to understand the different types of pricing used by resellers.

* **RETAIL PRICE:** Retail stores have very high expenses that include employees, rent, utilities, and inventory carrying costs. Most retail stores need to have a 100 percent markup on merchandise to make a profit over time. Therefore, retailers consider a wholesale price to be 50 percent (or less) of the suggested retail price (e.g., an item purchased for $100 wholesale would be resold at retail for $200).

* **QUICK-SALE PRICE:** The quick-sale price is the price bargain-hunters are looking for. You find these prices in wholesale clubs like Costco and Sam's Club, at outlet malls, and on the sale tables in retail stores. Because people go to eBay to find a bargain, the quick-sale price is often comparable to the eBay price.

* **DISTRESS PRICE:** Manufacturers, distributors, and retail store owners cannot afford to sit on nonperforming inventory; such items tie up their cash and monopolize shelf space needed for newer products that will sell for higher prices. Once merchandise reaches this point, it is often sold to closeout or surplus dealers and ends up in dollar stores, flea markets, and on eBay. Distress prices can be as low as ten cents on the retail dollar, or half (or better) off the original wholesale price.

Retail stores typically buy from distributors, although some buy direct from manufacturers. When a retail store owner buys merchandise, he is looking to *keystone* the pricing, or set his retail price at twice what he pays for the item. So if you are negotiating with a wholesale distributor, she might say something like this: "Here are the retail prices. We give you the keystone discount on your first one hundred items and an additional 10 percent if you pay cash." If the retail price was $10.00, your price would be $5.00 each in quantities up to one hundred, and an additional 10 percent off the wholesale price ($5.00 minus 10 percent [$0.50], for a final per-piece cost to you of $4.50) if you paid cash as opposed to getting thirty-day credit terms, where you pay your invoice within thirty days of delivery.

TYPES OF WHOLESALERS

There are several types of wholesalers, and we will explain shortly how to find these sources of merchandise. But first you need to understand who you are dealing with.

Importers

Importers may be large or small. A large importer generally sells in very large quantities, such as container loads or quantities of 5,000 to 10,000 at a time. There are, however, many small importers who buy large quantities and break them down into smaller lots. These importers may sell by the case or by the dozen, or may require a minimum-dollar order, such as $500.

Look in your local Yellow Pages under *Importers*. If you live in a small town or in the middle of the country, get a Yellow Pages directory from any large port city—such as New York, Philadelphia, Baltimore, San Francisco, Seattle, or Los Angeles—where you'll find a higher concentration of importers. You can use www.yellowpages.com or www.smartpages.com to locate importers as well.

Web sites like www.alibaba.com and www.globalsources.com link you with exporters from Asia. They are not vetted, though, so buyers beware. Suppliers are rated by the Web site, but do make sure to research a company before buying a large quantity. Global Sources used to have a separate service called Global Sources Direct. This was a service where you could get smaller lots of wholesale items. This service is not available quite as it was, but you are still encouraged to contact the suppliers directly for prices for smaller quantities. So don't be put off if you see a minimum quantity of 1,000 items or more.

Manufacturers

Manufacturers come in all sizes. The largest manufacturers, such as Sony, General Electric, Liz Claiborne, Revlon, and Cuisinart, will rarely deal directly with a reseller or retail outlet unless you are the size of Walmart or Sears. Instead, these manufacturers rely on distributors. There are however, thousands of small and medium-size manufacturers in the United States and overseas that will work directly with resellers. Some of them will even drop-ship to your customers. (We'll discuss drop-shipping in chapter 7.)

BIZ BUILDER

Whenever you buy from a manufacturer, you are as close to the source as you can get. This is always where the best pricing is.

Smaller manufacturers will often work directly with you while others work through manufacturer's representatives, or *manufacturer's reps*. A manufacturer's rep is usually a one- or two-person business that represents both domestic and foreign manufacturers on a commission basis. If you are talking to a large manufacturer or foreign exporter, ask if the company has a manufacturer's rep. This person will often sell goods to you at a lower price and in smaller quantities than a distributor will. Later in this chapter we will show you how to locate and contact both manufacturers and manufacturer's reps.

Distributors

There are two types of distributors—*master distributors* and *general wholesale distributors*. A master distributor is usually a sizable company that distributes for only one or two large manufacturers, or distributes only one product line, such as computers, apparel, furniture, or the like. Typically, a master distributor will not carry competing brands of the same product. For example, a master computer distributor might carry one brand of computers, printers, and monitors.

A general wholesale distributor buys products from various American and foreign manufacturers and resells them to distributors. Some specialize in certain products while others can, and often do, sell virtually anything.

Closeout or Surplus Dealers

Closeout dealers go by several names—closeout, liquidation, surplus, and overstock dealers—but they all do roughly the same thing. These dealers either buy distressed goods outright and resell them or act as consignment dealers for companies seeking to sell distressed merchandise. Remember that distressed merchandise consists of goods and products that a manufacturer, distributor, or retailer needs to get rid of quickly. Because of the subsequent low cost to resellers, surplus or distressed merchandise represents the majority of new items sold on eBay. Buying from closeout dealers is an excellent way to find goods to sell on eBay that will allow you to make a healthy margin.

It is important, however, to understand some of the terms that closeout dealers use. *Surplus*, *overstock*, and *shelf pulls* refer to new merchandise that did not sell. These items will typically still carry the original store price tags. Be very careful that you are not buying *returns*. You want to avoid purchasing an item a customer returned because it was broken, didn't fit, or was the wrong color—or perhaps was an expensive dress someone bought to wear to a party one night and then returned to the store the next day. I generally do not buy returns unless I can physically inspect them, which is rare.

The other category of closeout merchandise to avoid is called *seconds*. These are goods that have some type of manufacturing defect. These can be real bargains if you know what you are getting. However, I recommend holding off on purchasing seconds until you have more buying experience and can acquire and resell this merchandise effectively.

LOCATING WHOLESALE SOURCES

There are two basic ways to find the wholesale sources we've discussed so far:

* **THE INTERNET:** With every year that goes by, more and more companies are listed on the Web.

* **OFFLINE:** It is also very easy to find sources close to you by using traditional methods like the Yellow Pages and business directories and by visiting local wholesale merchandise marts or trade shows in cities near you.

Finding Wholesale Sources on the Web

There are several well-known wholesale search engines where you can perform a search online by product or manufacturer:

* **LIQUIDATION.COM** is one of the largest Web sites designed to help people locate dealers and distributors that sell surplus inventory to small resellers directly. You can search by individual products, such as shirts, cameras, or computers, or by brand name, such as Tommy Hilfiger, Nikon, or Dell. Or you can simply browse the listings that are available. Some are auctions; others are fixed-price listings.

* **GET THAT WHOLESALE** (www.getthatwholesale.com) is another great search engine for locating wholesale sources (Figure 6.1). In addition to offering a search feature, Get That Wholesale can connect you to dozens of major wholesalers who advertise on the site. Many of these advertisers are seeking eBay sellers to work with.

Figure 6.1 Get That Wholesale's Web Site

On the homepage of my Web site (www.skipmcgrath.com) is a link labeled *Wholesale Items.* From here you will see Top Ten Wholesale, a free wholesale search engine optimized for Internet resellers.

❋ **WHOLESALE CENTRAL** (www.wholesalecentral.com; Figure 6.2) lists several hundred wholesale vendors who pay to be hosted on this site.

Figure 6.2 Wholesale Central's Web Site

❋ **CLOSEOUT CENTRAL** (www.closeoutcentral.com; Figure 6.3), Wholesale Central's companion site, hosts dozens of closeout and surplus dealers.

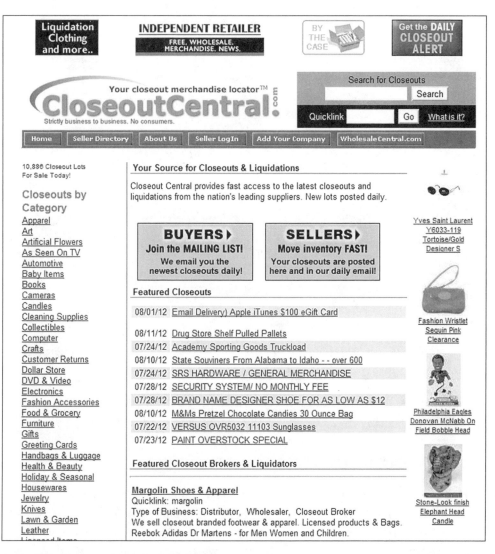

Figure 6.3 Closeout Central's Web Site

✴ **ALIBABA** (www.alibaba.com; Figure 6.4) is a pay-per-click site where manufacturers from China, Taiwan, Korea, and other Asian countries list their products. (The manufacturers pay for each clickthrough to their products or pay a monthly fee to be listed. It does not cost you anything to search this site.)

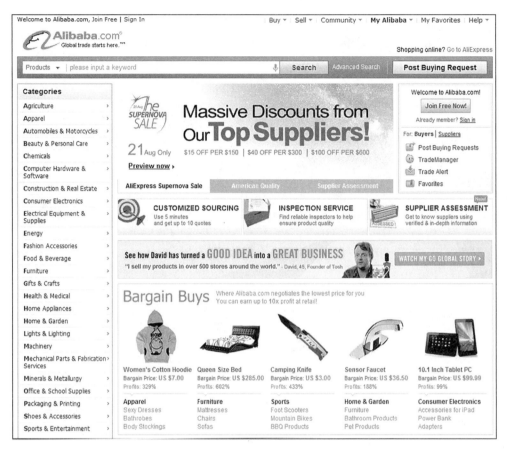

Figure 6.4 Alibaba's Web Site

Alibaba is a very powerful search engine, where you can find thousands of products. Many of the companies sell only in large volume, but if you are patient and keep searching, you can find plenty of sources that will sell in smaller quantities, suitable for the average eBay seller. One word of caution: *Anyone* can list products for sale on Alibaba, and there are many scam artists out there. If you look closely at the Alibaba site, you will see a link to Gold Suppliers. These are certain suppliers from China who pay a fee for more visibility on the site, but in exchange have to agree to an authentication and verification process from a third-party security service provider. They are not "preferred" suppliers, but you do at least know that they are who they say they are and are not a fly-by-night operation. To see the Gold Suppliers, go to http://chinasuppliers.alibaba.com.

✱ **GLOBAL SOURCES** (www.globalsources.com; Figure 6.5) is a large international pay-per-click Web site similar to Alibaba. In fact, you will find many of the same companies listed on both sites. Global Sources has had a close relationship with eBay, so you are more likely to find smaller wholesale quantities available from suppliers on this site.

Figure 6.5 Global Sources' Web Site

Merchandise Marts

Almost every large city in the United States has a *merchandise mart*. A merchandise mart is a building where various wholesalers—including small manufacturers, manufacturers' reps, and distributors—rent showroom space. (If you live in a small town or rural area, you will likely have to go to the nearest large city to locate one, although you can reach some by e-mail, telephone, and fax.)

These venues go by many names; some specialize in one kind of item while others feature all sorts of general merchandise:

* A *merchandise mart* typically showcases a wide variety of products, but most tend toward the low end in price.

* A *gift mart* usually specializes in gifts, collectibles, and small decorator and household pieces.

* A *design center* sells furniture, rugs, lamps, and decorator items.

* *Fashion centers* and *jewelry centers* that specialize in items of personal adornment are found in some cities, including New York, Chicago, and Los Angeles.

Whatever the name and the type of goods they carry, all these markets have one thing in common: They are not open to the general public. When you walk up to the information booth at a merchandise mart or design center, you will often see a sign that reads "Admission to the trade only." The word *trade* refers to retail stores, eBay and Web site sellers, and interior decorators. Depending on the venue, it can be somewhat difficult to gain admission. Some even insist that you own a retail brick-and-mortar store, although this is changing, as more and more companies conduct business on the Web.

You can locate a merchandise mart by doing a Google search for the term you are looking for: *merchandise mart, jewelry mart, design center,* and so on. This will usually bring up a list of markets by city. Just look for the one nearest you. You can often find local results by adding the name of your closest city to the end of the search—for example, *jewelry mart Chicago.*

When you approach the mart to go in, there will usually be a counter where officials are checking to see if you have a badge that was issued in advance, or the qualifications to obtain one onsite. To gain admission to most of these marts, you'll need to show proof of your business status, including a sales tax number, a registered business name, a commercial checking account, business cards, or company letterhead. If you followed our advice in chapter 1, you should have all of these. After the person at the front desk examines these, he will issue you a badge that you must wear while you are inside.

Once you gain entry, a whole new world of wholesale products opens up to you. Merchandise marts, gift marts, and wholesale trade shows (which we discuss next) are the best places to find new merchandise to sell. You will find dozens, even hundreds, of products that you will not come across on a Web search. Each dealer has a showroom that is much like a retail store, displaying all her products. Unlike what you can do in a retail store, however, you can't walk out with the items. When you enter each showroom, ask for a catalog and price sheet. As you walk around the room, you can refer to the prices for any items you see.

Most dealers at merchandise marts have minimum-order requirements. Sometimes it will be a case or a dozen units; sometimes it will be a certain dollar amount, such as $250 or $500. Unless the dealers are selling expensive merchandise like jewelry, the minimums will rarely be more than $500.

When you decide what you want to buy, return to the front desk and fill out an order form. You can pay by check or sometimes by credit card. Once you place a few orders with the same dealer, he will usually ship on credit.

Wholesale Trade Shows

Trade shows are just like merchandise marts, only larger. Trade shows move around the country, and there are different shows at various times of the year. Here in Seattle, where I live, the Seattle Gift Show is held every January and August. (If you go to the Web site for this book, www.skipmcgrath.com/3_weeks, you can find links I have posted to sites where you can find trade shows nearest your community.) Certain cities, such as Las Vegas, Los Angeles, Chicago, Dallas, Atlanta, and New York City, host dozens of specialized trade shows virtually year-round.

Getting into a trade show is much like gaining admission to a merchandise mart. The first time you register, the managers will want to see your business license or sales tax certificate, your business card, commercial checkbook, and so on. In many cities, once you register at the local merchandise mart, your name will be given to trade show companies coming into town and you will automatically receive tickets in the mail.

You shop at a trade show the same way you do at a merchandise mart. Browse the merchandise and place an order when you see something you like. The goods will usually be delivered within a week or so, unless you are seeing samples of products that are not yet available. For example, shows that run from July to October will often showcase merchandise the vendor plans to release in time for Christmas. Although you might place an order in August, the goods might not be shipped until early November.

When this happens, you will be asked for a small deposit with your order, and you must pay the balance before it is shipped.

Trade shows are an excellent way to see the newest merchandise on the market. When the Texas Hold'em poker fad was just getting started, I found a dealer selling complete Texas Hold'em poker kits, consisting of chips, cards, instructions, and the table covers you see in the casinos. I purchased a couple of cases and sold them quickly on eBay before everyone else jumped on the fad. They were so hot I was actually getting 50 percent over retail. Within a few months, everybody had them and the prices had fallen to 20 percent below retail. You could still make money at that price, but not nearly as much as when it was a new item.

Other Ways to Find Wholesalers

The final way to find local wholesale sources is through your local phone book or an online service such as Yellow Pages (www.yellowpages.com). The products will usually be broken down by category. For example, if you looked up *cameras*, you would see listings for *cameras, accessories*; *cameras, repair*; *cameras, retail*; and so on. Typically, at the end of each product listing, you will see an entry for *cameras, wholesale* or *cameras, wholesale distributor*. This is true for almost any product you can find in the Yellow Pages. If you live in a large city, there is often a special directory for the business community called the Commercial Directory or sometimes the B2B Yellow Pages.

Wholesale on eBay

The final place to find products to sell on eBay is on eBay itself. Almost every category on eBay has a subcategory called *Wholesale Lots*. Here you'll find companies (usually overstock companies) selling wholesale lots to the highest bidder. Make sure the seller has a good feedback rating, that the company is located in the United States (goods from overseas are often knockoffs, and it can be difficult to get your money back from an overseas vendor), and that you get a thorough and accurate description of the products being sold.

I once bought a pallet load of 7 for All Mankind jeans and made a ton of money reselling them individually on eBay. But then a few weeks later I bought a shipment of Burberry golf caps that turned out to be fake. I did eventually get my money back, but it was a lot of trouble and I was still out the return shipping.

A final piece of advice: Don't be an impulse buyer. Whether you are shopping on eBay, on a wholesale Web site, or through a merchandise mart or trade show, take the time to do some basic research to make sure there is a market for the product you are considering before placing a bid or an order.

POWER MOVES

- ❏ Once you select a product or product category that interests you, visit the various search engines mentioned in this chapter and run product searches to locate suppliers.

- ❏ Make a list of potential suppliers and begin contacting them to see if they work with small accounts. If so, ask about pricing and minimum-order requirements.

- ❏ If you live in a city with a merchandise mart or design center, visit it and register for admission.

- ❏ Call the convention bureau in your city (or the nearest large city) and find out if and when any wholesale trade shows are coming to town.

- ❏ Register to attend them.

CHAPTER 7

✦ WINNING WITH ✦ DROP-SHIPPING

DROP-SHIPPING IS AN INTERESTING and potentially profitable business concept. In the drop-shipping business model, you locate a wholesale vendor who will agree to ship his products directly to your customers. In the models we've discussed so far, you purchase an item, have it delivered to you, and then resell it on eBay. With drop-shipping, you first list the item on eBay at a price that is higher than the drop shipper's wholesale price. Once you make a sale and collect the payment, you then send a payment for just the wholesale cost to the drop shipper, who in turn ships the item directly to your customer.

The advantage of this business model is obvious. You do not have to risk any money buying products until the merchandise actually sells and you receive payment, and you don't need space to store inventory. Theoretically, if you found a vendor with hundreds of products to sell, you could list hundreds of items on eBay and each time an auction closed with a winner simply collect the money and send the payment and shipping instructions to the drop shipper. At first blush it sounds easy—a sort of unstoppable money machine. It can work, and it does work for many people. But like many things in life, it is not as simple as it sounds.

EBAY DROP-SHIP SUPPLIERS

If you do a search on Google for the term *drop shipper*, you will get several hundred results. There are dozens of companies that purport to have warehouses full of merchandise you can list on eBay—and then just sit back and collect the money, allowing them to drop-ship for you. When you visit their Web sites, you will usually see a sales pitch to sign up for a membership, although some of the sites offer free memberships if you register with them. The problems arise when you start examining the merchandise and the pricing.

Disadvantages of Drop-Ship Suppliers

True wholesale companies can sell only at low wholesale prices when they sell in bulk. Because their margins are much lower than a retailer's, they have to make a larger average sale to make a profit. Most drop-shipping companies buy from wholesalers and then mark the price up somewhere between wholesale and typical retail. On top of this amount, they will usually charge a special drop-ship fee of anywhere from $2 to $5 per item, plus the shipping charge. When you compare their shipping charges to those of UPS, you will often see that they are making another few dollars on the shipping as well.

Once you determine the final price (including all the special fees), search for the same product on eBay. You will often see the product selling for the same price or even less. This is because other eBay sellers are purchasing the same products from the actual wholesalers and therefore can sell them at much lower prices than you can using a drop shipper.

There are other drawbacks when dealing with a drop shipper, even if you can find items to sell at a profit. The primary one is customer service. Unfortunately, you are at the mercy of the drop-shipping company. If the drop shipper sends out the product late, ships the wrong product, or packs the product poorly and it arrives damaged, you are stuck with an angry customer who may leave you negative feedback. So even if you find a drop shipper with products that allow you to make a profit, you must still manage the relationship very carefully to ensure that the drop shipper is giving your customers the same customer service that you would.

Working with Drop-Ship Suppliers

Does all this mean you cannot make money drop-shipping? No, you certainly can, and many eBay sellers do—including myself. I have tried several of the general online drop shippers without success. The only success I have with drop-shipping is working directly with small manufacturers. Mostly I find these companies at wholesale trade shows. Admittedly it is a bit of work and hit or miss to find them—but they are there; when you find them, it is a really profitable way to work. Currently over 50 percent of my sales on eBay are from three small manufacturers that I work with.

If you can negotiate an exclusive deal with the manufacturer whereby you guarantee not to sell below the price they set, and they promise not to sell to any other eBay sellers, you are in great shape. This is the best way to work with drop shippers, as well as with any manufacturer small enough to be dealt with directly. If you get an exclusive deal, you know you're not going to end up being undercut in the market, and customers will not be shopping around to different sellers for the exact same item.

The fastest-selling and most popular products will be the hardest ones to profit from, because everyone else is selling them, too. The key is to look for those small niche or specialty products that very few people are selling. Instead of trying to sell digital cameras, for example, look for accessories, such as camera cases, batteries, flash cards, tripods, and so on. You will be far more likely to make money if you work around the margins than if you try to compete directly by offering top-brand consumer products.

I don't want to imply that there are no general drop-ship companies from which you can make a profit. It is just that I haven't tried them all, and traditionally this industry has been plagued by upstart companies that don't last very long, as well as by a number of scams.

In addition to general drop-shipping companies, there are also specialty companies that will often drop-ship. Again, the best way to find these are with a Google search— but you want to add the product name to the search term *drop-shipping*. For example, *drop-ship books, drop-ship Christian, drop-ship china, drop-ship art supplies,* etc. This will usually bring up a list of companies that specialize in those products.

DROP-SHIP MANUFACTURERS

You can also find thousands of small- and medium-size manufacturers that will agree to drop-ship goods for you. There are two ways to locate them: You can go through the wholesale section of the Yellow Pages (www.yellowpages.com) and contact the companies to determine if they will drop-ship, or you can pay someone to do this for you.

Worldwide Brands (www.worldwidebrands.com; Figure 7.1), an eBay-certified solutions provider, offers an online membership that costs $299 for life and locates and certifies manufacturers that will drop-ship, as well as genuine wholesalers who will work with online sellers. The listings in its online directory are updated weekly by the staff, who research the manufacturers and actually call them on the phone to confirm that they will drop-ship and to ask if they will work with eBay sellers. Visit the Web site for this book (www.skipmcgrath.com/3_weeks) to find a link to a special offer for Worldwide Brands membership for my readers.

Figure 7.1 Worldwide Brands' Web Site

I have personally used Worldwide Brands and can attest to the quality of the information. In just one hour of working with the directory, I was able to locate three manufacturers that would agree to drop-ship for me. I tried out all three of them. One manufacturer's product just wouldn't sell on eBay; another one sold sporadically (but at a nice profit margin); and the third product, a handmade steel barbecue grill, has been a steady producer of profits. We make about $90 on each one we sell and have sold as many as thirty in a single month. I have since found a line of digital photography lighting systems and accessories that are selling quite well. In this case, the small manufacturer readily agreed to drop-ship and he also gave me a semi-exclusive deal, so I would not face too much competition.

I am not going to kid you: Setting up these relationships can take a lot of research, testing, and hard work. But if you can make it work, drop-shipping really can be a money machine. Keep in mind, however, that in the long run you're much more likely to be successful with drop-shipping if you specialize.

POWER MOVES

❑ If you are interested in drop shipping, sign up with Wholesale Marketer for a three-week free trial, offered to readers of this book at www.skipmcgrath.com/3_weeks. Find products that interest you and then see what they are selling for on eBay, using the Completed Listings search option.

❑ Use the Wholesaler sections of the Yellow Pages to find manufacturers of products that interest you. Contact the manufacturers and ask if they will drop-ship for you.

❑ As you explore Wholesale Marketer and other potential drop shippers, maintain a list of products they offer that you believe you can sell for a profit. Once you are ready to begin selling, come back to this list and try listing a few of these items.

❑ Once you begin working with drop shippers, evaluate each one in terms of competitive pricing, reliability of delivery, customer satisfaction, and ease of dealing with returns and other customer service issues.

CHAPTER 8

✦ TYPES OF AUCTIONS ✦

WHEN EBAY FIRST STARTED, there was only one type of auction. All auctions ran for a specified period and ended at a specified time. The highest bidder at the last possible moment was the winner.

Now eBay offers several listing formats, as well as a Buy It Now add-on for auctions and strictly fixed-price listings. Before you begin to sell, it is important for you to understand all the different formats available to you—and to familiarize yourself with the unique advantages and disadvantages of each one. Most sellers use several formats, depending on what they are selling. For example, if you are selling a high-priced antique or collectible, you may want to use a Reserve Price Auction (RPA). Alternatively, if you purchased a wholesale lot of inexpensive toys just before Christmas, there are advantages to using a Multiple Quantity Fixed-Price listing. In this chapter, we'll explore each of the selling formats in detail.

AUCTION-STYLE LISTINGS

A typical auction-style listing works this way:

- ✳ The seller offers one or more items and sets a starting price.
- ✳ Buyers visit the listing and bid on the item during the auction's duration.
- ✳ When the auction ends, the high bidder buys the item from the seller for the high bid.

eBay uses a system of *proxy bidding*. Let's say a seller started an item at $1.00 and it's now been bid up to $9.00. eBay sets the minimum incremental bid at fifty cents ($0.50) for items priced between $5.00 and $25.00. Now assume that you are a bidder and you decide you would be willing to pay as high as $14.50 for the item being offered. You enter a bid of $14.50 and hit the button that says *Place Bid*. eBay now adds $0.50 to the current bid of $9.00, and displays the item's price as $9.50. No one else knows the top value of your bid—others can see only the current bid. Now another bidder comes along and bids $10.00. The bid price rises to $10.50 (her bid plus a $0.50 incremental bid from you), and she gets an immediate message that she has been outbid. If no one else bids, you will win the item for $10.50. As long as no one bids more than your $14.50 maximum, you will still win the item.

If someone bids more than your maximum, you will receive an automated e-mail from eBay that you have been outbid. You can let it go, or you can go back in and place a higher bid if you still want the item at a higher price.

Reserve-Price Auctions

Some auctions have a reserve price—a hidden minimum price—for the item. This is used to allow a seller to start an item at a low price that is sure to attract attention yet protect him from selling it at too low a price to make any money. A few points to keep in mind when it comes to Reserve-Price Auctions:

* Buyers are not shown the reserve price, only that the reserve has not been met.
* The seller is not obligated to sell the item if the reserve price is not met.
* The winning bidder must have the highest bid *and* meet or exceed the reserve price.

When you're bidding in a Reserve-Price Auction, bid as usual, entering the maximum amount you're willing to pay for the item. Watch the label beneath the current price to see whether the reserve price has been met. Until you see that the reserve price has been met, there have been no successful bids in the auction. Once the reserve has been met, the item will sell to the highest bidder when the auction closes. The *Reserve not met* label disappears once the reserve is met, and future bidders will have no knowledge that it was ever a Reserve-Price Auction.

If your maximum bid is the first to meet or exceed the reserve price, the bid displayed will automatically be raised to the reserve price. If your maximum bid doesn't meet the reserve, it will display the maximum amount you bid but the *Reserve not met* tag will remain until either you bid again and exceed the reserve or another bidder does so.

Second-Chance Offer

If you list an auction for an item and the bidding goes much higher than you expected, you may wish you could sell to all the other nonwinning bidders too. You can. If you have more of exactly the same item, you can send a second-chance offer to any of the nonwinning bidders to offer to sell the item to them for their highest bid. So let's say the winning bid was $120.00, but the next highest bidder was $119.00 and the one below that was $104.00. The person who bid $120 wins the item as the highest bidder. But you can send a Second-Chance Offer to the bidder at $119.00 and the one at $104.00 and any other bidders whose maximum bid was at a level you are willing to accept for the item. However, here is what you need to remember: They buy the item for the highest price *they bid,* not the highest bid on the auction. So when a Second-Chance Offer is sent to the second bidder, it is offering the item for $119.00. When it is sent to the third bidder, it is for $104.00. Neither bidder is obligated to accept your offer, and you cannot send more simultaneous Second-Chance Offers than you have items available for sale.

You set a duration for the Second-Chance Offer, and if the bidder does nothing, the offer just expires. However, if the bidder chooses to accept it, you will be notified and the bidder can pay immediately through eBay Checkout, as if he or she were the original high bidder. You will be charged a final-value fee for any accepted Second-Chance Offers. However, you do not have a separate listing fee, and you pay nothing to send the offers.

The Second-Chance Offer is a good option if the bidding goes particularly high. I have seen this happen when two bidders just go back and forth in a bidding war for an item that really isn't worth what they're bidding. However, if you get your Second-Chance Offer in immediately after the auction ends, you can hook the losing bidder before she goes looking elsewhere for the item.

BUY IT NOW AND FIXED-PRICE LISTINGS

Buy It Now (BIN) is an option eBay created for people who don't want to wait for an auction to end to purchase an item. The BIN option allows you as the seller to set a price at which you are willing to end an auction immediately and to sell the item to the buyer. One thing you need to know about the BIN option is that it usually disappears once an auction bid is placed. When you choose the Buy It Now option on a traditional auction listing (available for single-quantity items only), your item has two ways to sell:

* If a buyer is willing to meet your Buy It Now price before the first bid comes in, your item sells instantly and your auction ends.

* If a bid comes in first, the Buy It Now option disappears. Then your auction proceeds normally. (In Reserve-Price Auctions, the Buy It Now option disappears after the first bid that meets the reserve. In some categories, the Buy It Now price remains after the first bid.)

The purpose of Buy It Now is to make immediate sales. You set your BIN price at the upper end of what you would like the item to sell for. For example, say you are selling a pair of cowboy boots (yes, these are big sellers on eBay) in an auction with a starting bid of $49, and you hope to get at least $75 for them. You could set your

BIN price at $79 (or even higher). Now, if someone comes along and really wants those boots and doesn't want to take a chance on getting outbid, she simply clicks the BIN button in your auction. The auction ends and she is able to check out with eBay Checkout and pay you immediately.

There is one more option that can be used in conjunction with Buy It Now. This is called Best Offer. If you choose to use this option, a button will display on the listing page beneath the Buy It Now button. The buyer can use this to submit an offer lower than your BIN price, for your consideration. You can accept it, reject it, or send a counteroffer. Most savvy buyers who see the Best Offer option will use it. They know that you're willing to sell the item for less than the BIN or you wouldn't have added the option. You can have your settings auto-reject any offers below a certain threshold so you're not wasting time on lowball offers. If you use Best Offer, you should decide what your minimum "accept" price will be and then adjust your BIN price accordingly. A buyer who sees a BIN price of $50 and is able to "talk you down" to $43 using Best Offer thinks he got a much better deal than if you'd just set the BIN at $43. This can help you get excellent feedback and repeat buyers.

You should note that if you add the Buy It Now option to an auction, you must set the Buy It Now price at least 10 percent higher than the starting price. This is because eBay also has a specific fixed-price format (which we'll cover in a moment) that has different fees.

Fixed-Price Listings

In a *fixed-price listing,* you list an item for a specific price, just like a price you would see on any retail Web site. The buyer doesn't haggle as in Best Offer or bid as in an auction. Either the buyer pays the stated price or he looks for another item.

The great thing about fixed-price listings is that you can list as many identical items as you want for one listing fee. Then you just pay the final value fee to eBay for each item that sells. The duration for fixed-price listings can be longer than it is for auctions too.

For example, suppose you have fifty flashlights that you'd like to sell for $9.99 each. You would list them in a fixed-price listing with a quantity of fifty and a price of $9.99. Buyers could purchase any available quantity of your item at any time, without waiting for an auction to end. Fixed-price listings run for up to thirty days, but can be set to auto-renew if you want. The listing fee for fixed-price listings is the same whether you list one item or one hundred. The entire fee structure for fixed-price listings is different from auction-style listings. We talk about all the fees in chapter 10.

In order to sell with this format, you must:

✳ Verify your PayPal account, as we discussed in chapter 1

✳ Have a feedback rating of ten or above

✳ Sell the item for at least $0.99

SELLING SIMILAR ITEMS

As well as offering identical items at fixed price, you can also use a *multiple-variations listing*, where the items are very similar but not exactly the same. Typically, this is used to sell clothing, jewelry, or other categories of items where size, style, color, etc. may be the only difference among the items.

For example, you bought a lot of twenty pairs of Nike sneakers from a closeout dealer. You have three different styles and five different sizes. If you sold them using an auction-style listing, you would have to list all twenty items separately. However, if you use a multiple-variations fixed-price listing, you could put them all in one listing. You would enter the variations (style, color, size, etc.) and the quantity available in each. The buyer would use drop-down menus to select from the variations you have before he or she purchases the item. This can save you a lot of money because it is just one listing rather than twenty. In addition, just like with a regular fixed-price listing, sales can occur anytime, and they are just deducted from the total quantity of items available with those variations.

Lot Listings

In a *lot listing*, you sell similar items together (a record collection, a lot of same-size clothing, or the like) in one listing to one buyer.

For example, suppose you have fifty baseball cards that you'd like to sell together to one buyer for an average price of $1.99 each. To list the cards as a *lot*, you would first click the *Lot* tab in the *Quantity* section of the Sell Your Item form when you list your item, and enter 1 in the "Number of Lots" box and fifty in the "Number of Items Per Lot" box. You would then set the price at $99.50. The winning bidder will win all fifty cards.

Lots are very popular for children's clothing, because then the buyer pays only one shipping fee for the entire lot, rather than a per-item cost. If you have something low-cost and low-weight, like kids' clothing, lot listings can really improve your sales as a seller, plus it is much less work than having to make separate listings for each item.

PRIVATE AUCTIONS

When a seller creates a private listing, the winning buyer's user ID does not appear in the listing or in the listing's bid history. Only the seller is authorized to view all of the buyers' user IDs associated with that listing. This type of auction is typically used for items of an adult or sexual nature, or for celebrity auctions. Sometimes it's also used for expensive art and antiques, in order to help protect the identity of wealthy bidders. It is also used by sellers who don't want the items they've sold showing up on their Feedback Profile. Usually the screen will display the item title and its selling price beneath the buyer's feedback comment, but in a private listing auction, the screen just says "private."

EBAY STORES

eBay Store subscribers have their own pages where all of their items are listed. They can sort them into categories that then have links on the sidebar, which can include more information about their store, their branding, and so on. eBay Store subscribers have different fees than those of regular sellers, even when they are selling at auction versus fixed-price. I will talk more about eBay Stores in chapter 26, and will explain when it is worth your while to add this subscription, but you do not need it immediately. In fact, you would be wise to avoid it until you have been selling for at least ninety days.

The type of item you sell will determine whether you should sell at fixed price or auction. Also, look at the fees associated with both (we cover this in chapter 10) to determine which will be more profitable. Look at past listings for the same or similar items and you can typically see quite easily which format is more successful.

.... BEST PRACTICES ....

ADULTS ONLY

eBay does not list adult items in the regular section of eBay, and they will not come up in a search unless you log into the category Adults Only (located under the main category Everything Else). When you log into this category, an agreement will come up on the screen asking you to confirm that you are over eighteen years of age, that you will abide by the rules of the community, and that you will not hold eBay responsible for material you purchase in this category. You must have a credit card on file to prove that you are over eighteen to access this category.

POWER MOVES

❏ Spend some time on eBay looking at the various types of auctions. Analyze which types of auctions seem to be most popular/successful for different products.

❏ Think about the products you plan to sell, and which type of listing is right for each one. In your notebook, note which formats your competitors used and which ones appear to have been successful.

❏ If you plan on selling multiple identical items, study various multiple-item listings until you become comfortable with fixed-price listings, multiple-variation fixed-price listings, and lot listings. Make a list of what worked and what failed for other sellers.

CHAPTER 9

✦ LAUNCHING YOUR FIRST AUCTIONS ✦

YOU'VE GONE THROUGH THE PROCESS of bidding and buying on eBay, you've figured out how feedback works, and you've seen how to pay and get paid and how different sellers package and ship their goods. Now it's time to try selling. You are going to learn a lot more about selling techniques in the following chapters, but try launching a few auctions to get your feet wet. Throughout this chapter, I point out that we are going to cover some tasks, such as writing titles, in greater detail later on. You may wonder, "Why don't we do that first?" Here's why: I have found that actually going through the selling process a few times, even if you don't fully understand all the techniques, makes these methods easier to understand when you study them in detail. These first few auctions are like learning to ride a bike with the training wheels on. When you take the training wheels off, you will be glad you had the experience.

FINDING SOMETHING TO SELL

If you've been following my advice, you have researched products to sell and are well on your way to sourcing and/or ordering those items. However, for the purpose of this exercise, walk around your house, look in your garage and attic, and find a few items to sell that you don't need anymore. If you cannot find anything to sell around your house, then stop by a few garage sales this weekend.

Look for old golf clubs, nonfiction books in good condition, and small working appliances such as espresso machines, coffee machines, breadmakers, pasta machines, stand mixers, and so on. Try to find machines that are still in the box and have the instructions with them. These sorts of products are reliable sellers on eBay.

If you have small children, you probably have some clothes that no longer fit them. Assemble the clothes into a set of the same size and gender—for example, two pairs of pants, a jacket, and two shirts in boys' size three; or two dresses, two pairs of pants, and two sweaters in girls' size four. Sets of used children's clothing sell extremely well on eBay, and you can realize far greater profit on eBay than you would at a garage sale. Make certain the clothing is clean and in very good condition. Don't sell clothing with rips, tears, any stains, or excessive wear. Generally, items with big-name brands such as the Children's Place, Gymboree, the Gap, and Old Navy outsell all no-name clothing.

Another good category is used sporting, hunting, camping, and fishing equipment. For now, avoid large items like skis or hockey sticks, which could be difficult to ship.

PREPARING YOUR ITEMS FOR SALE

The next step is to take some digital photos of your items and upload them to your computer's hard drive. Make sure you take sharp, properly exposed photos, and that you shoot the objects without a lot of background clutter. (See chapter 15, on mastering auction photography, if you need some help in this area.)

Whenever you are selling something used, be sure to inspect it carefully and clean it well. Even though people know they are buying a used item, they don't want it to arrive all covered in greasy fingerprints or caked with dust and grime. Remember, they will be leaving feedback for you.

Once you have your items assembled, you need to weigh them and precalculate the postage. eBay has a shipping calculator that is very helpful. Unfortunately, it's not the easiest of tools to find outside of the Sell Your Item listing form. Go to the eBay Site Map (link at the bottom of any eBay page) and click *Shipping Center* under the *Selling Resources* heading in the middle column. The Shipping Center (see Figure 9.1) is a good page to bookmark. Currently, the direct link is http://pages.ebay.com/sellerinformation/shipping/shippingcenter.html, but that can change.

Click on *Shipping Tools* in the *Advanced Shipping* menu on the left side of the Shipping page and click on the *Shipping Calculator* option. You may have to click the same link again on the next page. Now you are finally at the Shipping Calculator. Bookmark this page too, because you will find you use it a lot. Currently the direct link is http://payments.ebay.com/ws/eBayISAPI.dll?EmitSellerShippingCalculator.

Enter the package type, size, and weight and then click *Continue*. Now select a city from the domestic sample rates (see Figure 9.2) that is about halfway across the country from you. I'm in Washington state, so I tend to use Denver or Houston. This will give you a good middle-ground cost estimate for shipping your item.

If a buyer is closer to you, your actual shipping cost could be a little lower. If the buyer lives farther away, it may cost you a little extra. But it does average out over time. Fixed shipping (as opposed to calculated shipping) is much easier for both the buyer and seller to deal with, so let's stick with that for now. Whatever cost you come up with, add 20 percent to cover the cost of your handling, shipping, and packing materials. If the postage comes to $3.90, you would add $0.78 ($3.90 x .20) for a total of $4.68. When you enter your shipping amount into eBay, you might want to round up to $4.70. (We will deal with calculated shipping and other shipping methods, such as UPS, later on.)

Welcome
News
How to Sell
Selling Resources
eBay for Business
Shipping Center
Seller Protection
Shipping Center Home
Shipping News
Shipping Basics
Overview
Order Supplies
Choose Your Service
Use eBay Labels
Beyond Basics
Spotlights
Priority Mail Send it in 2-3 days. LEARN MORE
Freight Resource Center
Shipping Calculator Test it out
Shipping
Shipping made fast and easy
From packing and weighing your item to confirming its delivery, learn how to make shipping as simple as possible.
SHIPPING BASICS
ADVANCED SHIPPING
See how to get started with these helpful resources
Learn about eBay Labels
See how eBay Labels helps make shipping from home easy.
Download the Shipping Made Easy PDF
Did you know?
You can get the latest updates about shipping policies and other related news on the shipping news page.
Go to shipping news

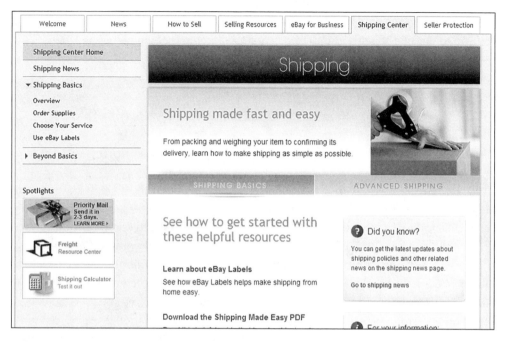

Figure 9.1 eBay Shipping Center

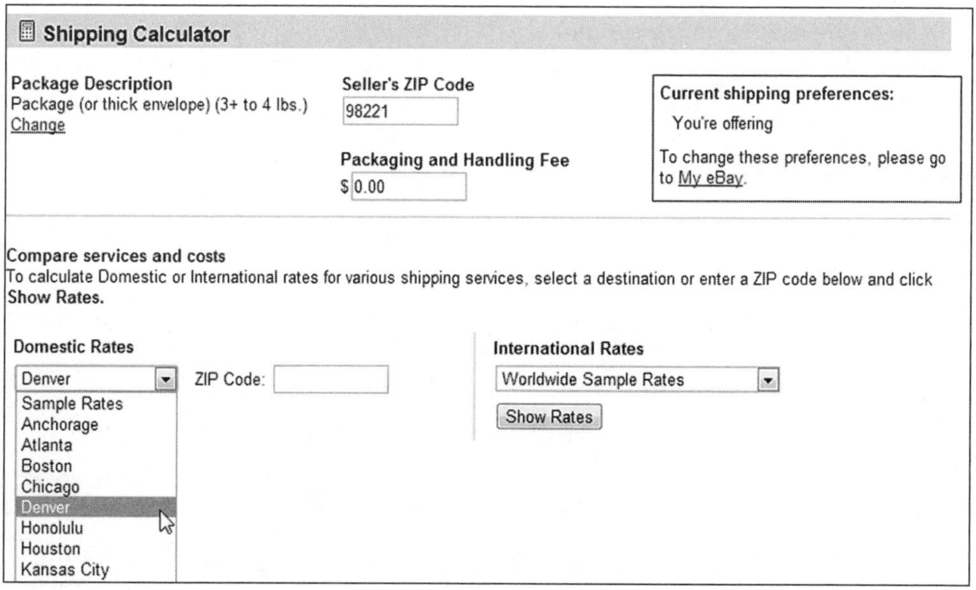

Shipping Calculator
Package Description
Package (or thick envelope) (3+ to 4 lbs.)
Change
Seller's ZIP Code
98221
Packaging and Handling Fee
$ 0.00
Current shipping preferences:
You're offering
To change these preferences, please go to My eBay.
Compare services and costs
To calculate Domestic or International rates for various shipping services, select a destination or enter a ZIP code below and click Show Rates.
Domestic Rates
Denver
ZIP Code:
Sample Rates
Anchorage
Atlanta
Boston
Chicago
Denver
Honolulu
Houston
Kansas City
International Rates
Worldwide Sample Rates
Show Rates

Figure 9.2 eBay Shipping Calculator

LAUNCHING YOUR FIRST AUCTION

Now go to any eBay page and click on the *Sell* tab at the top of the page (see Figure 9.3).

Hi, Skip! | Daily Deals
My eBay
Sell
Community
Customer Support
Cart
ebay
Browse by category
All Categories
Search
Advanced

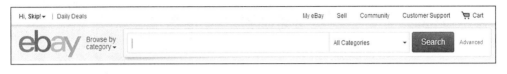

Figure 9.3 Top Menu of eBay Home Page

Step 1: Selecting a Category

eBay will initially present you with the "simple listing tool." If you use this, eBay will select your category for you, and you do not have nearly as much control over it. I personally don't like this. I want to look at the available matching categories and choose which is most appropriate myself, and I recommend you do the same. Click *Switch to advanced tool* on the top right of the page to get to the full version. I always recommend using the options that give you most control, so in this section I'm assuming you are using the advanced tool not the simple listing tool. If you do choose to go the simple route you will see slightly different pages from the ones shown in the following screenshots. That's okay, but understand that you will lose a lot of control and options for your listing and I discourage this for business users.

The first question you are asked using the advanced tool is "What do you want to sell today?" (see Figure 9.4). Here you can enter a UPC or ISBN that identifies your

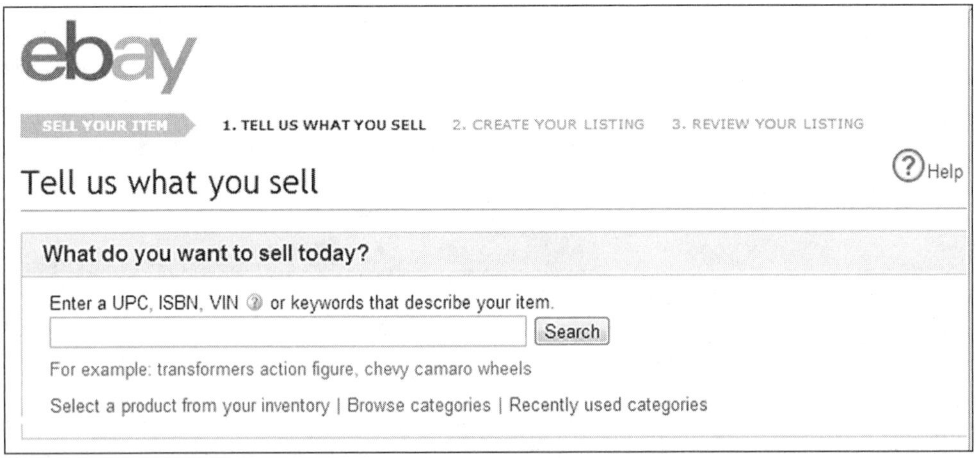

ebay
SELL YOUR ITEM
1. TELL US WHAT YOU SELL
2. CREATE YOUR LISTING
3. REVIEW YOUR LISTING
Help
Tell us what you sell
What do you want to sell today?
Enter a UPC, ISBN, VIN or keywords that describe your item.
Search
For example: transformers action figure, chevy camaro wheels
Select a product from your inventory | Browse categories | Recently used categories

Figure 9.4 Start of eBay's Category Selection Process

item (this is the number at the barcode); alternatively, if your item doesn't have a barcode, you should enter at least three or four keywords that describe your item to help find the right category. In this example, I am going to sell a Starbucks coffee mug that I picked up at the Pike Place market in Seattle. Seattle is the home of Starbucks and the Pike Place Market store is where Starbucks first started. These mugs are highly sought after. I paid $9.95 for this particular mug, which has been discontinued and is no longer sold. So my keywords might be *Starbucks Pike Place Coffee Mug*.

eBay uses the main category as a heading, and then shows you all the matching subcategories beneath it. In Figure 9.5 the three main categories are *Collectibles, Pottery*

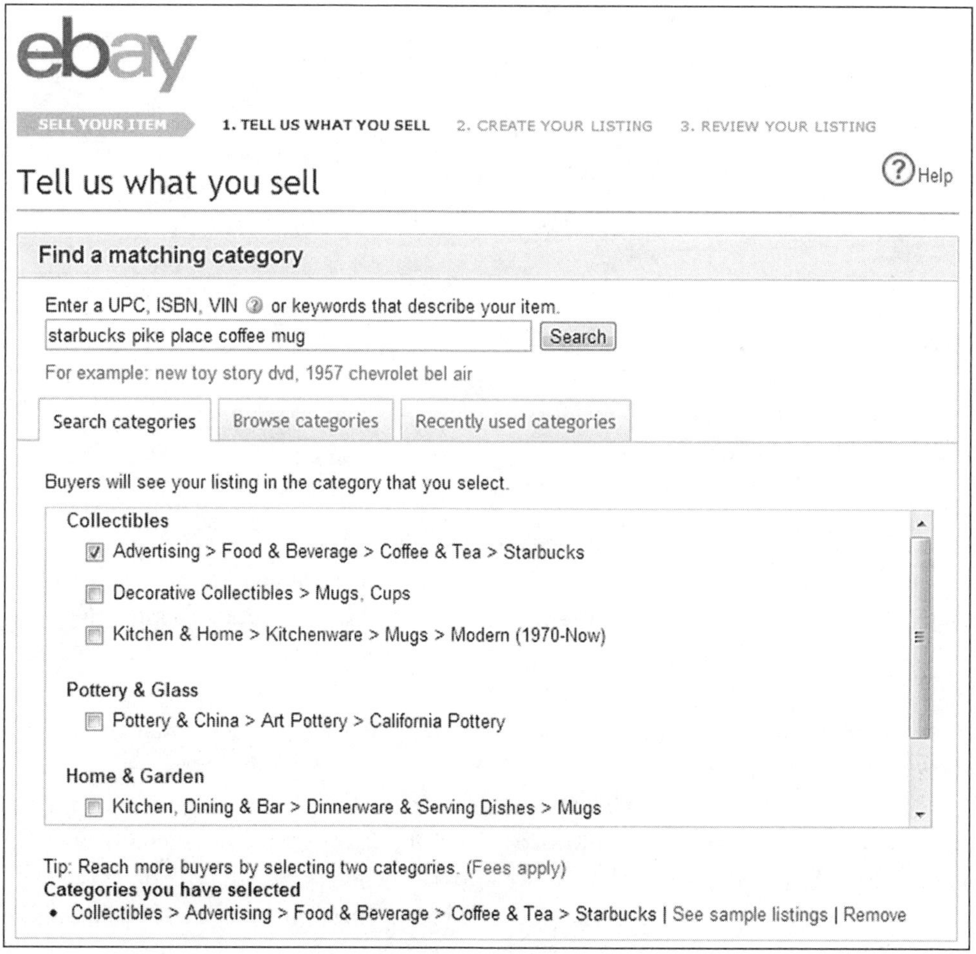

Figure 9.5 eBay Category Selection Page

& Glass, and Home & Garden. Select the category and subcategory that most closely fits the item you are selling (in my example it is pretty obvious since there is a specific subcategory for Starbucks collectibles). Once you select a category, you can use the link at the bottom of the page to See sample listings to make sure you made the right choice.

If you already know the category you want and it's not listed, you can use the Browse Categories tab to select each level of subcategory manually. Figure 9.6 shows how you would get to the same category we selected above but using the Browse Categories tab.

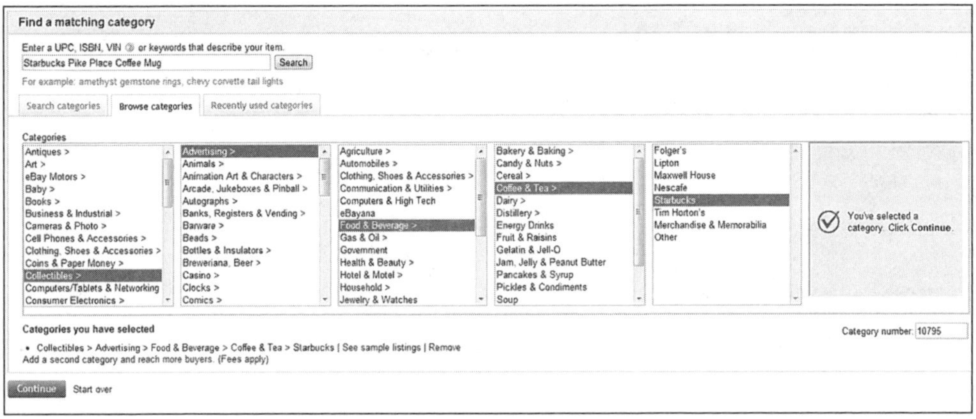

Figure 9.6 Using the Browse Categories Tab: Collectibles > Advertising > Food & Beverage > Coffee& Tea > Starbucks

You will also be given the opportunity to list in two categories. This is a special feature that costs a little extra. There are some situations where you will want to use this option, but let's ignore it for now. (We will cover this feature in detail in chapter 13.)

Step 2: Title, Pictures, and Description

After you hit Continue, you will be directed to the Create Your Listing page, also known as the Sell Your Item form (Figure 9.7).

You have the option of switching to the quick listing tool (Switch to quick listing tool at the top of the page), but I strongly recommend you stick with the advanced version. If you selected the quick listing tool on the category selection page, your option at the top of the page will be switch to advanced tool and you will miss out on a lot of options and control over your listing if you do not use the advanced version. So if you happen to be on the quick listing version at this point, go ahead and switch to advanced.

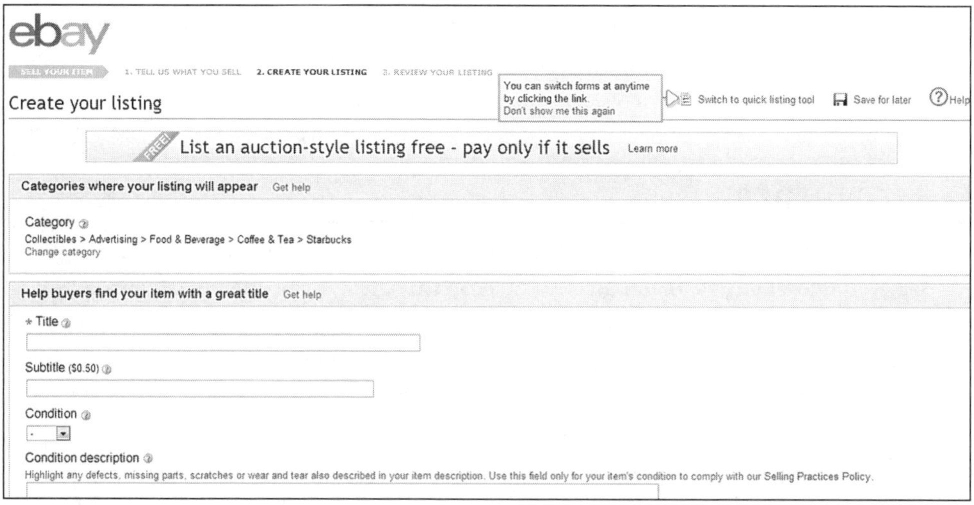

Figure 9.7 The Create Your Listing Page

First, you must write a title for your listing. Writing effective eBay titles is a real art, and one that we are going to spend some time on in detail in chapter 14. But for now, let's just go with a straightforward description: STARBUCKS SEATTLE PIKE PLACE FIRST STORE DISCONTINUED MUG. Write a headline that simply and accurately describes what you are selling. If the product has a brand name, be sure to include it. And keep in mind that you only get eighty characters. Here are some examples:

LOT OF SIZE 6 GIRLS ~ TOMMY HILFIGER ~ CLOTHES inc.
PANTS SHIRT SKIRT DRESS

HAMILTON BEACH 29881
HOME BAKER BREAD MACHINE
IN VERY GOOD CONDITION

BOB REVOLUTION ~ SE SINGLE STROLLER ~ ORANGE —
EXCELLENT CONDITION

PAIR OF BLACK HARLEY DAVIDSON ROAD KING
MOTORCYCLE SADDLEBAGS

COMPLETE SET OF WELL-MAINTAINED
OLD WOODEN WILSON GOLF CLUBS WITH BAG

Punctuation marks, like commas, tildes, and long dashes, may be used in these titles as well. Just remember that punctuation marks count as characters in each title's eighty-character maximum.

BIZ BUILDER

I like to use all caps in my titles, because it helps them to stand out from the other auction listings. Using all caps in eBay titles is not considered "shouting," as it is in Internet parlance. However, adding a few words in lowercase to an otherwise all-caps title can help that information to stand out.

Right below the title box you will see a box that says *Subtitle ($0.50)*. This is another eBay option, and a somewhat expensive one at that. I only use subtitles for very expensive items.

Now that we have our title, your next section is the item condition. First, select from the condition options in the drop-down menu. These will change based on the item type. For example, it may just offer *new* or *used*. In some categories (particularly electronics) you will see other options, including *new other* (typically used for an open-box, but otherwise brand-new item), *manufacturer refurbished, seller refurbished,* and *for parts or not working*. Select whichever option applies and be completely honest here. If you misrepresent the condition of your item you leave yourself open to returns where you pay the shipping and have to refund the full amount, including the shipping cost the buyer originally paid. Be honest, always. That is how you will build a successful eBay business.

If you select a condition other than *new*, you will see the *Condition description* box become available. Here you can give exact specifics about the condition. The information you enter here is displayed at the top of the listing page for your potential buyers to see. It is not a place to enter anything other than notes about the condition. If you're selling a dress with a mark on it, you could say "dime-size mark on bottom left by hem line. See photo." Or if your electronic item has a scratch, say so here. Equally, if you are selling a used item that is in perfect condition, it is entirely appropriate to say "no scratches or dings, flawless exterior condition." Think about what is most appropriate for your item condition that would help the buyer understand the exact condition of the item before they purchase. You do not want returns based on the item not being as described.

The next section is *Item Specifics*. The options vary by the product you select. It is vitally important to complete the Item Specifics, because they are used when buyers narrow down their search results. Also, if a buyer searches a term you didn't put in the title but matches based on your Item Specifics, your listing will still display in his results. Next you need to add your pictures. There are two tabs: Standard and Basic. Stick with the Standard version unless you are having issues with the files uploading. The Basic tab just is a much simpler uploading tool that doesn't give you as many options or as much control over changing the order of the photographs, etc. You don't get a preview of the files either.

Start by clicking on the *Add Pictures* button to enter eBay Picture Services (see Figure 9.8). From here, click on *Browse* to select a photograph from your hard drive. The top picture will become your Gallery thumbnail picture on the Search Results page.

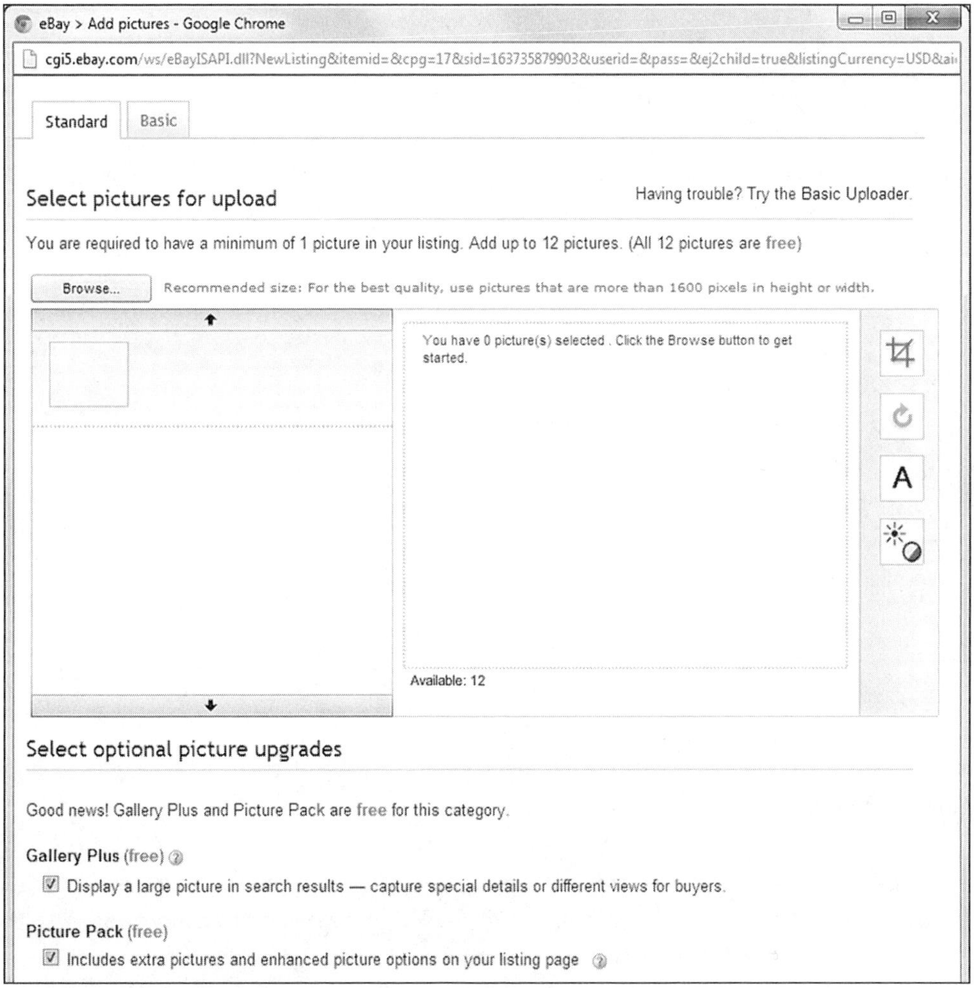

Figure 9.8 eBay Picture Services—Selecting Pictures for Upload

Repeat this process with any other photos you have. I always suggest including at least three or four photos of an item. Although eBay only requires you to have one photograph of the item in your listing, it does not charge for picture hosting so you can use up to twelve pictures at no cost. The more you can show a prospective bidder, the better. Below your photos, you will see *Select optional picture upgrades.* eBay used to charge for these (and for photos), but they are now free, so make sure to check both boxes for *Gallery Plus*, which makes it possible for the buyer to view an enlarged version of your Gallery picture right on the Search Results page, and *Picture Pack,* which includes a supersize and zoom feature that buyers love.

Once you have added your pictures, scroll down the page to the *Describe the item you're selling* box. If you look at Figure 9.9, you will see a box where you enter your text. Above it is a toolbar that looks similar to a Word document toolbar. Here you can select font and type size, as well as special formatting, such as bold, italics, underline, bullets, and numbered lists. This box is an hypertext markup language (HTML) generator: You type in normal text, and it generates the HTML code necessary to present your text as you wish it to appear on the Internet. There is no longer any need for eBay sellers to know HTML in order to change paragraphs, format text, and so on.

Figure 9.9 Item Description Box

Type your description into the box. Use a series of short paragraphs instead of one long one, since that's easier for customers to read. If you have specifications to list, then use the bulleted list or numbered list feature. Although eBay's *Sell Your Item* form has a good HTML editor that works like a Microsoft Word document, I prefer first to create my listing in Word and then to copy and paste the description into the editor.

This way I have a backup, should anything go wrong, as well as a record I can use again in future auctions.

When you're selling a collectible or a used item, your description should contain as many specifics as possible. These might include:

* The year and provenance of the item
* Item size (length, width, height, weight)
* Brand (such as John Deere, Coca-Cola, or Hard Rock)
* Name of series set, special edition, or collection (e.g., Coca-Cola Holiday Collection)
* The condition (new in box, mint, etc.), including possible flaws or scratches
* Material (such as porcelain, wood, or tin)
* Product type (sign, bottle, box, etc.)

So let's take a stab at describing my Starbucks mug.

This is a brand new—never used—Starbucks mug from the first Starbucks store in the world-famous Pike Place Market in Seattle. This is where Starbucks started and the store is still there today. It is one of Seattle's most popular tourist attractions and one of the busiest Starbucks stores in the world.

The mug is four inches high and three inches across and holds 12 ounces. There is a beautiful printed scene of the Pike Place Market printed around the mug with the words *Pike Place Market* and *Starbucks Coffee Co.* printed over the scene. Inside the rim of the mug is the legend: *The Birthplace of Starbucks Coffee.*

This mug is from the Skyline Series, the most collected series of Starbucks mugs since they were introduced in 1995. This mug was introduced in 2002 and discontinued in 2004. This mug is very hard to find and has sold for as much as $75 on eBay.

These mugs do not come up on eBay very often. Don't lose out to a last-minute sniper. Place your best bid now.

Shipping and handling is $6.90 via priority mail to any US destination. Please e-mail me for shipping costs to Canada and overseas.

I accept PayPal or credit/debit cards directly. I guarantee this item to be exactly as described or you can return it for a full refund within fourteen days. I post positive feedback for all buyers as soon as payment is received.

Thank you for looking at my item. Please e-mail me with any questions.

Notice that at the end of the description I specify my shipping cost, payment options, return policy, and feedback terms. The Sell Your Item process provides other opportunities to enter this data, but I always like to place it in the description as well—it helps reduce the number of e-mails I get asking the same basic questions.

Next you'll encounter eBay's *Listing Designer* feature (Figure 9.10). This is a template that can add borders and background art (called a *Theme*) to your listings. I tend not to use this option. Ten cents per listing isn't much, but it adds up. If you want to use one, pick a frame that complements the category where you're selling, or pick a generic one. There are some very garish ones, though, so be careful not to detract from the item you are selling.

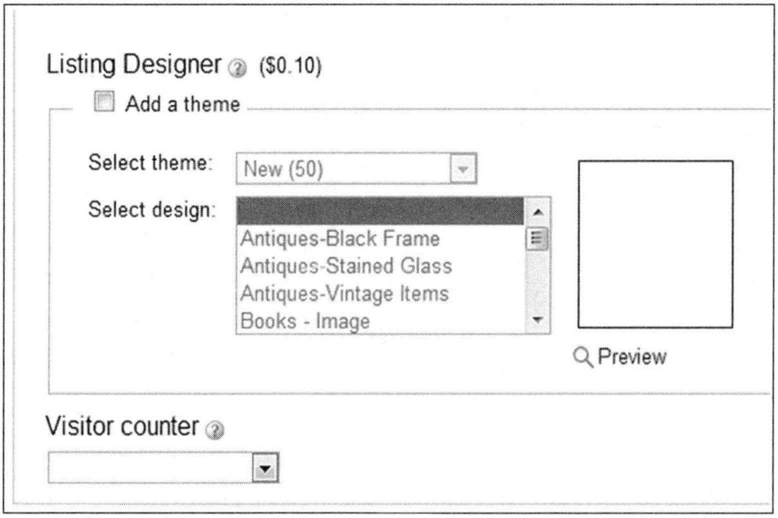

Figure 9.10 eBay Listing Designer Feature

Finally, at the bottom of the section, you can select the design of the visitor counter you want to use, often known as a "hit counter." The hit counter will appear at the bottom of your listing and will show how many unique users have opened your auction. This information is available in My eBay once your item is live. You can see both the number of views and the number of people who added your item to their "watch" list. A hit counter on an auction can be a double-edged sword. If there are many hits but few bids, it might turn off a potential bidder ("Why didn't all the others bid?"); if there are few hits, there isn't the immediate need to place a bid so that the item doesn't get snapped up by someone else. I tend to stick with the information given to me in My eBay, rather than put a hit counter on my listings.

Step 3: Pricing and Item Details

As you scroll down the page you will come to the *Choose how you'd like to sell your item* section. Here you will decide how you will price your item and what listing format you wish to use (Figure 9.11). Enter your starting price. When I was selling a Starbucks mug, I entered $9.99, which is what I paid for the mug. If you are selling a used item, make a low estimate of the value and use that as a starting price. In general, the lower your starting price, the more bids you will attract. Brand-name items usually attract more attention and bids.

If you are selling something obscure that has a high value, you have two options: You can set a low starting price and use a reserve, or you can set the starting price at the minimum you will accept for the item. We are going to cover listing and pricing strategies in great detail in the next chapter, so if you are unsure about what starting price to set, you may want to read ahead a little. Remember, however, that for now you are simply trying to gain some experience—not necessarily make a ton of money. You should be selling relatively low-cost items from your garage or attic. So I would suggest that you just go with a low starting price in hopes of attracting bids. If it doesn't sell, you haven't lost anything, because you haven't used any of the paid upgrades eBay offers during the listing process and your first fifty auction-style listings each month are free (until you upgrade to an eBay Store).

Looking again at Figure 9.11, you'll see that eBay offers two additional options: selecting a Buy It Now price (which we've mentioned before) and donating a portion of your proceeds to charity through eBay Giving Works. You can select a preferred charity to donate at least 10 percent of your proceeds to. This is automatically deducted and sent to the charity when the buyer pays you. There are a few bonuses to donating to charity. First, you get to deduct the amount given as a charitable contribution on your taxes. Second, you get an icon next to your item title on the Search Results page showing potential buyers that a portion of your listing's proceeds go to charity (which can net you the sale over another seller of the same item). Third, eBay gives you a credit for the portion of basic fees that corresponds to the amount you are giving to charity. If you donate 10 percent, you get 10 percent of the fee credited to you. Donate 20 percent and you get 20 percent of the fee credited, and so on.

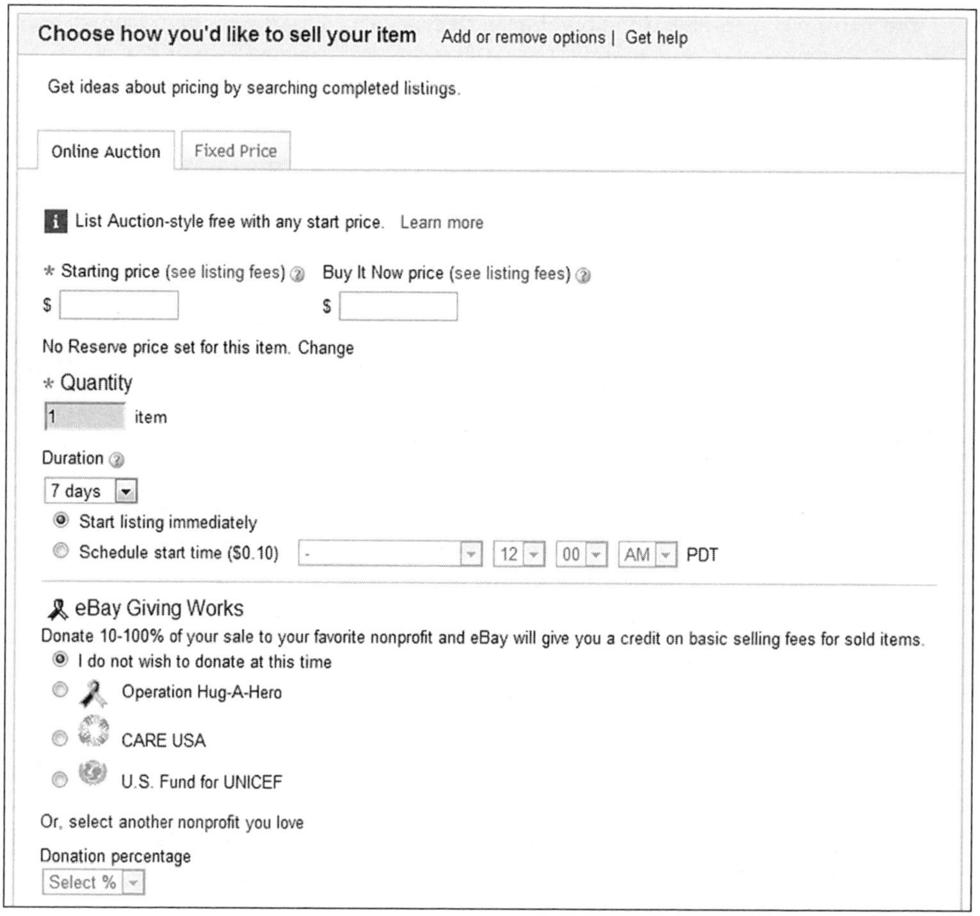

Figure 9.11 Pricing Your Item

Below the starting price is the item quantity. You'll notice the box is grayed out and the quantity is *1*. The only way to change this is to add the option for "lots" (i.e., selling a group of items in one listing to one buyer). To do this, click the *Add or remove options* link at the top of the section and check the box next to *Lots*. Now the grayed-out box becomes *Number of lots* (and it still says *1*) but there is an additional box next to it that says *Items per lot*, and this is where you enter the number of items you are selling within the lot. You don't need to worry about this at all unless you decide to sell in lots.

Next you are asked to set the duration for your auction. A drop-down menu offers several choices: 1, 3, 5, 7, or 10 days. We will use a 7-day auction for this example (which is also the default).

Now you are given the option of starting the listing immediately or scheduling it to start at a later time (called *Scheduled Listing*). Unless you happen to be uploading at the optimal time for your item (we'll talk about this later), I strongly suggest you pay the 10 cents for *Scheduled Listing.* You can select the time and date you want it to start.

Step 4: Payment and Shipping

The next section addresses the payment methods you will accept (see Figure 9.12).

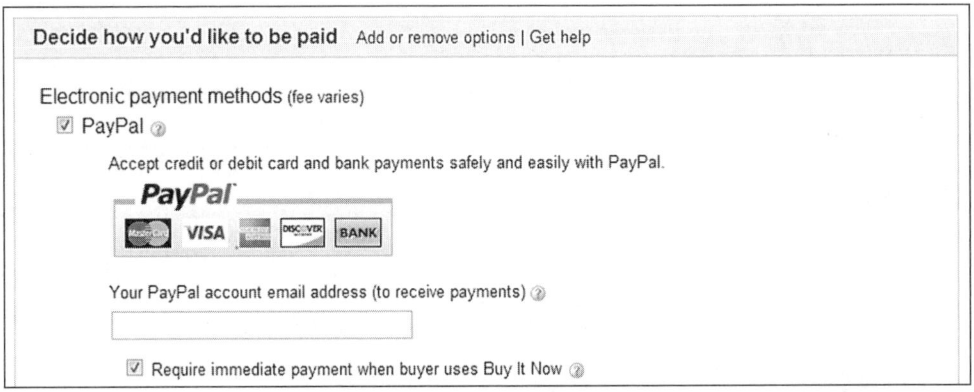

Decide how you'd like to be paid Add or remove options | Get help

Electronic payment methods (fee varies)
☑ PayPal ⊚

Accept credit or debit card and bank payments safely and easily with PayPal.

PayPal
MasterCard VISA   DISCOVER BANK

Your PayPal account email address (to receive payments) ⊚

☑ Require immediate payment when buyer uses Buy It Now ⊚

Figure 9.12 Selecting Payment Methods You Will Accept

All eBay sellers are required to offer PayPal. Your other additional options are ProPay, Skrill, Paymate, or accepting a credit/debit card through your own merchant credit card account. At least 90 percent of buyers will pay via PayPal, either using their account or using their credit/debit card through PayPal's payment processor. You really don't need to worry about the other options. eBay payments are all electronic to help curb fraud issues and also so the buyers will get their items faster (waiting for a check to clear can be frustrating). So checks, money orders, bank-to-bank transfers, Western Union, or MoneyGram, are not allowed on eBay (except for certain categories in eBay Motors and Adults Only, which have their own restrictions).

The next section on the *Sell Your Item Form* is your shipping information (see Figure 9.13). If you want to offer international shipping, you will need to add that to the form. Click on *Add or remove options* next to the section title, then select the checkbox for *Show international services and options*, then click *Save.* Now you will see an international shipping box beneath the US shipping section. There are several issues involved in international shipping, which we will explore later on. For the time being,

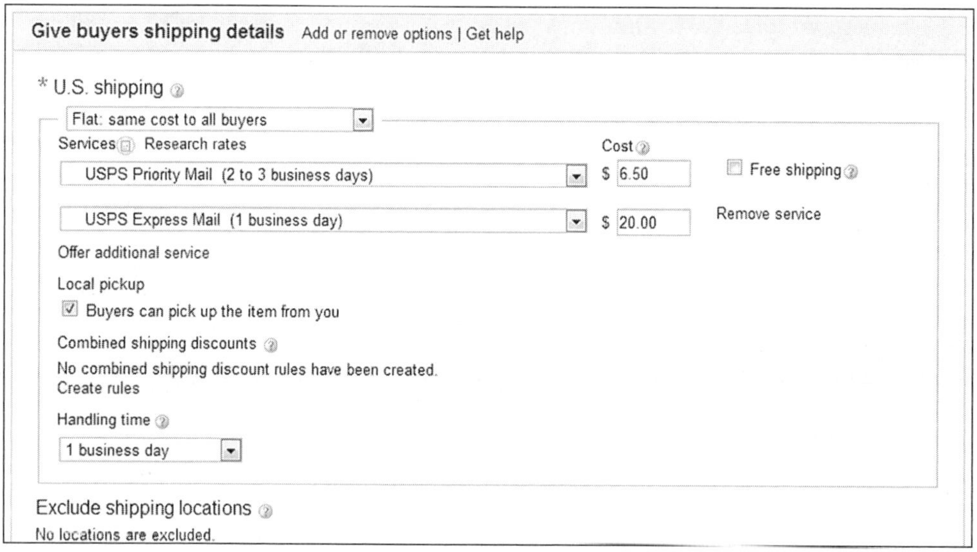

Figure 9.13 Entering Shipping Information

I suggest that you stick to the United States and Canada if you do decide to include international shipping at all.

Using the drop-down menu, you may select either flat-rate or calculated shipping. There are times when I use calculated shipping, but most eBay PowerSellers and Top-Rated Sellers prefer to use flat-rate shipping amounts for reasons of economy and convenience, both for the buyer and the seller. It also means your shipping price shows up on the search results page even if the buyer isn't signed in because it's not based on where the buyer lives. It can be a big bonus if you have good shipping prices in comparison to your competitors. It also makes it easier to create combined shipping rules where you automatically set discounts for multiple purchases from the same buyer and paid on the same invoice.

BIZ BUILDER

If you select *calculated shipping*, eBay inserts a box in your auction where a bidder can enter her zip code and eBay will calculate the shipping cost to her location. If you select *flat-rate shipping*, you set the shipping price and enter that amount into your listing.

Remember the Shipping Calculator I mentioned earlier? The *Research rates* link on the shipping details part of this screen will take you right there. You can select the services through the Shipping Calculator and the shipping rate will be automatically added to your listing. This can be useful, because if you use calculated shipping, you can add a per-transaction handling fee, but the buyer won't see it separated from the actual postage cost.

Use the *Offer additional service* link to add more options. Always put the cheapest shipping method at the top, because this is the one eBay will use on the Search Results page. I've seen many sellers put the fastest (and therefore most expensive) shipping method first, which makes it look to buyers like the seller is gouging on shipping. They never get as far as clicking on the auction to see that there are actually cheaper shipping options.

You can also set up combined shipping rules. You may choose to discount $1.50 from each additional item's shipping cost, or you could go the other way and say it's the full shipping cost of the highest auction and then $2 per additional item. Make sure whatever rules you set mean that your shipping cost is still covered! You can offer combined shipping without setting up rules; just enter your discount and requirements in your description and have buyers contact you directly with what items they are wanting to bid on to get a combined shipping quote. However, I recommend setting up the rules because it makes it easier for the next item you list, and also it means you get fewer e-mails from buyers asking about shipping quotes. If a buyer comes across your auction very close to the end time, you may not see his e-mail with enough time to respond before the auction ends. Most buyers prefer to see the combined shipping discounts on the listing page so that they know the total of what they will be paying before they bid.

Next you must select a handling time from the drop-down menu. This is the amount of time between when the buyer pays you and when you mail the item. If at all possible, choose *one business day*. When we get to looking at detailed seller ratings (DSRs) and how to minimize the negative impact, you will see that if you use one-business-day shipping and upload tracking information to eBay to prove that you shipped within that limit, your DSR for shipping time is automatically five stars (the highest rating). The buyer cannot change it. This is very important, because many buyers consider "shipping time" to be how long it took to get to them, rather than how long it took for you to get the item into the mail. So this easily negates any potential issues from buyers who don't understand this DSR.

Once you have a history of sales through eBay, your listings can qualify for Fast 'N Free promotion from eBay. This promotion adds a logo to your listings to indicate the ones that offer free expedited shipping (such as USPS Priority Mail) and one-business-day handling. Based on the history of your item deliveries in the past, eBay must be confident in estimating that the item will arrive within four days for your listing to display the Fast 'N Free logo to that particular buyer. Some buyers will see it, some will not, based on the history of how long it actually took for your items to reach buyers in the same region as this buyer. Until you have a history of transactions, the logo won't show. It is important to make sure eBay has historical data of your shipping times, so always make sure you upload the tracking number to My eBay if it is not automatically filled in for you.

Next on the shipping information screen you will see the *Exclude shipping locations* area (Figure 9.14). I recommend you exclude countries that have a high record of fraud and, if you are not offering international shipping, exclude all international regions. The advantage of adding an excluded location is that buyers with primary shipping addresses in that country will not even be able to bid on your auction (once you set this in the Buyer Requirements in the next section). Figure 9.14 shows the regional exclusions available. You can use the *Show all countries* link next to a region to exclude only certain countries from that region, if you prefer.

You can also exclude post office (PO) boxes. If you ship exclusively via UPS or FedEx, rather than by the USPS, you cannot ship to a PO box, so make sure to exclude those locations here.

Finally, you are presented with *Item Location*. To be clear, this does *not* say "Seller location." If your items are in a warehouse in Arizona and that is where they ship from, then that is the zip code you enter here. For the most part, it will be your home location, though. eBay requires you to put in the actual zip code rather than the town name. For example, I live about two hours from Seattle. Once upon a time, I could put Seattle as my location. Now it has to be the exact town I live in.

Step 5: Buyer Requirements and Return Policy

Buyer Requirements Buyer Requirements are automated blocks you put in place to prevent buyers with these specific features from bidding on or buying your items. These can be very useful, but are also limiting, so use them wisely. When you click on

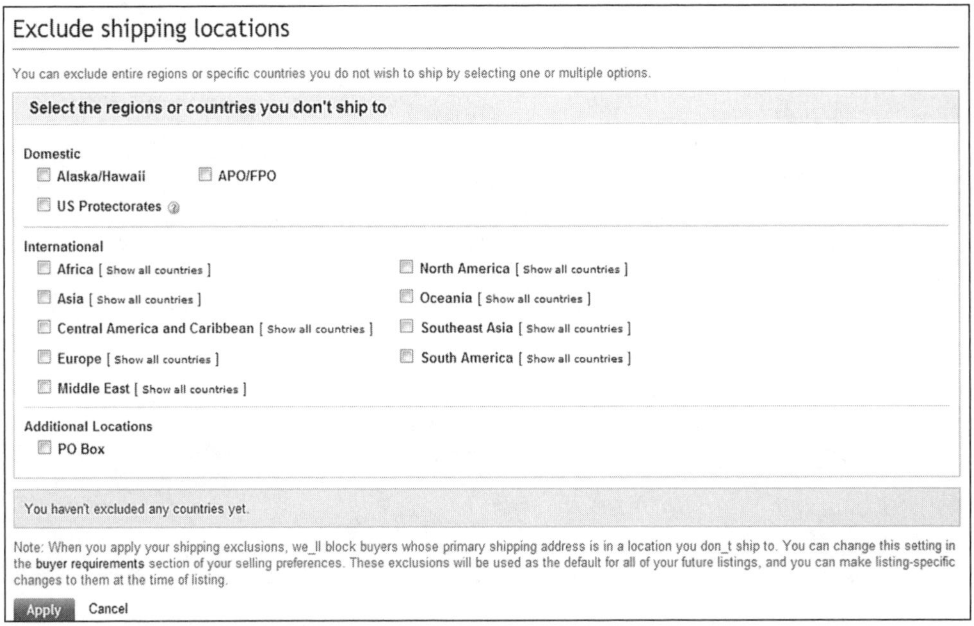

Figure 9.14 Excluding Shipping Locations

Change Buyer Requirements you will see all of the options to set up your rules (see Figure 9.15). These will apply to all of your listings.

Your options are to block buyers who:

* Don't have a PayPal account

* Have received *X* unpaid item case(s) within *X* months (This is when the buyer commits to purchase an item but then doesn't pay and the seller initiates an *unpaid item* claim with eBay and the dispute is ended in the seller's favor.)

* Have a primary shipping address in countries that I don't ship to (This is a very useful option if you don't offer international shipping or specifically don't want to ship to certain countries.)

* Have *X* policy violation reports within *X* months

* Have a feedback score equal to or lower than *X*

* Have bid on or bought my items within the last ten days and met my limit of *X*

Each of these *X*s is a place for you to fill in a number onscreen.

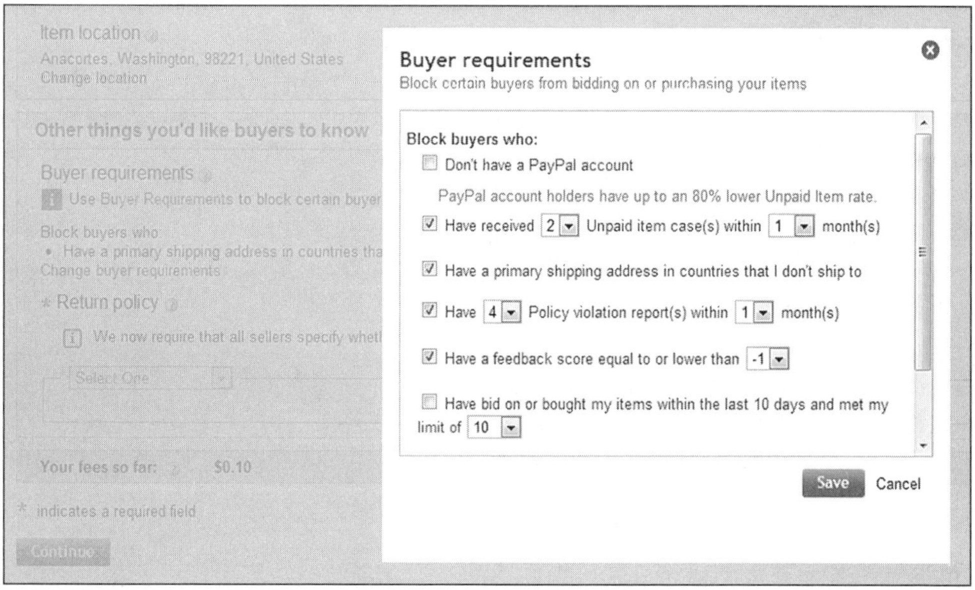

Figure 9.15 Changing Buyer Requirements

You can always exempt a specific buyer from these requirements if you want to. For example, if someone is registered in the United Kingdom, but is visiting family in the United States and wants to buy from you, she may be blocked by your Buyer Requirements because her primary shipping address is in the United Kingdom. However, since she wants you to ship to her family's address in the United States, you could choose to unblock that particular buyer while keeping the Buyer Requirements set for all other buyers. You do this using the *Buyer Block Exemption List* (http://pages.ebay.com/services/buyandsell/biddermanagement.html). It's also a prominent link in the *Selling Activities* section of the eBay Site Map.

Return Policy After your Buyer Requirements comes your Return Policy. You must select either *Returns Accepted* or *Returns Not Accepted* from the drop-down menu (see Figure 9.16). If you indicate that you accept returns, you will then be given extra options so you can select the specifics of your returns policy.

Select the time frame in which returns are accepted, who pays for return shipping, and any other details you want to specify. Once you enter data in these fields, this information will be saved for all future listings. So if you are selling something that will follow a different policy, be sure to change your Standard Return Policy before launching the next auction.

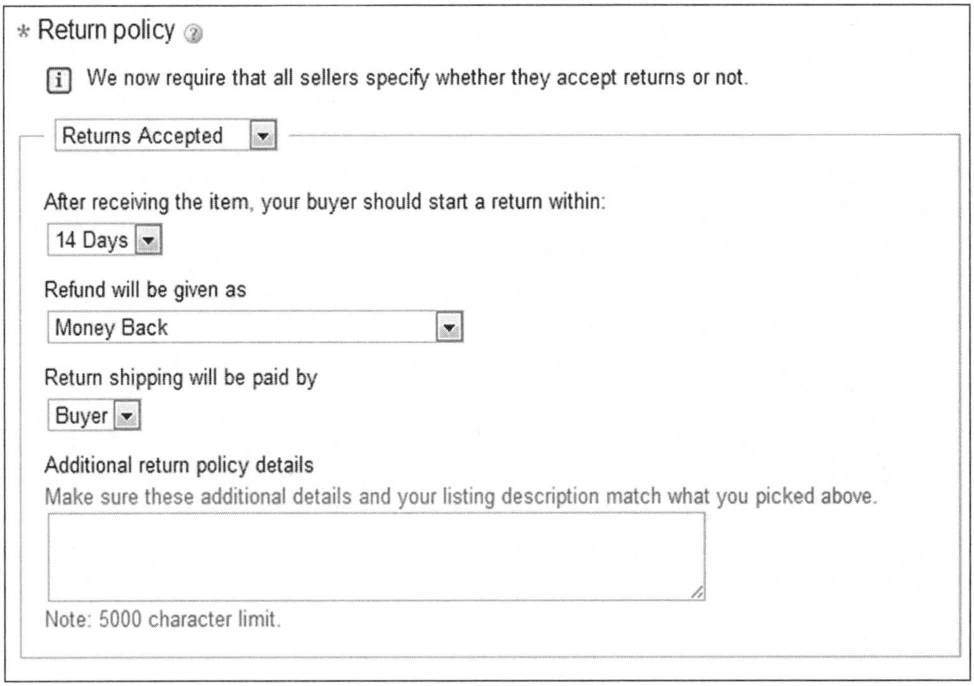

Figure 9.16 Your Return Policy

I always offer a fourteen-day money-back guarantee. This is required for Top-Rated Plus status and also gives you a boost in the Best Match search results. I offer thirty-day returns on some of my products too. But the minimum I offer is fourteen days. I would rather deal with a return than a buyer deciding they're going to find a bogus reason to dispute the transaction with eBay.

Step 6: Promotional Add-ons

Once you click *Continue*, you will go to the final page of the *Sell Your Item* form. Here you are given the opportunity to select eBay promotional options under the heading *Make your listing stand out* (see Figure 9.17).

There are three options regarding the display of your listings: *Gallery Plus,* which enables a buyer to enlarge your thumbnail image on the search results page and actually view the other photos you have uploaded for that listing; *Subtitle,* which we covered earlier (here eBay will try one more time to get you to spend the extra 50 cents to use it); and *Bold,* which we will talk about next.

The Bold add-on costs $2. When you select this option, your listing's title appears in boldface in bidders' search results pages. eBay offers strong statistical evidence that using the Bold feature increases the number of hits a listing receives, the number of bids submitted, and the final price the item commands. If you are auctioning something that is likely to sell for $50 or more, this option will usually pay for itself. If you're anticipating less than that amount, I would not use it.

Next, eBay will show you how your listing will display in the search results (see bottom of Figure 9.17). This is a good time to look at your title and see if it is eye-catching. How does your image look as a thumbnail? If you need to make any changes, click *Edit listing*. *Do not* hit your browser's back button. Depending on your browser, you may lose the information you have already entered on the previous page.

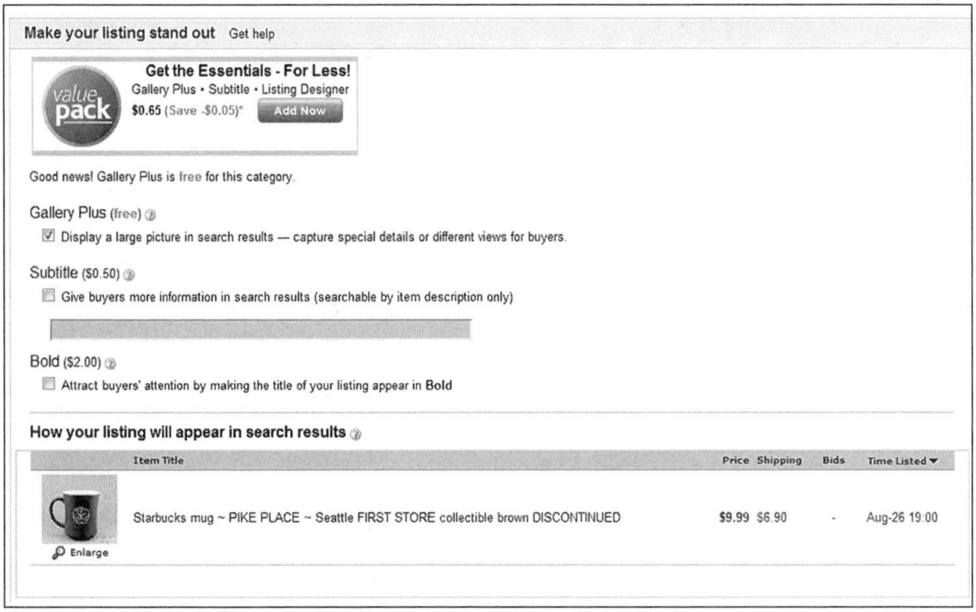

Figure 9.17 Promotional Add-ons and Listing Preview

Below the image of how your listing appears in the results, you will see a section titled *Recommendations for your listing*. Typically, this includes an offer for international shipping, or maybe just shipping to Canada, or for making a portion of your listing a donation to charity, and so on. For the most part, you can ignore these. You should have made your decisions about these details while you were creating your listing, so this shouldn't make any difference to you now.

Step 7: Review and Submit Your Listing

After you have launched dozens of auctions, you will be able to review your listings and fees very quickly.

Be sure to examine the fees eBay will charge you (Figure 9.18). In this auction, my listing fee (insertion fee) came to a whole 10 cents, because it is one of my first fifty auction-style listings of the month. If I were past that point, it would have cost me 35 cents. If you recall, the cost of this mug was $9.95; if I add $0.10 to that, I get my true cost for launching this auction on eBay: $10.05. If the mug sells, there will also be a final value fee of 9 percent that eBay charges, which includes the shipping cost in calculating the final value. (You can read more about fees in chapter 21.) Because I expect this mug to sell for at least $25 (with $6.90 shipping), the final value fee should be somewhere around $2.87 ($25 +$6.90 = $31.90; and $31.90 x .09 = $2.87). My PayPal fee is 2.9 percent of the total amount the buyer pays (including shipping) plus a per-transaction fee of 30 cents, so that fee should be about $1.23 ($31.90 x .029 = $0.93; and $0.93 + $0.30 = $1.23). So my total actual cost for selling this on eBay is $9.95 (item cost) + $0.10 (eBay listing fee) + $2.87 (final value fee) + $1.23 (PayPal fee) = $14.15.

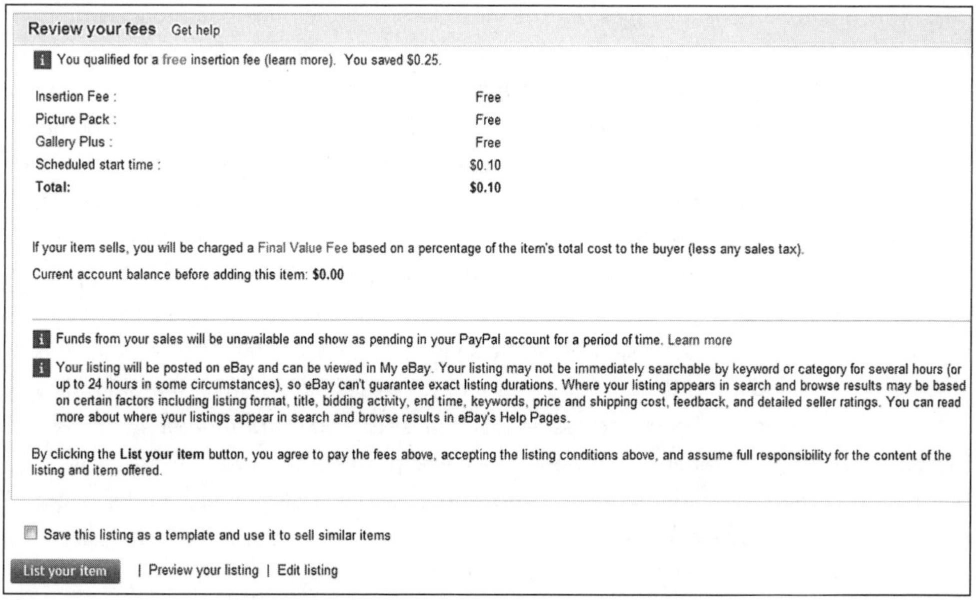

Figure 9.18 Review Your Fees

If the mug sells for $25, my profit will be $10.85. It took about ten minutes to create and launch the auction, and it will take another fifteen minutes or so to communicate with the buyer about payment and to pack and ship the box.

If this were an item you always carried in stock and were selling repeatedly, check the box for *Save this listing as a template and use it to sell similar items* just above the List Your Item button. Now you can use that template to launch identical auctions in less than a minute. In chapter 23, we are going to show you how to use outside services to automate your auctions too.

Click on *Preview your listing* at the bottom of the page (see Figure 9.18) to see how your auction will look. Click *Edit listing* if you notice anything that is wrong. This will take you back to the previous page of the Sell Your Item form without losing the options you've selected on this page.

Once you are satisfied, hit the *List your item* button and give yourself a pat on the back. Now the fun starts.

THE LIFE OF YOUR AUCTION

Don't be surprised if your auction receives few bids—or even no bids at all—the first few days. This is normal. Most auctions see the most activity in their final four hours, with furious bidding in the last few minutes. The advantage of having your auction up for seven days is that a lot of people will have a chance to consider your merchandise. Those who are interested will add the auction to their *watch list*, waiting until the right moment to place their bid. Other sellers use automated programs, called sniping software, which will not place their bids until thirty seconds before the end of the auction. You can track the number of views and watchers from the Active Selling section of My eBay.

Don't be surprised if your used household items bring far more money than you would have expected. If you are selling an old pasta machine at a garage sale, you might have thirty or forty people look at it during the day. On eBay, the keyword *pasta machine* is searched more than 2,000 times a day. I was cleaning out some old boxes in the attic last year and I came across an RCA transistor radio from the early 1970s. I think it cost about $25 when it was new, which was pretty expensive in those days. I put fresh batteries in it and it worked! I know people collect old radios, and I thought I might be able to get $30 or $40 for it on eBay. I placed it on eBay in a seven-day auction. It received over fifty bids and sold for $212!

And the Starbucks Pike Place Mug? I just sold my last one for $78.

POWER MOVES

❏ Locate a few items from your attic or garage that you can use for your first listings. Make sure to clean them so that they're in good shape for selling.

❏ Take some digital photographs of your items. See chapter 15 if you need advice on how to do this effectively.

❏ Determine a price point for your merchandise. Do some research on eBay to determine the average selling price for your products.

❏ Follow the steps outlined in this chapter to launch your first auctions. Take note of any questions that arise regarding headlines, descriptions, pricing, and so forth. We'll cover these topics in greater detail later on in the book.

CHAPTER 10

✦ LISTING AND PRICING STRATEGIES ✦

HERE'S AN INDISPUTABLE FACT about eBay: Low starting prices for auctions attract more bidders. The typical eBay bidder scans the category and search results pages for two things: low prices and items that already have bids. So getting that first bid is all-important, because it drives more traffic—and, therefore, more bids—to your auction. (We'll discuss the reasons why in a moment.) Therefore, where you set your starting bid is a critical decision, fraught with anguish and uncertainty. In this chapter, we'll go over different pricing strategies for different types of listings, as well as the best days and times to begin and end your auctions.

GENERAL PRICING STRATEGIES

The risk in setting your starting bid price too low is that if you don't get many bidders, you may end up giving your treasure away for a song. Conversely, if you set the price too high, you may not attract any bids. Setting the opening bid price is something of a black art. This is a decision that takes some experience and research. If you are selling hot or popular items that routinely attract a lot of bids, it is usually safe to set a low minimum bid. If you are spending money on eBay's optional features to attract attention to your listings (we will cover these features in the next section), it is probably safer to set a low starting price, so that your auction will receive more hits.

The problem arises when you are selling an item that is not well-known or lacks a popular brand name.

Remember: The starting bid is only important to attract those first few bidders. Once the bidding starts, the current bid price will appear next to your title on the search results page. eBay's research shows that a sizable percentage of sellers will scan the search results page, looking for items that already have bids on them. For some reason, buyers feel more secure bidding on an item that has already received at least one bid. In response to this buyer behavior, some unscrupulous sellers will have a friend place a bid on their item (with no intention of buying the item) just to record that first bid. This is a prohibited practice called *shilling* and can get you kicked off eBay permanently.

Many experienced PowerSellers list their items at cost. Their reasoning goes like this: Their cost is lower than the item's value, and therefore will attract bids. At worst, they will recover what they paid for the item and will only lose out on the eBay and PayPal fees.

Other sellers argue that you should set the opening bid at the minimum price you will accept for the item. However, this strategy has a drawback: A smaller percentage of your auctions will actually receive bids. This is okay if you don't have a listing fee and aren't using any of eBay's paid features, but after your first 50 auction-style listings (or if you upgrade to an eBay Store subscription), you will pay an insertion fee per listing. (See chapter 21 for more about insertion fees.) I usually use my cost as the starting price.

RESERVE-PRICE STRATEGIES

We covered the basics of Reserve-Price Auctions (RPAs) in chapter 8. An RPA is an auction-style listing where you start the bidding at a low price but establish a hidden reserve price—the minimum amount for which you are willing to sell the item. eBay charges special fees for RPAs. Table 10.1 presents a summary of these fees.

TABLE 10.1 Reserve-Price Listing Fees

Reserve Price of Listing	Fee
$0.01 to $199.99	$2.00
$200.00 and up	1% of reserve price (up to $50)

I rarely use RPAs for auctions under $50. But I almost always use them when listing an expensive item (over $200) at auction—unless I'm selling an extremely popular product, like an Apple iPod, which is likely to attract many bids and likely to reach the desired price without a reserve.

Reserves are controversial on eBay. If you visit the message boards, you will see plenty of negative comments about them, mostly from buyers who have no experience with selling. While no one keeps official statistics on things like this, there is plenty of anecdotal evidence suggesting that a large percentage of eBay members will not bid on an item with a reserve.

Personally, I have not run up against this kind of resistance in my auctions. In fact, I sell several items in the $200 to $500 price range, and I have actually garnered more sales with reserves—not fewer.

BUY IT NOW PRICING

Buy It Now (BIN) is an eBay feature that allows a bidder to end an auction immediately by purchasing at a fixed BIN price. The BIN price is usually only displayed until the first bid is placed, and then it disappears. On Reserve-Price Auctions, the BIN price is available until the reserve is met. In some categories, the BIN price will remain even past the first bid or after the reserve is met. BIN auctions exist to attract impulse bidders or to capture that one bidder who must have exactly what you are selling and cannot risk losing it to a higher bidder.

You can use the BIN option for free if you are eligible for the free insertion fee for the first fifty auction-style listings per month. Once you exceed those fifty listings (or if you have upgraded your account to include an eBay Store), the fees in Table 10.2 apply.

TABLE 10.2 Buy It Now Fee Schedule

Buy It Now Price	Fee
$0.99 to $9.99	$0.05
$10.00 to $24.99	$0.10
$25.00 to $49.99	$0.20
$50.00 or more	$0.25

If you list a BIN price, avoid starting the auction too low. Otherwise, someone will simply bid a very low price and the BIN option will disappear. One benefit of BIN is that it works to establish a value in a bidder's mind. I like to set my BIN price at slightly above the item's value. If I start an item at $19.99 that I think will sell for $29.00, I usually set the BIN price a little higher, say, at $33.00. eBay requires your BIN price to be at least 10 percent higher than your starting bid.

FIXED-PRICE LISTINGS

Fixed-price listings have a completely different fee structure from auctions, and they are a lot more complicated. We will look at the fees in chapter 21, but suffice to say it is quite different. The advantage of a fixed-price listing is that you can list something for a longer duration (up to thirty days) and it is much more similar to a Web site sale. You set the price and the buyer decides if she wants it at that price (if so, she then clicks Buy It Now) or not (if not, she just moves on to look for another item). There is far less risk of your listing ending up on a potential buyer's "watch" list and forgotten about until after the duration is ended. But at the same time, there is less of a sense of urgency to bid immediately.

The biggest advantage of fixed-price listings over auctions is that you can list as many items as you want in that single listing. Each time an item sells, the buyer pays, you ship the item, and it is automatically removed from the total number of items you initially allotted. The listing ends at the end of the duration you set (for multiple-item listings, you will always want to use thirty days and quite possibly with the "Good 'til Canceled" auto-renew option), or when the inventory you listed gets to zero. The longer you keep the listing active, the more visibility you get in "Best Match" for having already received sales. Plus, why would you want to end a listing before you have to if you still have inventory? It is cheaper to use a thirty-day listing than relist every seven days for a month.

The other advantage of a fixed-price listing is the option to list similar items with specific variations in the same listing. Let's say you sell garden art. You have butterflies, dragonflies, and birds and you have small, medium, and large in each style. You could set a Variations listing so your buyers could select the size they want and then from the styles you have available in that size, or vice versa. Variations listings are used a lot in clothing listings, where the items might be identical except for size. Or you may have the same style shirt in five different colors and four sizes. Not a problem in a Variations listing. And each time an item sells, eBay automatically manages your inventory so a buyer cannot select a combination that you do not have.

THE BEST TIMES TO LIST AND END AUCTIONS

eBay offers five choices of auction duration: 1, 3, 5, 7, and 10 days (only fixed-price listings get the 30-day option). How long should your auction last? This is an area where many PowerSellers and Top-Rated Sellers disagree, and there isn't really a hard-and-fast rule.

One theory is that the shorter the auction the better, because people don't like to bid on auctions that have a long waiting period until they end. Auctions attract impulse buyers. These types of bidders will definitely seek out shorter auctions. This is especially true if you are selling common products that are always available on eBay, such as children's clothes, low-cost jewelry, leather jackets, digital cameras, MP3 players, designer brand-name goods, and the like.

If you are selling something of a collectible nature, as opposed to a readily available product, you will want to expose your auction to as many people as possible over the longest period of time. Collectors tend to be more careful and will shop diligently for specific items for their collections. For rare collectibles, then, I recommend the 10-day auction.

The more important decision is this: On what day should my auction end? Different types of people shop at different times. The most popular primetime television shows are on Monday, Tuesday, and Wednesday evenings, meaning fewer people may be shopping on eBay at those times. Young people are usually out Friday and Saturday nights. Older folks who stay home spend a lot of time on eBay during the day and on Saturday evening, because it's usually a lousy TV night. Table 10.3 spells out the best and worst days to end an auction.

TABLE 10.3 Best Days and Times to End Auctions

Day	Rating	Comment
Monday	Good	A lot of people surf eBay at work. After the weekend, they need their "eBay fix." Monday evenings are also very good.
Tuesday	Worst	Tuesday statistically receives the lowest number of bids on eBay.
Wednesday	Poor	According to studies, Wednesday is not quite as bad as Tuesday, although it is still not a great day to end an auction.
Thursday	Fair	Thursday is not a bad day to end an auction in the spring and summer, because people going away for the weekend may place bids on Thursday before they leave.
Friday	Fair	Ending your auction Friday before 6:00 p.m. may attract bids from students and young people who are not usually home on Friday and Saturday evenings.
Saturday	Good	Weekend days are usually more profitable than weekdays, probably because more people have time to shop.
Sunday	Excellent	Sunday evening is the period of highest bidding activity on eBay. If your auction ends at about 11:00 p.m. Eastern time, you will maximize your bidding activity.

The auction duration you select determines which day your auction will end. I personally prefer to launch my three-day and ten-day auctions on Thursday evenings, so they end on Sunday evening. Between 4:00 and 6:00 p.m. PST (between 7:00 and 9:00 p.m. EST) seems to work best for me, but you should experiment based on the types of products you are selling. Remember: eBay time is Pacific Standard Time, so you have to add three hours to calculate the time on the East Coast. Forty-four percent of the US population lives in the Eastern time zone, and 69 percent live in the Eastern and Central time zones combined. So be careful not to allow your auctions to end too late in the evening in the Central and Eastern time zones.

Another factor to consider when choosing which day to end your auction is *where* your auction will appear.

When bidders perform a search or go to the listings page for a category, they are given several choices of how the auctions are sorted, including *Time: newly listed* and *Time: ending soonest*.

If you place a three-day auction on a Friday, it will appear in a prominent location several times over the weekend, which is the time of highest bidding activity. On Friday it will show up near the top under *Time: newly listed* and on Sunday it will show up near the top in *Time: ending soonest*.

The default search results sort order is *Best Match*, which is an algorithm eBay has created to try to match what the buyer is looking for with the best item and seller of that item. There are many things you can do to boost your Best Match placement, but the proximity to the end of the auction duration is a factor, even in this sort order.

Having said all of this, once you have settled on a product or category of products to sell, you will want to run your own tests to determine the best time to list and end auctions for the products you are selling. Some products seem to sell at different times. I used to have a product that I sold to businesses. When I tested various ending times, the optimum was Monday and Tuesday between 11 a.m. and 1 p.m. (Pacific Time).

WEEK 1

POWER MOVES

☐ Go to http://pages.ebay.com/help/sell/fees.html and become familiar with the complete eBay fee schedule. Bookmark this link and be sure to check it before listing an item. This will help you understand your potential costs when deciding on your pricing strategy.

☐ Do a completed listings search for the product you plan to sell. Select the *Price: highest* first as the sort order to display the search results. Look at the items that sold for the most money, and open the auctions to see on what days and at which times they ended.

CHAPTER 11

✦ BUILDING GREAT FEEDBACK ✦

I HAVE HEARD SOME EBAY USERS remark that feedback isn't all that important and comment that "No one reads that stuff." Nothing could be further from the truth. While eBay novices often overlook the feedback factor because they don't understand it, veteran buyers will almost always check the seller's feedback before placing a bid. If they see comments like "Product not delivered," "This guy is a fraud," or "Terrible seller," they will never purchase your merchandise. Once you have hundreds of feedback posts, you can survive the occasional negative feedback comment. As a new seller, you need to have an outstanding feedback rating, brimming with positive comments, to quickly grow your eBay business. To attain that outstanding feedback rating, you'll need to provide impeccable customer service. In business circles, there's an old saying that, if you want to keep your customers happy and coming back, "You should not just service your customers; you should delight your customers."

Customer service encompasses each interaction with everyone from potential bidders to those who win your auctions or buy from your eBay store. Always answer a bidder's and/or buyer's e-mail as quickly as possible. Whether the customer is praising your product or complaining, whether he is offering his input or asking a question, he deserves an answer—especially on eBay, where feedback really counts!

THE VALUE OF FEEDBACK

In the first chapter, we introduced you to the concept of feedback on eBay by comparing it to a shopping mall where, outside each store, customers could post comments about the store's products and customer service on a large board, and store personnel were not allowed to remove or change the comments—they were there for all to see before entering the store. Would you look at the messages before shopping at the store? Of course you would. Well, this is the role feedback plays on eBay. Everyone gets to see a review of your customer service and integrity *before* placing a bid on your item.

There is a second element to feedback called *Detailed Seller Ratings* (DSRs). These are one-star to five-star ratings on four aspects of the transaction that are considered the most important to buyers. They are:

- Item as described
- Communication
- Shipping time
- Shipping and handling charges

These ratings are in addition to the feedback comment and are completely anonymous. Your Feedback Profile shows the average rating for each DSR item over the last twelve months. eBay tracks your low DSRs (one or two stars), and if you have too many of these low DSRs, you get your listings demoted in the Best Match search results.

If you follow my advice about writing your item description (see chapter 14) and if you are always quick to respond to questions from buyers, you shouldn't have any trouble with the first two items on the ratings list ("Items as described" and "Communication"). The problems tend to come with "Shipping time" and "Shipping and handling charges." Theoretically, "Shipping time" should be the time it took from when you received cleared payment until you got the item into the mail. However, a lot of buyers consider "Shipping time" to be how long it took for them to receive the item. "Shipping and handling charges," in my opinion, shouldn't even be a DSR matrix because if buyers didn't like the price for shipping, they shouldn't have bought from you. Still, we can't change that policy, but we can work it to our advantage.

Getting Automatic Five-Star Ratings on DSRs

Amid controversy about the fairness and accurate use of Detailed Seller Ratings, eBay has figured out a way to get sellers to do exactly what eBay wants. They entice sellers to follow optional policies and in return they give the seller an automatic five-star rating on certain DSRs. These policies aren't crazy, though. They make a lot of sense.

Communication

eBay would rather automate everything these days rather than build buyer-seller relationships (after all, you might end up selling to them off of eBay's platform). So, for "Communication," they actually mean lack of direct communication. You will receive an automatic five-star DSR for "Communication" if:

- You have a one-business-day handling time specified in your listing and you upload tracking details to My eBay (the delivery confirmation number is fine) within that handling time. If you use eBay Labels, this is automatically done for you once you pay for the shipping label through PayPal.

* You do not have any buyer-initiated or seller-initiated e-mails in My Messages. This doesn't include invoice requests. Specifically, it refers to questions. The idea is that you should have all necessary information in your listing so that the buyer doesn't have to contact you; eBay doesn't want you contacting them and building a buyer-seller relationship that could continue outside of eBay's platform.

* Neither you (the seller) nor the buyer has requested contact information for the other through eBay. There is an option available to retrieve a phone number for the other person if you need to contact him or her and are not getting a response through My Messages. In this case, though, it could be a work-around to be able to contact the buyer directly to offer to sell future items off of eBay without using My Messages. So it is not an option for you if you want the automatic five-star DSR.

Shipping Time

eBay wants to be competitive with Amazon, which offers free two-day shipping to prime members. It's hard to compete with that when sellers can set their own shipping time and cost. This is one DSR you absolutely want to get the automatic five-star rating on, since so many buyers rate shipping times inaccurately:

* Have a one-business-day handling time and upload tracking information to My eBay within that time.

* Use a shipping service that gets the item to the buyer within four business days. This is why I use USPS Priority Mail or UPS Ground. Typically, both are delivered within three business days, even from where I live in the far northwest part of the country.

Shipping Cost

eBay wants you to give free shipping to buyers, because that makes eBay more competitive with Amazon (its biggest competitor), which offers free shipping on all orders over $25 and free two-day shipping on any size order for Amazon Prime members. But eBay can't force you to offer free shipping, so they offer you an automatic five-star DSR for "Shipping and handling charges" if you do.

You will need to do your own research to determine if it is worthwhile to incorporate the shipping cost into your item price. You also get a boost in the Best Match results if you offer free shipping, so in a competitive marketplace it can be well worth it. Make sure that you check the "free shipping" box in the shipping section of the Sell Your Item form if you are offering it; otherwise you won't get credit for it in either Best Match placement or DSRs. You can offer other paid services. So you could offer free Priority Mail shipping, but then also offer UPS 2-Day Air and Overnight shipping for a fee. This is particularly useful during the holiday season. Granted, if the buyer picks one of the paid services, you won't get the automatic five-star DSR, but you will still get the boost in Best Match.

The only DSR you cannot get an automatic five-star rating on is "Item as Described." But if you write a complete, honest description of all of your items, you should never have a problem with this one, unless you ship the wrong item!

You can see how you are doing on DSRs by looking at the Seller Performance Numbers in your Seller Dashboard (in the *Account* tab of *My eBay*), as shown in Figure 11.1. You will automatically see twelve months of data, but you can adjust this to a shorter period if needed. You can also run reports to see if there are patterns in the DSRs you're receiving (e.g., a particular product seems to consistently get a lower "Item as Described" DSR, or "Shipping Time" is always rated lower when the item is sent to a particular geographic area).

Seller performance numbers		Updated daily ⓘ
12 months (09/01/11 - 08/31/12) ▾		Transactions: **270** See your reports
Average detailed seller ratings	**Your average**	**Low ratings (1s and 2s)**
Item as described	4.96	0.00% (0)
Communication	4.97	0.00% (0)
Shipping time	4.96	0.00% (0)
Shipping and handling charges	4.97	0.00% (0)
Buyer Protection cases		**Your percentage (count)**
Opened cases		0.00% (0)
Closed cases without seller resolution		0.00% (0)
Performance numbers are from transactions with buyers in the United States.		

Figure 11.1 Detailed Seller Ratings in Seller Dashboard

The most critical part to watch is the *Low ratings (ones and twos)* column. The maximum number of low ratings (either one- or two-star) allowed for each individual DSR is three. However, once that is met, it converts to a percentage. So getting three low ratings for a particular DSR isn't going to kill you. But you then are allowed a maximum of 1 percent low ratings for "Item as Described" and 2 percent for the other DSRs. Be aware of these numbers and do your best to fix any trends you see or repeated concerns you notice. You are considered "below standards" if you do not meet the DSR minimums. This affects your search placement and your eligibility for Top-Rated Status and fee discounts, etc.

The point of mentioning all of this is to show you how important feedback really is. So how do you get an excellent feedback rating? By delivering quality products quickly, efficiently, and honestly. If you are looking to make a quick buck or stage a "hit-and-run" action, eBay is not the place for you. You can build a hugely profitable and legitimate business on eBay without cheating or misleading anyone. I know—I have done it.

There will always be a few rogue customers who claim they never received their product, or you were too slow to deliver it, or they were unhappy with what they received. We all know the customer is not *always* right. My recommendation for dealing with such problem buyers is simply to offer a thirty-day, no-questions-asked refund. Offering a bidder a refund can head off negative feedback posts.

Once you have a decent Feedback score (over one hundred), you can tolerate the occasional negative feedback comment. But, until then, you should take the long view and remember that you are trying to build a long-term business that can generate thousands of dollars in income. Don't take issue with a $9.00 item that someone was unhappy with. Just refund the buyer's money and move on.

HOW TO BUILD FEEDBACK QUICKLY

Here are some tips to build your feedback rating quickly:

* Sell low-cost items, such as baseball cards, stamps, or inexpensive pieces of costume jewelry, for $1 each. You won't make much money, but you can sell dozens, even hundreds, of items in a short time and quickly build your feedback numbers.

* Your e-mail signature to buyers should contain the current *Leave Feedback* link. As of this writing it is: http ://cgi2.eBay.com/aw-cgi/eBay-ISAPI.dll?LeaveFeedbackShow. (Note that eBay often changes its links. See eBay's site map for the most current link.)

* Here is an interesting statistic from eBay: Only 45 percent of buyers bother to leave feedback. Many sellers add a personal touch by including a handwritten thank-you note when they fulfill an order. Such notes should thank buyers for their business, encourage them to contact you with any questions or concerns (give them your direct e-mail address here), and remind the buyer that you left positive feedback for them. I include the following preprinted note in all my packages:

> Thank you for your business. I have posted positive feedback for this transaction. I would greatly appreciate it if you would leave feedback for me too. If there is anything wrong with your order, please contact me immediately and I will do my very best to correct the problem or make it right.

* I include my e-mail address, Web site, and phone number after the message, and then sign each note. These notes are printed on 4-by 5-inch colored stock. I have them sitting next to my shipping station (see chapter 17) so that it is easy for me to grab one, sign it, fold it in half, and insert it into the box.

    This is a nice, neat way of getting around eBay's requirement that you don't contact the bidder via electronic means (by My Messages or phone). You are, however, encouraging buyers to reach out to you. eBay cannot control your putting a note in the parcel encouraging a buyer-seller relationship, so this is definitely something I encourage if you are looking to get the automatic five-star "Communication" DSR.

* Create a little giveaway of some kind. One woman I know who sells autographs and other paper memorabilia wrote a short article on how to spot fakes. She inserts a copy of the article in each shipment she sends out. I offer a link to a free report about selling on eBay (which just so happens to be posted on my Web site, which encourages the buyer to visit my site, which also has products for sale on it). My daughter-in-law once received a special-occasion dress she had bought on eBay for her then four-year-old daughter; with it came a little plastic baggie with some princess stickers and a few little stick-on jewels and some glitter. It probably cost the seller about 25 cents to put together. It had a sticky label on the outside saying, "Some fairy dust and jewels for your little

princess, from mine." Years later, my daughter-in-law still remembers this seller, and she is still on her "saved sellers" list on eBay. Just use your imagination and you can probably come up with several ways to surprise and delight your customers.

✳ Customers sometimes forget to leave feedback after they receive the product because it has been a week or so since your last e-mail and your message is buried in their e-mail files. At this point, you have to decide if it is worth giving up the automatic five-star Communication rating to actually receive feedback and ratings on the other DSRs. To combat this "out of sight, out of mind" effect, check that your item has been delivered (the tracking number will be next to the item in your *Sold* section of My eBay). Then send an e-mail that includes the *Leave Feedback* link. Your e-mail could say something like this:

> By now you should have received your unique baseball batting glove.
>
> I hope you have had a chance to try it out. If you have any questions, or if there are any problems with your order, please e-mail me immediately.
>
> I enjoyed doing business with you and I have left positive feedback for this transaction.
>
> > Best regards,
> > Sammy Sosa
>
> P. S. If you would like to leave feedback about our eBay transaction, please go to: http://cgi2.eBay.com/aw-cgi/eBayISAPI. dll?LeaveFeedbackShow

✳ An e-mail like this reminds your customer to leave feedback. I have tested this type of e-mail and it has increased my feedback response by at least 20 percent.

✳ Another way to increase your positive feedback quickly is to be overly generous in posting your feedback. If the buyer didn't send PayPal payment until seven days after the auction ended, so what? I still post a nice feedback notice. If someone cancels or doesn't follow through, I rarely bother leaving feedback, although I do file an unpaid item request to recover my fees (we cover this in detail in chapter 20). Ask yourself: How many times have I misplaced an e-mail or had an emergency to deal with and forgotten about everything else? Not all slow payers are nonpayers. Sometimes, people really do forget. Why make an enemy, particularly since you cannot leave negative feedback for buyers, but even if they don't pay, they are still able to leave neutral or negative feedback for you?

I remember the story of one poor lady who had a heart attack. Before this incident, her feedback rating was over 500, with a 100 percent positive rating. While she was recuperating from her heart attack, several winning bidders who hadn't heard from her left brutal negative feedback comments. A week or so later, her daughter sent all of them e-mails explaining the situation. Surprisingly, several of the buyers didn't believe her. They continued to send abusive e-mails and complaints to eBay. It took copies of the woman's surgery report and a letter from her doctor to get the negative feedback comments removed.

CUSTOMER SERVICE DOS AND DON'TS

Always respond quickly and clearly to questions from eBay bidders and buyers. If I have auctions running, I check my eBay messages at least three times a day, and always a few minutes before the auction closes in case bidders have any last-minute questions. If you fail to answer e-mails quickly, you may receive negative comments, such as "Unresponsive seller" or "Ignored my repeated inquiries" in your feedback file. You will almost certainly also get a lower rating for the "Communication" DSR.

Look at your *Active Selling* section of My eBay. You will see a big red notification if there is an unanswered message related to that listing. This is harder to track when you have hundreds and hundreds of items, but it's worth scanning through at least once a day, particularly as auctions come to a close.

Keep your answers short, courteous, and to the point. Provide all relevant information and be friendly; however, don't get bogged down in long e-mail conversations or let the customer lead you on an irrelevant tangent. Your time is money.

All your business policies as they relate to shipping, payment, feedback, and so forth should be written in a clear, personable style and specified at the end of each of your item descriptions. You want to convey your policies without listing a set of rules that turns people off. It is also helpful to explain why you have certain policies. For example, if you only ship via Priority Mail, you might want to say something like:

We use Priority Mail for all shipments under five pounds. Priority Mail costs less than UPS and includes free boxes and shipping materials, so we don't have to charge you for those or build in a hefty handling fee.

SHORTCUTS TO SUPERIOR SERVICE

When it comes to customer service, you need to balance time, efficiency, and courteousness to maximize your working potential. One way to save time is to create a folder in your e-mail program called "prewritten messages," in which you store template messages for answering common questions like these:

* When was my item shipped?
* Did you receive my payment?
* How long does shipping take?

You'll create additional prewritten messages customized to fit your particular product as you continue to receive similar questions and comments from customers.

It is much easier to send out a prewritten e-mail than to write a specific answer to each inquiry. However, to prevent your e-mails from sounding like form letters, add a personal touch whenever possible. Use the person's name if you know it, or her eBay user ID if you don't. Always "sign" your name at the bottom.

You have the option to create "auto-answers" for your eBay listings. This is designed to answer the common questions without the buyer having to actually contact the seller. eBay has its own system for pulling information from your listing to answer certain questions; however, you can add your own if you want.

To do this, go to My eBay and click on the *Account* tab. Select *Manage Communication with Buyers.* Here you can see what eBay will automatically send to your buyers. You can add a message to the Buyer Checkout e-mail (to make it more personal) and also to the e-mail sent when your order is updated with the shipping tracking information.

In addition to this, you can choose to turn off the eBay automated question-and-answer service, or to customize it. Click *edit* next to *Manage questions and answers* and you can choose specific questions to show from eBay's standard list, or scroll to the bottom and add your own questions and answers. Some buyers love the Q&A system because it means they don't have to contact you (this also preserves your automatic five-star "Communication" DSR). Others find it impersonal and may contact you anyway. That is okay too. If that happens, never just refer them back to the Q&A page. So what if the person really wants to hear your shipping policies directly from you? It takes you a few minutes and shows this potential buyer that you are a real business with real customer service. Sometimes that's the only reassurance customers need. They want to know that you are legitimate—it has little to do with whatever question they asked. So always be polite, even if it is a really stupid question that has been answered in your listing description and in your Q&A section already.

BIZ BUILDER

Amazingly, giving out your telephone number can actually save you time. I've started listing my phone number in my e-mail signature. Sometimes a phone call can clear up an issue in much less time than it takes to send several e-mails back and forth. Also, the fact that you list your phone number enhances your credibility and reduces suspicion.

NEGATIVE FEEDBACK

While you are still a new seller trying to build up your feedback rating, *be very careful about leaving neutral or negative feedback for others.* Most of the time, it is better not to leave any feedback at all than to leave negative feedback.

True, eBay is a community. If someone is a crook or taking advantage of people, then you have a responsibility to leave appropriate feedback. However, you don't want to start a "feedback war" over something that was poorly shipped unless the seller is being really unreasonable. There are, unfortunately, some "crazies" out there. If your feedback angers someone, she could potentially bid on your auctions, not pay you, and then leave negative feedback for you as revenge (remember, sellers cannot leave negative feedback for buyers, so this isn't as crazy a scenario as it sounds). Yes, if the buyer doesn't pay, you can go through the dispute-resolution process and, if the buyer receives an *unpaid item strike*, the negative feedback will be removed. But it can do a lot of damage to your current sales while that process is ongoing. (This process is covered in detail in chapter 20.)

If you suspect that someone is violating the community guidelines, you may be better off reporting it via e-mail to the eBay Trust and Safety team. (Click on the link to the *Security Center* at the bottom of any eBay page.) If eBay suspends the violator, he will not be able to leave you negative feedback.

Once your feedback score is over one hundred, the occasional negative feedback won't hurt you that badly. Until then, I would suggest that you not leave negative feedback for someone else unless her actions are truly egregious.

If I am about to buy something, I always read the feedback details for a seller who has more than one negative comment. When someone leaves negative feedback for you, you get to make a response. I once read a negative comment from someone whose order was wrong and late. The seller's response was: "I screwed up! It doesn't happen often, but this one was my fault." I was so impressed by the seller's honesty that I didn't hesitate to buy from her.

FEEDBACK REMOVAL

Getting eBay to remove a negative feedback comment is extremely difficult. There are only certain circumstances under which the comment may be removed, such as if a buyer uses personal details in the feedback (your name, phone number, etc.), if eBay is issued with a court order to remove the feedback, if the feedback was from an international bidder and solely referenced customs charges or delays, if the buyer didn't pay for an item and received an unpaid item strike for it, etc. The full details are available at http://pages.ebay.com/help/policies/feedback-removal.html. There is one other option called *Feedback Revision*. If the buyer leaves negative feedback, let's say because the item didn't arrive, and then a couple of days later it arrives and the date of mailing shows the seller did actually ship it on time but it got delayed in the mail, the buyer may want to change the negative comment. The seller can initiate the Feedback Revision process until thirty days after it was initially posted. This allows the buyer to change the feedback rating (positive, negative, neutral), the comment itself, and also the buyer's DSR ratings (in this case, the buyer could change his Shipping Time DSR from a two-star to a five-star rating, since it wasn't the seller's fault that the package was delayed).

Here's the catch—there is a limit to the number of feedback revisions a seller can request. It is currently five revision requests per 1,000 feedback comments received per twelve months, so this is not an alternative to creating a good eBay experience for your buyers; it is only to address occasional mistakes made by either the buyer or seller.

If you have exceeded your maximum Feedback Revisions, or if the buyer won't change his feedback, you should still leave a follow-up comment. Go to the eBay site map and click on *Reply to Feedback Received* under the *Feedback* heading. This will allow you to select the transaction and leave a comment explaining what happened. Remember, the seller who responded that he messed up? Mistakes do happen. So if this happens to you, acknowledging it and explaining how you fixed it will help instill confidence in other potential buyers.

If you are going to reply to feedback, make sure you write a specific comment for each feedback comment. The numbers on your Feedback Profile are hyperlinks. So a potential bidder can click just to see the negative or neutral feedback comments that have been left for you. There's nothing worse than doing this and then seeing feedback replies from the seller of "Deadbeat buyer" for every single one. Buyers understand that mistakes happen. They also understand that a seller who always blames the buyer, no matter what the issue, is not typically someone they want to do business with.

BUYER FEEDBACK VERSUS SELLER FEEDBACK

On your Feedback Profile, there are separate tabs for *Feedback as a buyer* and *Feedback as a seller*. This is valuable for the following reason: Suppose you're interested in bidding on an item, and you see that the seller has a feedback score of thirty-five. When you look more closely, however, you notice that most of the feedback comments are from *sellers,* for merchandise the seller of the item you're interested in has *purchased*. His feedback for items he's *sold* may be quite low or even nonexistent. Therefore, you, as a buyer, may be wary of purchasing from this seller, since he hasn't shown he is a trustworthy seller on eBay yet. I know this will hamper new sellers—but all of us were new at one time. Most PowerSellers and Top-Rated Sellers worked very hard to build their rating over a long period.

You can also view the feedback a member has left for others on the tab *Feedback left for others.* I like to see what kind of feedback sellers leave for other people. Someone who leaves a lot of negative feedback is less likely to get bids from me. Those who complain about others all the time are not really the type of sellers I want to support.

In the end, building positive feedback is all about honesty, good shipping terms, and customer service. If you are honest in your descriptions and provide good customer service, your feedback rating will climb rapidly.

POWERSELLER AND TOP-RATED SELLER

Feedback is critically important to your continued success on eBay. One of your first goals should be to reach Top-Rated Seller status. This takes a minimum of ninety days, but it is the work you do right at the beginning that sets you up for hitting this goal as quickly as possible.

You've heard me use the term PowerSeller as well. The programs are similar but have different requirements.

For many years, the PowerSeller program was the only option. It was based far more on sales volume than on customer service standards. However, that program has morphed over the years, but still it is rooted in the sales volume. The Top-Rated Seller (TRS) program was launched to focus on customer service and experience combined. You don't need as high sales for TRS as you do for the PowerSeller program, but your customer service standards have to be higher than they are for a PowerSeller. You won't see eBay advertise PowerSeller status anywhere except on your Seller Dashboard. However, eBay does advertise your Top-Rated Seller status if you qualify for this program.

PowerSeller Requirements

To be a PowerSeller you must have:

* Ninety days as a registered eBay user.
* Ninety-eight percent positive feedback rating.
* A minimum average 4.6 out of 5.0 stars on each of the Detailed Seller Ratings.
* The rate of one star or two stars on the DSRs can be no more than 1 percent for the "Item Not As Described" DSR, and 2 percent for all other DSRs. You are allowed three instances of a low rating for each DSR before eBay looks at the percentage.
* Minimum sales of $3,000 and 100 transactions within the last twelve months.

The DSR requirements are based on the last three months if the seller has over 400 transactions in that period of time. If not, the DSR average and rate of one or two stars is based on the last twelve months.

The benefits of being a PowerSeller include:

* Priority customer support.
* Unpaid-item protection (you can receive a credit for the listing upgrades you used on certain listings if the buyer didn't pay, in addition to getting the final value fee credit and the relist credit).
* Discounted shipping rates from USPS and UPS.
* Special promotional offers only for PowerSellers.

eBay used to offer fee discounts to PowerSellers, but this is now strictly for Top-Rated Sellers.

Top-Rated Seller Requirements

To be a Top-Rated Seller you must:

* Have ninety days as a registered eBay user.

* Have $1,000 in sales and one hundred transactions over the last twelve months to US buyers.

* Keep your rate of one star or two stars on the DSRs no higher than 0.5 percent of all of your DSRs for any individual DSR category. For sellers with over 400 transactions in the previous three months, this is calculated on the previous three months' DSRs. If you have over 400 in the last twelve months, it is calculated on the previous twelve months' DSRs. If you have fewer than 400 transactions in the last twelve months, it is calculated as a fixed number rather than a percentage. You are allowed a maximum of two instances of a low (one- or two-star) rating on each of the DSRs.

* Upload shipping tracking information to eBay within your stated handling time on 90 percent of your sales.

The benefits of becoming a Top-Rated Seller are:

* The ability to qualify your listings for Top Rated Plus (I'll explain this in a moment).

* Increased visibility in the Best Match search results.

Top Rated Plus Seal

The Top Rated Plus seal is displayed in the item and seller information box on the top right of your qualified listing (see Figure 11.2). It is only available to Top-Rated Sellers, so it shows that you adhere to all the Top-Rated Seller customer service requirements. But it also means that this particular listing offers fourteen-day (or longer) money-back returns and also uses one-business-day handling. If your listing qualifies for Top Rated Plus, you get a 20 percent discount on the Final Value Fee for any items sold from that listing. That discount adds up very quickly.

Remember, though, you still have to adhere to the Top-Rated Seller requirements. So if you specify one-day handling but then don't get the tracking information uploaded within that time, you are going to end up losing your Top-Rated Seller status and any discount you would get from Top Rated Plus; plus you'll lose the extra boost in visibility in Best Match. So make sure you only put one-day handling on listings for which you can control when the item goes into the mail.

For example, if you use a drop-shipper for some of your items, the item may be in the mail within one business day, but it depends on when they provide the tracking information to you so you can upload it to eBay rather than when the item is actually confirmed to be in the mail. So if you don't upload the tracking information until into the second business day, that counts as a hit against you on the Top-Rated Seller requirements. To keep your Top-Rated Seller status, you have to upload tracking information within your handling time for 90 percent your sales, so it is better on drop-shipped items to lose the 20 percent final value fee discount but ensure that the tracking information is uploaded within the handling time and that you keep your Top-Rated Seller status.

You should strive to become a Top-Rated Seller as quickly as possible. Use the customer service strategies I've recommended, use the options that will give you an automatic five-star DSR rating wherever possible, and build up your sales volume so you can reach this level as soon as you can after you are eligible by longevity on the site (ninety days).

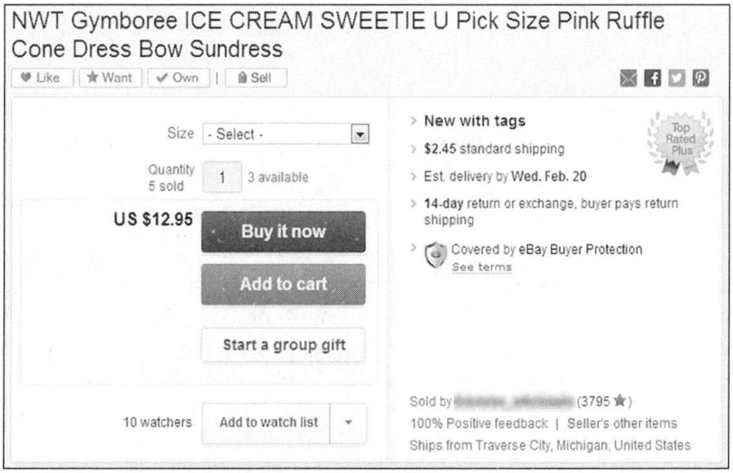

Figure 11.2 Top Rated Plus Seal on Listing Page

POWER MOVES

❏ Go to the eBay site map and click on the links under the heading *Feedback*.

❏ Bookmark (add to Favorites) the links you will use most often, such as:

- Follow up to Feedback left for others

- Leave Feedback for a member

- Leave Feedback for a transaction

- Reply to Feedback received

❏ Regarding the auctions you launched in chapter 9, make sure you leave positive feedback for them and include a personal note in your parcel that encourages buyers to leave feedback, as well as providing buyers with your direct-contact information.

❏ Sell a series of inexpensive items for the purpose of quickly building your feedback rating.

❏ Consider sending a follow-up e-mail to buyers who have not left feedback. Always include the Leave Feedback link in your e-mails to buyers.

❏ Set up a folder in your e-mail program for prewritten messages. Create template messages for answering common questions you receive. Go to Manage Questions and Answers (in the Account section of My eBay) to customize eBay's automatic Q&A system, add your own questions, and customize the formula e-mails eBay sends to buyers during the checkout and postsale process.

CHAPTER 12

✦ WRITING YOUR SUCCESS PLAN ✦

IN THE INTRODUCTION, I asked you to evaluate your personal definition of success. This is an important concept. Now that you understand some of the basics involved in running an eBay business, it is a good idea to ask yourself the following questions: What are my goals? How much time do I want to devote to eBay? How much money can I make given the time and resources I have to commit?

Most people starting a business write a plan and establish their goals before they start. However, before you attempted that, I wanted you to have a better understanding of how eBay works and what is involved in selecting a product to sell. Now that you understand the work and costs involved, you're ready to put together your business plan.

In the business world, almost every company has a business plan that its executives continually revise and update as the business develops. For selling on eBay, you don't need a full-blown business plan with financial statistics and detailed marketing strategies, but you do need to set some basic goals and map out a series of steps to help you reach those goals. As we conclude Week 1 of this three-week program, we will focus on the basics of setting some realistic objectives and writing a success plan to guide you through the next stages of developing your eBay business.

EVALUATING YOUR EARNING POTENTIAL

The first question you have to answer is how big you want to be, or, put another way, how much money you want to make. If you already know what you want to sell on eBay, this is a much easier question to answer—your anticipated revenue depends on the price point or the final value of what you will be selling. Let's do some simple math to demonstrate this point.

If you are selling a product with an average selling price (ASP) of $50, and the item costs you $30, you will make an average of $20 on each successful auction (less eBay and PayPal fees). (For the sake of these examples, we're not dealing with fees and shipping here.) So if your goal were to make $3,000 a month on eBay, you would have to close 150 auctions a month ($20 x 150 = $3,000). Experienced sellers will successfully close (or convert) as many as 70 percent of all their auctions. So, you would have to launch about 215 auctions a month—or just over 50 auctions a week—in order to close

150 auctions successfully (150 ÷ 215 = 70 percent). (Note: a month has 4.3 weeks.) Alternatively, if you were selling a $100 item for an ASP of $160, you would make $60 an auction. Now you would have to convert only 50 auctions a month to make the same amount of money ($60 x 50 = $3,000).

BIZ BUILDER

If you focus on selling higher-value merchandise, you will make more money for the same amount of work. The key to moving "up market" is to thoroughly research a product to make sure there is a market for it and that you can buy it at a price where you can make money selling it on eBay. Remember—you make money when you *buy*, not when you sell.

So if you haven't yet researched and selected a product or products to sell on eBay, now is the time to complete these tasks. You first must determine what you are going to sell and what your average price points will be before you can start setting concrete goals and crafting a business plan.

SETTING GOALS

I know plenty of people who are successful in life and in business who do not create formal, written goals. But I know far more who *do*—and, on average, they tend to be much more successful.

Written goals serve several purposes. Long-term goals give you a vision of where you want to be in the future; short-term ones provide the stepping stones to get there.

To be useful, your goals should be both specific and achievable. A goal "to become a millionaire within three years" is both vague and difficult to achieve, unless you already have $500,000 in assets. A better goal would be "I want to achieve Top-Rated Seller status within four months, Silver PowerSeller status ($36,000 or 3,600 transactions within the last twelve months) within eighteen months, and Gold PowerSeller status ($120,000 or 12,000 transactions per year) within three years."

If you want to relate your goals to income, you could set up steps like these:

1. Earn $1,000 a month by (date)
2. Earn $3,000 a month by (date)
3. Earn $5,000 a month by (date)

TYPES OF POWERSELLERS

PowerSellers are Top eBay Sellers who average consistently high volumes of sales from month to month, maintain a high percentage of positive feedback, and comply with eBay's policies. PowerSellers are divided into six tiers based upon sellers' yearly sales or transaction totals. (eBay considers a transaction to be a unique sale. If a buyer purchases ten things from you in one go, that is still only one transaction.) Certain benefits and services vary with each tier. eBay automatically calculates sellers' eligibility each month, based on the previous twelve months; if you qualify, you will be notified of your status via e-mail and in the Seller Dashboard in My eBay. For the Bronze level you must meet both the sales and the transaction totals ($3,000 and one hundred transactions). However, for each other level it is an either-or situation. This means that if you sell low-cost, high-volume, you are still eligible for PowerSeller status. eBay uses yearly totals too, so that sellers don't get penalized for slower periods. Some sellers specialize in Christmas items and will meet PowerSeller requirements just in the months of November and December and then will find the summer months are comparatively slow. Other sellers are steady sellers year-round. This makes it more fair to all sellers.

The following are sales criteria for each PowerSeller tier:

PowerSeller level:	Bronze	Silver	Gold	Platinum	Titanium
Yearly sales:	$3,000	$36,000	$120,000	$300,000	$1,800,000
Transactions:	100	3,600	12,000	30,000	180,000

Once you establish your primary business goals, you should set subgoals, or a list of tasks that have to be completed to get you there.

Your first set of tasks should be a list of all the things you have to do to set up and organize your business; we covered these in chapter 1. These might include getting your state sales tax number, opening your business checking account, verifying your PayPal account, and so on. You should make a complete list of all these tasks and treat them like individual goals.

Next, you will want to set specific business goals. This will involve determining how many auctions you will run and how often. You should also set your goals for reaching certain metrics such as conversions, sell-through rates, and average selling price.

DEFINING *METRICS*

Metrics is a term that means "standards of measurement." There is an old saying in business that goes like this: "If you can't measure something, you can't control it." Some of the more important metrics in eBay selling are:

- **CONVERSION OR SELL-THROUGH RATE:** This is the percentage of auctions you close versus the number you listed. If you listed a hundred items and successfully closed sixty-five with a sale, your sell-through rate would be 65 percent—or you might say you "converted" 65 percent of your listings.

- **AVERAGE SELLING PRICE (ASP):** This is the average price of all the items you listed that sold (ASP does not include listings that did not sell).

- **GROSS MERCHANDISE SALES (GMS):** GMS is the total dollar value of your sales for the month (or week, or year, and so on).

- **GROSS MARGIN:** This is the amount you made on your sales after taking into account the cost of the items you sold, your eBay listing and selling fees, and your PayPal fees.

There are many other, more detailed metrics that eBay sellers track on a daily, weekly, and monthly basis; however, they are all variations or extensions of the ones specified above.

The purpose of establishing goals is twofold: First, you want to set targets to achieve. Second, you want your progress in reaching these targets to be measurable.

Remember that goals can have a numerical value, such as "dollars earned," and/or an accomplishment value, such as "Completed Phase I of my product research." But all goals must have a time value (the date by which they are to be accomplished) to be meaningful.

Here are some points to help you set and achieve your goals:

* **KEEP MOVING FORWARD.** Never look back, except to learn from your mistakes.

* **FOCUS YOUR ENERGY.** Don't be distracted by other issues and businesses.

* **HONE YOUR SKILLS.** Practice and experiment for success.

* **INCREASE YOUR KNOWLEDGE.** Read everything you can find that relates to your business and your goals.

* **MANAGE YOUR TIME AND YOUR ENERGY.** Set aside some time for yourself, your family, and your friends. Otherwise, you're likely to burn out.

* **SURROUND YOURSELF WITH POSITIVE PEOPLE.** Don't listen to those who say you can't be successful.

* **MOST OF ALL, HAVE FUN!** If you enjoy what you're doing, you're more likely to work hard and be successful.

YOUR BUSINESS PLAN

Now that you have your goals specified, it's time to write your business plan—or, as I like to call it, your *success plan*. You have already done most of the work by establishing your goals. Your business plan is nothing more than a statement formalizing these goals in writing:

* What business you are in
* Where you want to go with this business
* What resources you will need to get there
* What will determine your success

You might be tempted to skip this step—or take mental notes rather than write down the details. That would be a mistake. The act of writing this information down in an organized fashion will help clarify your thinking. If you are starting a business with your spouse, you should create this plan together and discuss each of the points. If you are married or living with someone and are doing this alone, you should still discuss your plan with your significant other to get his feedback and to make him part of your success plan.

My wife and I have been running a successful eBay business for over thirteen years, and I am good friends with several of the top PowerSellers on eBay. We know—and they know—that there is no "quick fix" to success on eBay. If someone tells you she has the "instant secret to success on eBay," and that you can "make $5,000 a month by working only a few minutes a day," she is trying to sell you something. Furthermore, she has probably never actually sold anything on eBay. Yes, you can make $5,000 a month on eBay (and even more), but you cannot accomplish this with just a few minutes of work a day. Now that you know what is involved in launching auctions, part of setting your goals is assessing the amount of time and resources you can devote to the business. If your plan is realistic and you see progress week after week, you will be encouraged to keep pursuing your goals.

I am doing my best to reveal all the tips and tricks I have learned over the last thirteen years to help you succeed. However, none of these takes the place of planning, research, and hard work. Now that you understand the basics of selling on eBay and how the system works, take the time to set your goals, write a plan, and create a schedule for success. In Week 2, we are going to delve into the advanced systems and techniques that will save you time, reduce your costs, and help you launch professional-looking listings to ensure that you build a long-term profitable business.

POWER MOVES

❑ In your eBay binder, write down short- and long-term goals for your business. Determine how much money you are looking to make and how much time you can realistically devote to achieving your goals on eBay.

❑ Review your research and estimate the average selling price of your product(s). Using the formula discussed in this chapter, calculate how many auctions a week you would need to launch to reach your monthly goals.

❑ If the number of auctions you need to launch to reach your goal will take more time than you can realistically devote to your business, reassess your product selection. Do additional research, if necessary, to come up with alternative products to sell.

❑ Either with your partner or alone, turn your goals into a formal business plan. Keep updating and revising this plan as your business develops.

WEEK 2

PUTTING YOUR AUCTIONS TO WORK

By now you have organized your business, completed your product research and determined what you want to sell, and even taken steps to acquire the products. You have launched your first eBay auctions and have worked through the steps of getting paid, communicating with customers, and delivering the product. You may even have earned a few feedback comments. Now it's time to start building and refining your skills to make your fledgling business a success.

In Week 2, we're going to focus on specific ways to improve your auctions and grow your profits on eBay, including driving customers to your auctions by using strategic category selection, writing listing titles and descriptions that sell, improving the effectiveness of your photos, and using listing upgrades to promote your auctions across eBay. In addition, we'll discuss how to increase profits by selling internationally and how to minimize your costs and maximize your buyers' confidence. Finally, we'll explore how to monitor and revise your listings so they are as successful as possible, and we'll review the steps you need to get paid in a timely fashion.

You have already encountered some of these choices and tasks as an eBay seller. We'll now discuss these topics in greater detail and we'll reveal how to set up processes and systems so you can run your business like a pro, saving you both time and money—and boosting your profits.

CHAPTER 13

✦ CATEGORY SELECTION ✦

CATEGORY SELECTION IS IMPORTANT for several reasons. While 80 percent or more of eBay buyers find items by *searching,* that still leaves about 20 percent who locate products by *browsing.* Browsers are usually looking for particular kinds of items, so they tend to browse by category, and they're generally impulse buyers (as opposed to searchers, who come to eBay looking to buy something specific). This impulsiveness can prompt unexpected sales or increased bidding activity, which, as we discussed in Week 1, can generate more interest from *all* potential bidders.

When a buyer searches a particular keyword (or group of words), eBay offers refinements to help her narrow down the search results to exactly what she is looking for. The first option she sees is the category selection. On the left sidebar, she is presented with a list of major categories and subcategories within them and a number in parentheses next to each category. This tells her how many items matching her keywords are listed in each of these categories. As you might imagine, the category with the most matches is the one listed first.

For example, a buyer might search for a *3T dress,* but might get so many results that she then narrows it down to the *Baby and Toddler Clothing* category within *Clothing, Shoes, and Accessories,* then *Girls-Clothing (Newborn to 5T),* then *Dresses,* then *3T.* If your item is miscategorized, neither this searching buyer nor a browsing buyer will see it.

In this chapter, we'll discuss how to drive more traffic to your listing by choosing the most strategic category for your item, as well as when to list it in more than one category and how to take advantage of pre-filled item information from eBay's product catalog.

THE MANY CATEGORIES OF EBAY

To date, eBay has thirty-five main categories and more than 20,000 subcategories. Table 13.1 spells out the main eBay categories.

TABLE 13.1 Main eBay Categories

Antiques	Consumer Electronics	Pet Supplies
Art	Crafts	Pottery & Glass
Baby	Dolls & Bears	Real Estate
Books	DVDs & Movies	Specialty Services
Business & Industrial	eBay Motors	Sporting Goods
Cameras & Photo	Entertainment	Sports Memorabilia,
Cell Phones	Memorabilia	Cards & Fan Shop
& Accessories	Gift Cards & Coupons	Stamps
Clothing, Shoes	Health & Beauty	Tickets
& Accessories	Home & Garden	Toys & Hobbies
Coins & Paper Money	Jewelry & Watches	Travel
Collectibles	Music	Video Games
Computers/Tablets	Musical Instruments	& Consoles
& Networking	& Gear	

eBay gives you some flexibility in choosing categories, but the item must somehow be related to the category you are selling in. Selecting the optimal category and subcategory (for simplicity's sake, going forward we'll refer to both collectively as "categories") for your item is important because you want your item to be listed where other similar items can be found. Remember: You are trying to reach browsers, impulse buyers, and searchers who narrow down their categories, so you need to list your goods where they are looking.

Before you list your item, do some research. Search for items on eBay that are similar to yours and pay attention to which categories they are listed in. Try several different keyword searches and see if you find particularly active categories (those with more than 5,000 auctions). Think creatively about your item. For example, maybe the hand-thrown potter lamp you first thought belonged in Antiques/Decorative Arts is better suited for Home & Garden/Home Decor. (To see which category an item is listed in, just look at the top of the item listing, as illustrated in Figure 13.1.) Look at the page-view counters and numbers of bids for similar items listed in different categories. Select categories where other sellers are conducting successful auctions.

eBay will suggest the most likely categories for your item when you enter the keywords in the category search at the beginning of the *Sell Your Item* form. It's

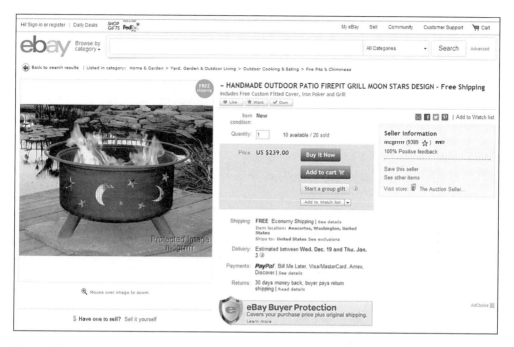

Figure 13.1 Listing Categories to Get to Fire Pits

entirely up to you if you want to use one of these categories or a different one that your research has suggested would be better.

Before listing your item in any category, follow these simple steps: First, browse through all of eBay's categories and write down which ones you feel are relevant to your product. You should be able to find at least three to five possible fits. Next, write down the number of auctions currently under way in each of those categories (this information will appear next to the category name). If there are fewer than 5,000 auctions underway when you check a category out, you may consider it *inactive*.

I consider categories with over 5,000 auctions to be *popular* and those with over 20,000 to be the *most popular*. Some categories have over 100,000 auctions going at any one time. Using this ranking system, rate the categories you have chosen for your product.

I recommend listing in the most active categories because they get the most traffic. If you put your product in an inactive section of eBay, you may get few or no bids. Avoid categories with less than 1,000 auctions, unless your product is highly specialized to that category. You should also note that if you're selling using a fixed-price listing, the final value fee varies based on the category, so a lower-priced category is usually a better option (so long as it meets the "active" test). The different category fees for fixed-price listings are detailed in chapter 21.

Never list in a category that doesn't show up on the left sidebar of the search results page for a search of that item. However well you might think it fits in a different category, you will lose a significant number of potential bidders if they never see your item.

LIST IN TWO CATEGORIES

eBay has another helpful feature called *List in Two Categories*. Listing in a second category is a great way to reach more eyeballs and generate more bids for your item.

For example, an old tray table from China could fit in both Asian Antiques and Antique Furniture. By listing in both locations, you can attract browsers in each category.

Listing in two categories incurs an additional expense, and I use it only for items that I expect to sell for over $50. When you list in two categories, eBay doubles your insertion fee (listing fee), as well as the fees for most listing upgrades (bold, gallery plus, and so on). The optional Scheduled Listing fee and the final value fee are not doubled. eBay claims to have research proving that listing in two categories will, on average, increase final values by 17 percent. If you are selling an expensive item, this can be quite profitable. When you select that second category, be sure to select a highly active one with plenty of auctions. This will get you more bang for the extra buck you are spending.

EBAY CATALOG

Items with model numbers, ISBNs, UPCs, and other standardized ways of identifying the item are typically required to be listed using the eBay Catalog (unless the item isn't already part of the Catalog). When you enter keywords about the item to select a category you will instead see "matching products" for you to select from. The easiest way to see if your item is already in the eBay Catalog is to use the product identifier (ISBN, model number and brand name, etc.). You don't have a choice of category for items in the eBay Catalog.

When you get to the Sell Your Item form you will see pre-filled item information already completed by eBay (including a title, a stock photograph, and a technical description about the item). You do not have to use eBay's suggested title, the stock photo, or the description. In fact, I recommend you change these so your listing isn't identical to hundreds of other sellers' unless it's a new item that really doesn't need an additional description. If your item is used, you may not use the stock photograph as your thumbnail photo (i.e., your first photograph). Instead, you must upload an image of the exact item you are selling.

This feature is a huge time-saver. I once had a large lot of new (remaindered) books to sell on consignment for a friend. I was able to open an auction listing for one of the books, type in the ISBN, add a couple of lines about the original cost, enter the condition of the book, and launch the auction in less than ninety seconds. In fact, using the pre-filled information from the eBay Catalog, I was able to launch thirty auctions in about forty-five minutes. If the items had been used I would have had to upload a photograph too, but that adds only a minute or so.

POWER MOVES

❏ Take some time to go through any categories relating to the products you plan to sell. Explore the various subcategory listings, including the number of auctions in each one.

❏ If you are going to sell books, music, or movies, go to the eBay Customer Support tab at the top of any eBay page and type in *eBay Catalog*. This will bring up a link to an excellent tutorial on how to use this feature.

CHAPTER 14

✦ WRITING AUCTION TITLES AND ✦ DESCRIPTIONS THAT SELL

THE TWO MOST IMPORTANT FACTORS in attracting bidders to your auctions and closing the sale are the item's title and item description. The title is what potential bidders see when they perform a search or browse through the categories. The item description is your sales pitch—a description of what you are selling and why the person reading it should bid on it or buy it. In this chapter, we will look at what constitutes a good title, how to use keywords to show up in more search results, and how to write a benefit-rich item description that closes the sale.

THE TITLE

The title is the single most important item in your listing. An arresting title has the power to "get the eyeballs" (eBay slang for getting people to view your item). The title should immediately attract potential buyers to your listing—if you get someone to click on your title, your odds of getting a bid or making a sale have just gone up by about 100 percent.

When a buyer performs a search or clicks on a category, she is presented with a page listing about fifty listing titles (the buyer can choose to view up to 200 listing titles per page). The potential buyer scans the list, looking for something that catches her attention. Making your title stand out in this list is critical to your success.

Viewed this way, a title is nothing more than a collection of words designed to stop your potential buyer's eyes from scanning the page, and instead linger long enough for him to eventually click on your listing. To accomplish this, the title must first contain a keyword that describes the item the buyer is looking for. It should also be compelling, right to the point, and state or imply a benefit to the buyer.

Keywords

The single most important criterion for titles is the use of relevant keywords. According to eBay, over 80 percent of bidders find items on eBay by using the search feature. Therefore, your title should be as precise as possible—yet also contain specific keywords that will make it come up in the greatest number of searches. Look at this title:

JERRY RICE ~ SIGNED ~ FOOTBALL JERSEY
FROM 49ERS 1988 SEASON – No Reserve

This is an excellent title for several reasons. First, it exactly describes what is being offered. Second, it is rich in keywords. It would come up in a search for the following terms:

* Jerry Rice
* Football
* Football jersey
* Jerry Rice signed

* 49ers jersey
* Jerry Rice 49ers
* Signed 49ers jersey

eBay allows eighty characters (including spaces) in a listing title. This one uses seventy-seven. Here is another example of a keyword-rich title:

NWT TRUE RELIGION DESIGNER WOMENS
SKINNY DARK BLUE JEANS, SIZE MEDIUM M 30 x 31

A woman searching for designer blue jeans might type in several combinations of keywords such as: blue jeans, designer blue jeans, True Religion (a popular brand name), blue jeans medium, jeans M, dark blue jeans 30, Skinny jeans, True Religion skinny jeans 30, etc. Any of those keyword combinations would bring this listing up in a search. This title also uses all eighty characters. (Note that to remain under this character count, the seller has used the abbreviation "NWT" for "New With Tags." See Best Practices on the opposite page for a list of abbreviations frequently used in listing titles.)

Sometimes you need to describe the condition of an item in the listing title:

JOHN STEINBECK 1937 1ST EDITION ~
OF MICE AND MEN ~ MINT w/ ORIGINAL DUST JACKET

The word "mint" tells the buyer this book is in perfect, like-new condition—something every book collector searches for.

Notice that I use all caps in my titles. Experience has shown that all-caps titles will generally stand out better in a list of auctions than will those with a combination of upper- and lowercase letters.

Because people are searching for products by keyword, it is extremely important that you use correct spelling. If you are selling a Staffordshire plate and spell it *Stafordshire*, your auction will not come up when bidders use the eBay search feature to find items.

Hot-Button Words

Years of research by direct marketers has proven that certain words have the power to make people act. If you have room in your title, after including all the relevant keywords, you should try to include *hot-button* words in your title. These are words that motivate people and increase interest. Table 14.1 lists some of the best-performing hot-button words.

Be reasonable and accurate with your choice of words. Your credibility is on the line. If a title makes a buyer click on your listing and it's immediately obvious that the bidder is being misled, you have just written a check that you can't cash. Potential bidders will just hit the back button on their browser and move on. You have just seconds to grab and keep their attention, and if they are in any doubt, they will move on.

Remember that eBay gives you eighty characters to get your point across. Use every one of them as if it were a valuable piece of real estate.

ITEM DESCRIPTIONS

Once a person clicks on your listing, you have the opportunity to sell to her—and your description is your best sales pitch. The first goal of your item description is credibility. Your item description must inspire trust, so forget about making irresponsible, wild

TABLE 14.1 Hot-Button Words

BREAKTHROUGH	SECRET	SUCCEED	TOP-SELLING
MAGICAL	LOVE	GAIN	UNIQUE
REVEALING	ENORMOUS	MONEY	FREE
NEW	BEST	SALE	HOT ITEM
ACCOMPLISH	EARN	STUNNING	UNUSUAL
FAVORITE	MORE	HOW-TO	PERFECT
SECURITY	WEALTH	PROUD	VALUE
SAVE	PROTECT	HEALTH	UNBELIEVABLE
STUNNING	DAZZLING	PROSPER	AWESOME
PERSONAL	EXCITING	FUTURE	BEST
OUTRAGEOUS	INCREDIBLE	EASY	HARD TO FIND
YOU	FREE	EXTREME	BEST ____ ON EBAY
ANNOUNCING	FEAR	FATE	
WARNING	IMAGINE	SUPER DEAL	

claims. If your item descriptions are too far-fetched, overuse adjectives, or make unfounded claims, you will sow doubt in prospective bidders' minds. Although the item description is basically a sales letter, it is important to strike a balance between compelling copy and silly or outrageous claims.

One way to inspire trust is to accurately describe your product, including any shortcomings. If a product has a flaw, mention it. If the product is new but the box is damaged, be sure to inform prospective buyers about this. If a product is perfect except for a small scratch, tell bidders and show them a photo of the scratch.

If you select "used" for the item condition, you will have an option to add an *item condition note.* This is a new feature for eBay that puts information about the condition (in addition to "new," "used," and so on) at the top of the listing page. This is optional, and it remains to be seen how many sellers will actually use it, but whether you use the item condition note or you enter a more detailed description of the condition in your item description, it is important information to convey to the buyer before he bids.

Just the Facts, Please

You have no limit to the length of your description; however that doesn't mean you should ramble on. It's important to break it up into bite-size chunks for your potential buyer or they will just lose interest and click away. The first part of your description should be no more than an accurate portrayal of the product. Describe what you are offering before you start to *sell* it. You want to be very specific. Include model number, size, weight, color, and any attachments or accessories—any information that will help bidders understand exactly what they are about to bid on or buy. There should be no confusion about the product.

It is critical that this information be contained in the first paragraph of the description. If bidders have to scroll through the entire page to find out exactly what is included in the listing, you risk their clicking away to something else. If there are a lot of specifics, you might use a bulleted list to make it easier to scan.

Know Your Audience

Before you start writing your description, decide who you are writing to. If you are selling baby clothes to stay-at-home moms, your item description will be quite different than if you are selling software to computer techies. Look at your niche market and try to picture your customers. What are their likes and dislikes? What are they looking for? How old are they and what sorts of jobs do they generally hold? What are their hobbies and interests? What makes them tick? Do they have plenty of disposable income? Are they seeking quality—or a bargain? The tone of your description should reflect all the facts and benefits you emphasize.

What's the Benefit?

In my description, I like to talk about the product's *benefits* next. Words mean something. Use their power to convey the benefits that readers will enjoy when they buy your item.

To do this, first list all your item's benefits in a separate word-processing document or on a sheet of paper. Then arrange them in order of priority (for your target customer). Now, start describing the first benefit—and move down your list until you've exhausted every benefit of your product.

Be sure here to write about the product's *benefits*—not its *features*. For example, "This barbecue grill has two height settings" is a feature. Compare it to this statement: "This barbecue grill has two height settings, an upper setting to cook slowly so your food doesn't burn and a lower setting to sear your meat instantly for the best taste." The benefits here are "so your food doesn't burn" and "sear your meat instantly for the best taste."

A successful sales pitch appeals to the base desires and self-interest of the customer. When composing a sales pitch, attention to psychology counts more than attention to writing style. What do people want? They want to be loved or liked. They want to be rich. They want to look better. They want to be successful. They want to feel that they have just scored an incredible bargain. They want to believe they are doing some good in the world. These are the factors that Madison Avenue advertisers consider when conceiving big-budget ad campaigns. However, you don't need all their talent and experience to write great item descriptions. You just have to keep in mind who you are selling to and what stimulates people to buy.

I once bought a wholesale lot of Tommy Hilfiger polo shirts from an overstock dealer. I thought I was getting a mixed lot of shirts. When they arrived, they were all large and extra large, and all of them were black. I was really annoyed; however, I now owned the shirts and had to make the most of them. I reasoned that men who wore large and extra-large shirts were probably a little thick around the waist. So I wrote an item description that first described what I was selling. In the second paragraph I said:

> I love these black polo shirts. They have the classic "Tommy" look—rich and elegant, and the black tends to hide my middle-age paunch. When I wear my Tommy Hilfiger black polo shirt, my wife says I look thinner.

Now, I wasn't lying. It is well known by fashion designers that black is slimming. In fact, my wife did say I looked good in the shirt. I got top dollar for the entire lot—several customers bought two or three shirts at a time. (I offered free shipping to anyone who bought two or more.)

Potential buyers want to know what your product will do for them, and they do not need a lot of useless distraction. Again, your item description must appeal to the profile of the buyer, must display your professionalism, and must promote a feeling of trust in you as the seller.

All the romancing you can do with a product is based on the product's real or perceived benefits. If I can't come up with enough benefits, I will often do a Web search for the product to review the advertising that others have done. You don't want to plagiarize the consumer advertising copy, but you can certainly get ideas from it.

White Space and Boldface

I'm constantly frustrated on eBay by listing descriptions that appear in small type and go on and on in one long paragraph. See Figure 14.1 for an example. This is a screenshot from an actual auction. The description is fairly well written, but because it's all run together in one long paragraph, it is somewhat hard to read. Breaking the description into three paragraphs with white space separating them would dramatically improve this description's readability.

People tend to scan a Web page looking for something that grabs their attention. Instead of one long paragraph, I recommend using a series of short paragraphs of three or four sentences each. Make lists, use bullets, and highlight important information with boldface type. Just don't overdo it. If every other word is in bold or all caps, you lose the impact.

By using short paragraphs and lists, you create *white space* in your auction. This makes it easier for people to scan the page to find the information they want.

The other major auction killer is *reverse* or *drop-out* type. This refers to featuring white or light-colored type against a dark background. It may look artistic, but it can be difficult to read. If you are selling anything to people over age forty-five, this factor is very important. As people age, their eyes require more light and greater contrast to see well. An older person will have a difficult time reading yellow type on a black background. Remember this if you choose to use templates from companies other than eBay, whose backgrounds may be darker.

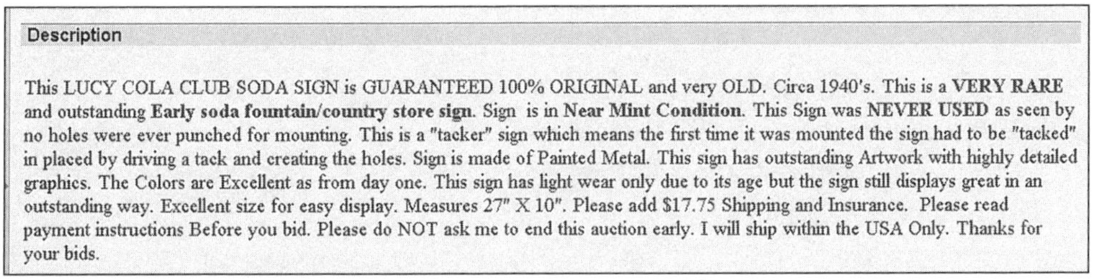

Description

This LUCY COLA CLUB SODA SIGN is GUARANTEED 100% ORIGINAL and very OLD. Circa 1940's. This is a **VERY RARE** and outstanding **Early soda fountain/country store sign**. Sign is in **Near Mint Condition**. This Sign was NEVER USED as seen by no holes were ever punched for mounting. This is a "tacker" sign which means the first time it was mounted the sign had to be "tacked" in placed by driving a tack and creating the holes. Sign is made of Painted Metal. This sign has outstanding Artwork with highly detailed graphics. The Colors are Excellent as from day one. This sign has light wear only due to its age but the sign still displays great in an outstanding way. Excellent size for easy display. Measures 27" X 10". Please add $17.75 Shipping and Insurance. Please read payment instructions Before you bid. Please do NOT ask me to end this auction early. I will ship within the USA Only. Thanks for your bids.

Figure 14.1 Sample Auction Description

Type size is another factor. If you are selling body jewelry to teens, they probably won't have difficulty reading eBay's small, default type size. But if you are selling products that older customers might want to buy, remember that many people over forty need bifocals or reading glasses. Therefore, a larger type size may be more effective. To increase the type size in your auctions, in the Sell Your Item form, select the larger type size in the HTML editor.

Increase Bids with a Call to Action

Salespeople have an old saying: "If you want to make the sale, you have to ask for the order." I have worked in sales and sales management, and I can tell you that statement is 1,000 percent correct. I cannot tell you how many times I have seen a salesperson go through a perfect product presentation and then conclude with a weak statement, such as "Well, what do you think?" You don't want to take the time to write a terrific item description only to water it down with an ineffective final statement. Instead, ask for the sale: "Don't be knocked out by a sniper bidding at the last second. Place your best bid now so you can enjoy a sizzling steak on your new barbecue this weekend."

I always end my auctions by asking for the bid. This is known as a *call to action.* Think of all the direct marketing pieces you've received in the mail over the years. Didn't all of them end with something like this: "Don't let this once-in-a-lifetime opportunity pass you by. Call now!" You need to end your auction with a similar punch.

THREE QUICK WAYS TO DISCOURAGE BIDDERS

There are three common errors that eBay sellers make, all of which discourage bidders:

1. They write short, incomplete descriptions.
2. They use large colorful type or many colors of type.
3. They write payment, shipping, and return policies that sound like jailhouse rules.

At least once or twice a day I will surf eBay and come across an auction that includes a statement like this: "If you don't pay right away I will report you to eBay." Who would want to do business with this kind of seller?

Last is the drill-sergeant mentality. This refers to people who spell out their shipping, payment, and return policies in harsh language, often in all caps. Here is one I saw recently:

> *I SHIP ON TUESDAYS AND THURSDAYS SO GET YOUR PAYMENT IN BY THOSE DAYS OR WAIT UNTIL THE FOLLOWING WEEK. I ACCEPT PAYPAL ONLY. DO NOT SEND A CHECK. IF YOU DO I WILL THROW IT AWAY AND RELIST THE ITEM.*

It is important to spell out your payment, shipping, and return policies. However, the policies should be realistic, and they should be written in friendly language that *explains your policies,* instead of *dictating them.*

Here is another example from an actual auction. This seller had a feedback rating of just over 50 percent with twelve negative comments. (Incidentally, by eBay's current standards, this seller would not be allowed to sell on eBay anymore with that feedback rating; in addition, you are no longer allowed to charge separately for insurance).

> *I ship everything by priority mail on Monday and Friday. I charge the priority mail rate plus $2.00 to pay for box and packing material. I don't guarantee anything. If you want insurance the extra cost is $5.00. I know it*

doesn't cost that much to insure a package but I have to wait in line and fill out forms at the post office and keep the forms until a claim is made and that is a big pain but I will do it for $5.00.

This seller is doing everything he can to tell me he doesn't want my business. If the tone of his e-mails to customers is anything like his policy statement, it is no wonder he has poor feedback. If someone pays on a Monday night, he won't ship until Friday and the parcel likely won't arrive until the following Tuesday or Wednesday. The whole point of paying for Priority Mail is to get something quickly.

In contrast, the following is an auction description we use to sell a line of expensive decorative fire pits. Others are selling similar items much cheaper, yet we tend to outsell our competition. Notice how we appeal to the prospective bidder's desire for quality and how we communicate the product's benefits. Also note the use of white space, the call to action, and the inclusion of shipping and payment details.

THIS IS THE WORLD'S BEST, SOLID-STEEL HAND-FORGED OUTDOOR WOOD-BURNING FIRE PIT.

THIS FIREPIT RETAILS IN UPSCALE MAIL ORDER CATALOGS FOR $399.

Free Shipping to 48 States—Sorry we cannot ship to Alaska or Hawaii

I am including a free $29 value cover when you buy this firepit from my eBay Store.

Perfect for barbecues, backyard gatherings, camping, or a quiet romantic evening at home. Our fire pits are handcrafted from durable cold-rolled steel and **INCLUDE A BBQ GRILL, A POKER FOR STIRRING COALS AND A SPARK-ARRESTING SCREEN** *to let the fire die down safely.*

Unique flame cut-out western broncos provide ventilation and add to its unique charm. Creating the perfect complement for your backyard couldn't be easier. Natural rust patina finish, no assembly required. This is not a mass-produced product. These are made entirely by hand in a small forge by master craftsmen.

These fire pits are normally only sold in high-end mail order catalogs like Smith & Hawken and Orvis for $399.

The firepit is 31" x 31" x 17" and weighs 41 lbs. so it's not going to tip over. (Total shipping weight with poker, grill, and cover is 50 lbs.)

It is not just a firepit; it also has a removable grill top so you can cook steaks, burgers, hot dogs, and more on it. Just think how good steaks would taste cooked on this grill over some real mesquite wood.

THIS IS THE BEST FIRE PIT I HAVE EVER OWNED.

I have owned several firepits of different designs and have always been disappointed. They either allow sparks to float out or they smoke too much. Most of them are so poorly made, you are lucky to get one or two seasons out of them. OUR FIREPITS ARE HEAVY, DURABLE 3MM COLD-ROLLED STEEL AND WILL LAST FOR A LIFETIME.

When I found this firepit, I bought one for myself. The very first evening we had friends over, I sold two to them on the spot. This is absolutely the best firepit on the market—bar none. The top cover is a very fine mesh so large sparks don't fly out. THE CUTOUTS IN THE SIDE PROVIDE PERFECT UPWARD VENTILATION. The smoke really goes UP. It doesn't blow around sideways, so you can sit close to it and get all the warmth. With a good roaring fire, you can sit 6 or 7 feet back and still feel the warmth.

Also, if you live in an area where open fires are banned, you can still use this model, because it qualifies as a COVERED GRILL.

I am sorry, but we CANNOT SHIP TO ALASKA, HAWAII, OR CANADA. Please note: We do not stock these because of the size and weight. They are drop-shipped directly from the forge. Shipping can take as long as 5-6 days to the East Coast. Sorry, but we cannot ship this item overseas.

I am going to go out on a limb and offer a money-back guarantee on the cost of the pit and the outbound shipping. Keep it for 30 days and use it for a few fires. If you are not completely satisfied, send it back (at your expense) and I will refund all of your money including the shipping cost. Your only risk is the return shipping cost. I know you will love this thing and I don't really expect to get any back, but I will stand behind my guarantee if I do.

We have an excellent feedback rating and strive to keep it that way. Your complete satisfaction is our first priority. Please visit our About Me Page to learn more about our company, our feedback, and to see our other auctions.

After reading all this, you may worry that writing successful item descriptions is difficult or a lot of work. It's not, once you get the hang of it. Take your time crafting effective auction descriptions as you are getting started, and after a while you will find that it becomes second nature.

POWER MOVES

Titles

❏ Sit down with a notebook and a pen and write out as many keywords as you can think of for your product.

❏ Now do a search on eBay for those keywords. Write down the titles that appeal to you. Open those auctions and look at the corresponding hit counters. Determine which titles appear to get the most hits.

❏ Using the above information as a guide, begin creating your own attention-grabbing titles.

Descriptions

❏ List every benefit of your product in a separate document. Now write a sentence about each benefit and how it relates to a buyer.

❏ Once you have done this, list your item for sale. In the description field, first include all the facts about the product that you are selling. Fill in the rest of the description with the benefit statements you created.

CHAPTER 15

✦ MASTERING AUCTION ✦ PHOTOGRAPHY

AS AN EBAY SELLER, you need to take sharp, attractive photographs. Photography is one of those skills that can take years to learn well. Fortunately, digital cameras—with all their automated features—have made this task much simpler. In this chapter, we will look at the equipment and software you will need to take digital photographs and upload them to your auctions. We'll also discuss powerful techniques for taking photographs that sell, and the most efficient ways to host and upload your pictures.

DIGITAL CAMERA SELECTION

Your first task is to select a good digital camera with all the features you will need. There are hundreds of digital cameras on the market, and new models are coming out every week. The trend today is toward higher and higher image quality. This is expressed in the number of pixels or megapixels a camera can resolve. The higher this number (or the greater the resolution), the more expensive the camera.

eBay requires all item photos to be at least 500 pixels on the longest side, and prefers this number to be at least 1600 pixels. When bidders enlarge or zoom in on your picture, you want to make sure they can see the details clearly.

For items that are not well-known (clothing, collectibles, etc.) details are important. eBay Picture Hosting Services can handle photographs of up to seven megabytes (MB) in size each, so you don't need to worry about a photo being too high-resolution. (A megapixel is ten million pixels.) I usually shoot at the "medium" or "high" resolution setting for a typical digital camera. A three-megapixel camera will suffice, but most cameras these days are far higher than that, so you should have no worries about not having an image whose resolution is high enough. Try to do all of your editing at once. Multiple saves in JPEG (.jpg file extension) format compresses the quality, so the fewer intermediate saves the better. You can use other file formats, but JPEG; it's the best optimized for the web and typically will load the quickest. You can find out more about uploading pictures on eBay's page "Adding Pictures to Your Listing."

Here are some of the features you will need in a camera used for auction photography:

* **TRIPOD SCREW:** Almost all cameras include a standard tripod screw mount at the bottom. It is very important to use a tripod when taking auction photographs to avoid the blurred images that occur when you hold a camera by hand.

* **MACRO SETTING:** *Macro* is the photographic term for the ability to focus very close to an object. Typically the macro feature will allow you to focus as close as 3 or 4 inches (8 or 10 cm) from the subject. This is important for photographing small objects or showing details, such as the original manufacturer's price tag or a maker's mark on pottery or silver.

* **WHITE BALANCE ADJUSTMENT:** We will talk about *white balance* in detail shortly. Basically, this is how you adjust a camera to account for the different "color temperatures" of light. (The color reflected from an object will vary subtly, depending on the type of lighting.) Almost all cameras have an automatic white balance adjustment feature, but you want to make sure you get one that allows you to manually choose between daylight, fluorescent, halogen, and incandescent settings.

* **EXPOSURE ADJUSTMENT:** The light meter in a camera can be fooled by bright backgrounds. Since you'll often be shooting against a white background, especially when using a light tent (see page 172 for more about this), you need a camera that can adjust for this exposure.

* **OPTICAL ZOOM:** Digital cameras come with *optical zoom* and/or *digital zoom*. Digital zoom is essentially only zooming in on an image (as you might do with a photograph on a computer screen). Digital zoom does not preserve the resolution of the image when it is zoomed in. Therefore, make sure your camera has a basic optical zoom feature. You can tell if it does by pushing the zoom button and seeing if the lens actually moves in and out. If not, the camera is only using digital zoom.

* **APERTURE PRIORITY SETTING:** The ability to select a small lens opening (aperture) allows you to achieve what is called greater *depth of field*. Greater depth of field means that there is a wider range in which the material you are shooting will be in focus.

Nikon, Sony, and Canon all make fairly low-cost cameras that fit these criteria. Since models change so rapidly, I'm not going to recommend any specific model. Just make sure to look for the features I've specified.

TAKING PHOTOGRAPHS THAT SELL

A complete course on digital photography is a subject for another book. Instead, I have organized the most important information as a series of tips. If you want to learn more about digital photography, there are several books on the market that run the gamut from beginner to advanced. For a handy, basic book aimed at the auction photographer, check out *Online Auction Photo Secrets,* available through my Web site (www.skipmcgrath.com).

Use a Tripod

Unless you are shooting outdoors or using a flash, digital cameras tend to use a very slow shutter speed. With a slow shutter speed, typically under 1/125th of a second, most people cannot hold a camera steady enough to prevent blurring. Using a sturdy tripod will allow you to shoot all the way down to 1/30th of a second with good results. Make sure your tripod has an adjustable head that will rotate the camera both horizontally and vertically. A quality tripod can cost as much as $100, but I have found that most large photo stores often have good—even professional-quality—secondhand tripods for as little as $20 to $30.

Focus Carefully and Correctly

I see out-of-focus pictures on eBay every day. One reason for this is autofocus malfunction. Most digital cameras project a laser or infrared beam onto the object being photographed and measure the reflection to determine the focus. Problems may occur when large objects allow the beam to spread out, or when something reflective on the object itself "fools" the autofocus feature.

The other issue is depth of field. Have you ever looked at a photograph where the subject is in focus and the background is all fuzzy? Depth of field is the focal distance, from near to far, in which a camera can focus. The aperture, or lens opening, on a camera adjusts to allow more or less light into the camera. When the lens opening is large, the camera has a very narrow range of focus. When the opening is small, the focal length is longer. This effect is magnified when you are shooting very close up, such as when you are photographing small objects.

The aperture can be set manually on most digital cameras. Lens openings are marked as a series of numbers that range from 3.5 to 16. The higher the number, the greater the depth of field you will have. This is critical when shooting up close with the macro function, because the macro function also limits the depth of field for technical reasons I won't get into here. If I am shooting an object close up, I typically use an aperture of 8 or higher. With automatic digital cameras, when you set the aperture at a high number, the camera compensates for the reduction in light by slowing down the shutter speed. This is why you need a tripod. If you try to hand-hold a camera at a slow shutter speed, you will almost always get a blurry photo.

Finally, using your camera's aperture priority mode to narrow the lens opening can improve the performance of your autofocus, if you are using that feature, by improving your depth of field.

Use Soft Lighting

Sunlight or direct light from a bulb or a flash may create hot spots and reflections in your photos. If you are shooting outside, you should shoot in bright shade or on a cloudy day. If you have a north-facing window, this can often produce very nice, diffused light. If you are using lights, you can either purchase white plastic light covers to diffuse the light or use a light tent (essentially a cube where all sides are covered in diffusing fabric except the front, which you shoot into).

You can view and learn more about the different types of light tents at www.EZAuctionTools.com. They start at around $30 to $40 and go up to $200 for the complete sets with lights.

Avoid Clutter

Try to photograph only the object you are shooting. Placing an object on a table with other stuff in the background will distract from your subject. If you use a light tent, this is easy. However, you will sometimes have to photograph large objects that do not fit in the tent. In this case, be sure to clean up the background as much as possible. If you are shooting a computer, for example, remove everything from the desk it's on and hide the wires or any other distracting objects. If you are shooting a car, drive the car to a park where you can shoot it with grass and trees in the background, instead of shooting it in your garage or driveway.

If you are shooting apparel, you should invest in a dress form or mannequin. Place the mannequin against a wall draped with cloth that contrasts with the color of the clothing and diffuses any shadows.

Avoid Underexposure

If you are shooting against a white or bright background, or are shooting outside in bright light, you camera's automatic light meter may "read" the surrounding light instead of your object, underexposing the image. Most good digital cameras include an over/underexposure compensation adjustment feature. If you are shooting against a white background, such as in a light tent, try adjusting your camera's exposure setting to +1 or even +1.5. This will prevent the subject of your picture from appearing too dark, as your camera adjusts to the white background (a case of underexposure). One way you can tell whether you are underexposing your pictures is if white backgrounds appear gray in the photographs. If this happens, or if your objects are just too dark, then try adjusting the exposure compensation until the white looks truly white.

Use the Correct White Balance

Different types of light have different wavelengths. Without getting into a discussion of optical physics, this means that you have to adjust your camera for the type of light you are using. If your camera is set on *daylight* and you shoot with an ordinary household lightbulb, your photos will appear yellow. If you shoot with a fluorescent light, your photos will appear blue-gray. You can purchase daylight bulbs—ordinary lightbulbs with the same wavelength as daylight—from almost any grocery or hardware store. They are even available in the modern compact-fluorescent bulbs, which do not get hot like regular incandescent bulbs and last a lot longer. Any modern digital camera should have a white balance setting. Just set your camera for the type of light you are using: daylight, halogen, indoor incandescent lightbulbs, or fluorescent lights.

Get Close

Getting close to your subject will produce a better photo. It is easier to focus accurately when you are close, and you'll capture more of the object without the distracting clutter.

The best way to learn to take good photos is to practice. Read your camera's instruction manual from cover to cover, and experiment with all the controls and functions until you are comfortable with them. Fortunately, with digital cameras you don't have to spend a fortune on film and developing to learn how best to use your camera.

MANAGING YOUR PHOTOS

Image management is the term used by eBay sellers for editing, storing, and uploading photos.

When shooting a colorful item, try placing a piece of colored cloth or craft paper behind the object. Pick a color that matches one of the minor colors—not the main color. For example, if you were shooting a blue teapot with a gray or yellow trim, you would use a gray or yellow background paper. This is a trick used by professional photographers; it will give your photo an image of greater depth and will allow the main color to "pop," or stand out, in the photograph.

Editing Software

Most digital cameras come with photo-editing software. I happen to like Nikon's the best. You can set it so whenever you plug your camera into the computer, the program automatically opens and you can import your photos with one click. If you own an Apple computer, you have iPhoto, which is one of the best all-around photo-editing and management programs on the market. PCs come with Windows Live Photo Gallery, which isn't bad either. Both have similar features, are free with your computer, and are easy to use.

There are also a number of software programs you can buy to perform these functions. There are some very advanced (and expensive) programs available, such as Adobe PhotoShop; however, there are functional and less expensive programs available as well. If you go to www.shareware.com or www.tucows.com, you'll find a number of free image- and photo-management programs you can download (just type *photo editing* into the search box). One of the best is Serif Photo Plus. The download is free; the company makes money selling the support and training tools, which cost far less than most expensive programs and are excellent. There is a paid version, but the free one has all the tools you will need.

Whichever program you use, you should be able to easily plug your camera into your computer, import the photos, give them file names so you can organize them, and then edit and crop the images. Any software program you choose should allow you to adjust the brightness and contrast of your photographs. This is a real time-saver, because then you don't have to reshoot your products.

Storing and Uploading Your Images

Once you have your photos edited and named, you need to create a folder on your hard drive called *eBay Photos* (or something similar). Within this folder, you should create subfolders for the various product categories you are selling. Simply name and file your photos in the appropriate folders, so you can easily find them when you are ready to upload them to your listings.

Once you have your photographs stored on your computer's hard drive, you need to import them into your listings. eBay allows you twelve images per listing for free. You just upload them when you complete the *Sell Your Item* form. This also optimizes the images for eBay Mobile, so buyers purchasing through their cell phones and tablets will see the pictures correctly displayed for that device (the way it displays in the mobile version is different from the way it appears on the Web site).

Another way to host your photos is with a Web site. If you already have a Web site, you can simply upload your photos to your site, labeling each one with a separate URL (uniform resource locator, or the "address" of the photo) and then insert the URL of the specific photo into each auction. I don't recommend this option. Not only is it is time-consuming, but you also have to pay for the Web space and need FTP (file transfer protocol) software to upload your photos.

Managing Photos with Auction Management Services

In chapter 23, we are going to cover auction management services. A good free one to start with is Auctiva.com (they also have subscription levels). Other popular services are Vendio (www.vendio.com) and InkFrog (www.inkfrog.com). All of these companies will host your images as part of their service. In addition to photo hosting, you'll get numerous features so you can automate your auctions as well. In my opinion, this is the best option if you plan to launch fifteen or more auctions a week.

Here's how it works: You simply upload your images to the Web site of the auction management service, where they are subsequently stored (you can also organize them into folders). When choosing an image for your auction, simply double-click on or check the appropriate photo. The auction management service inserts the URL of the particular image into your auction. When the auction launches, eBay looks for those images at the named URL, and they are displayed in your auction every time someone clicks on it. Make sure you select a Gallery image (which will be the thumbnail that shows on the search results page) so the URL is fed constantly to eBay. Each of the auction management services offers this "gallery picture" option. Once you start using an auction management service, you will appreciate the speed—and therefore the time-saving aspects—of hosting your photos this way. You will also enjoy the additional benefits such as templates, automated customer e-mails, shipping calculators, and inventory management tools that come with the service. These do come at a cost, though, so you can happily stick with eBay's Picture Services through the Sell Your Item form until you can justify the cost by the amount of time you will be saving.

POWER MOVES

❑ After selecting the camera you are going to use for your auction photography, spend some time familiarizing yourself with the instruction manual. Pay special attention to the size settings, white balance, macro (close-up) feature, manual focus, and aperture priority settings. Once you understand how all the features work, take some practice shots. Upload them to your computer and use whatever image editing software you have to crop, rotate, and resize the photos.

❑ Don't forget to use a tripod. This is very important.

CHAPTER 16

✦ PROMOTING YOUR AUCTIONS ✦

EBAY OFFERS SEVERAL OPTIONAL features to help you drive potential buyers to your auctions. While a few of them are free, most come with a fee. The key to using these features effectively is to make sure they are appropriate to the type and value of the auction you are running, and that the cost provides a good return on investment (ROI).

Now that you have enhanced your listings with photographs, descriptions, and titles that sell, the next step is to attract more buyers to your listings. In this chapter we will explore how to take advantage of various free promotional tools and evaluate the performance and ROI of those that are fee-based.

FREE PROMOTIONAL TOOLS

Obviously, free tools provide the best return on investment. eBay offers promotions from time to time, including free listing days (sometimes category-specific), where you may list as many items as you like with no listing fees, free subtitles, etc. You can learn about these and other opportunities on the Announcements page, accessible from the link at the bottom of the eBay Homepage (under the Community heading). All announcements from the prior two weeks are posted in chronological order, with the most recent at the top. You should check this list first thing every morning, since free listings and listing discounts are typically offered on very short notice—usually one day or less.

EBAY PAID PROMOTIONS

eBay offers you various listing upgrades, each for an additional fee. Let's take a look at each one. Fixed-price listings that run for the same length as auctions (3, 5, 7, or 10 days) have the same listing upgrade fees as auctions (in most cases). However, listing upgrade fees for both thirty-day and Good 'Til Canceled fixed-price listings are more expensive. The first number in parentheses below next to each listing upgrade name is the fee for auction-style listings and fixed-price listings running for 3, 5, 7, or 10 days. The second number is the price for thirty-day fixed-price listings. These fees are completely different if you have an eBay Store subscription, which we will cover in chapter 26.

Subtitle (Fee: $0.50, $1.50)

A subtitle is just that—a second title that appears in slightly smaller print just below your auction title on the eBay Search Results page. A subtitle can provide descriptive information about your item that buyers will see when browsing through categories or viewing search results. (Words included in the subtitle do not come up when buyers perform a basic search, however.) Subtitles are limited to sixty-five characters. Because of the cost, you only want to use a subtitle for items where you expect the profit margin to easily cover the expense. For example, if you were selling a product with a projected profit margin of less than $5.00, the subtitle would represent 10 percent or more of your profits. If you anticipate that the cost of the subtitle will equal more than 10 percent of your profit margin, the feature may not be worth its cost.

A subtitle allows you to spotlight features or benefits that may not fit in the title field but would be of interest to potential buyers viewing a list of items. It may contain additional information about what you are selling, such as "accessories included," or may include information about outstanding benefits, special offers, and so on. I find that subtitles make your listing stand out somewhat from the other listings around it. In fact, according to eBay, listings using subtitles are 18 percent more likely to sell. Here is an example of how I use a subtitle:

> COWBOY STYLE, HANDMADE SOLID STEEL FIRE PIT & BARBECUE
> GRILL—No Reserve
>
> Free poker, grill & spark arrestor. Free shipping with Buy It Now

Bold (Fee: $2.00, $4.00)

This feature presents your listing title in boldface type, making it stand out from other listings. This is one of my favorite options, because it's a proven producer. eBay's own research has shown this feature to increase final values by an average of 21 percent. At a cost of $2, as long as you are listing an item that will sell for over $25, this is the single best promotional tool in terms of ROI.

Gallery Plus (Fee: $0.35, $1.00)

The small thumbnail photo next to your listing title on the search results page is your Gallery image, and this is free (and required by eBay). For an extra $0.35, you can get an *enlarge* tag below the thumbnail, which shows buyers that they can enlarge your photograph to 400 x 400 pixels (the thumbnail is ordinarily 96 x 96 pixels) by hovering the mouse over the image. This is not really a necessary option unless you're selling something where the thumbnail doesn't really show off the features. For example, if you're selling a set of items together, this may increase the chances of the buyer clicking through to your auction.

It is worth noting that Gallery Plus is free for both auction-style and fixed-price listings in the Collectibles, Art, Pottery & Glass, and Antiques categories. If your item is being sold in one of these categories, go ahead and check the box for Gallery Plus when you upload your images. If it is free, it is worth using—your competitors will be using it.

Value Pack (Fee: $0.65, $2.00)

Value Pack is a combination of features. It includes Gallery Plus, Listing Designer, and Subtitle. We mentioned Listing Designer in Week 1 (the option to add a theme border around your item description). It costs 10 cents for auctions and 30 cents for thirty-day fixed-price listings. If you were to buy all of these three features separately, your total would be $0.95 for auctions and $2.80 for thirty-day fixed-price listings. So if you're planning to use all of them anyway, this is a better deal, but if you're not planning to use them all, you could end up paying more than you planned.

10-Day Duration (Fee: $0.40, Free)

This feature costs 40 cents for auction-style listings but is free for fixed-price listings. If you have a collectible item, a one-off, or something like that, you would be wise to use a 10-day duration to enable more potential buyers to see it. I rarely use 10-day fixed-price listings, though.

International Site Visibility (Fee: $0.10 to $0.40, $0.50)

If you are specifically marketing to an international audience, paying for International Site Visibility is probably worth the cost. This will place your auction in the main search results for searches on international eBay sites (such as eBay.ca, eBay.co.uk, eBay.au, etc.). The fees are tiered, based on the starting price for auction-style listings, and are flat-rate for fixed-price listings, no matter what the duration. (See Table 16.1.)

This replaces the need to list the item specifically on the international eBay Web site, which would cost far more, and allows you to promote a one-off item to both international and domestic buyers without the risk of it getting bids on two separate listings when you have only one item.

Despite what eBay says about the performance of its various promotional tools, you should test each one yourself on your own listings. eBay's numbers are averages over all types of products in all price ranges. You need to see what works for you and for your product(s).

TABLE 16.1 Fees for International Site Visibility

Starting Price	Auction Fee	Fixed-Price Listing Fee
$0.01 to $9.99	$0.10	$0.50
$10.00 to $49.99	$0.20	$0.50
$50.00 and up	$0.40	$0.50

Set up a spreadsheet that lists your auction items and which, if any, promotional features you used. Now create columns for hits, bids, final values, total fees, and net profits. Try running auctions with various combinations of options in order to gather a variety of data. In no time at all, you will be able to determine the optimal combination for your particular product(s). Keep this spreadsheet in your reference binder so that you may access it when you are considering using these features.

POWER MOVES

❑ Visit the eBay fees page at http://pages.ebay.com/help/sell/fees. html. Expand the listing to show all the fees and print out a copy. Having this information at the ready when you are deciding which promotional items to use will save you time and help you make better decisions.

❑ Create a spreadsheet for market testing. After every listing ends, record the options used, the number of hits, number of watchers, number of bids the auction received, and the final outcome—no sale or the final value. Use this information to assess the performance of your auctions with and without various upgrade combinations.

CHAPTER 17

✦ SHIPPING, HANDLING, ✦ AND INSURANCE

POOR SHIPPING PRACTICES are a leading cause of negative feedback on eBay; they are specifically addressed by two of the Detailed Seller Ratings (DSR). eBay buyers have come to expect that they will receive their purchases intact and professionally packaged. What you charge buyers for shipping is also important, because that influences their expectations and feedback. Therefore, your challenge as a seller is to provide quality packaging and shipping at a low enough cost that it will be attractive to buyers.

In this chapter, we'll discuss the advantages of the various shipping carriers; ways to save on shipping costs, supplies, and insurance; and how to automate the process and set up a convenient and efficient shipping station.

SHIPPING WITH THE US POSTAL SERVICE (USPS)

More and more eBay sellers are using Priority Mail to ship their items. For items that weigh less than six pounds, Priority Mail is competitive with UPS. UPS becomes cheaper between five and six pounds.

USPS provides free boxes, envelopes, and labels for Priority Mail. When you add on the cost of shipping materials, Priority Mail is not that much more expensive than Parcel Post—and it's a lot cheaper than UPS for small packages, for which you have to provide your own boxes. Even if purchased in large quantities, 12-by-12-by-12-inch (30cm^3) boxes can cost as much as $0.90 each. When you buy them in small quantities, they can cost as much as $1.50 each.

Priority Mail offers both a simple flat-rate option and the by-weight, zoned system. Flat-rate packaging includes envelopes and various box sizes. The flat-rate envelope is the cheapest rate you can get for the envelope. However, the by-weight Priority Mail price may be lower than the flat-rate for that box size, based on the weight and destination of your parcel. So it pays to do your research and see which is cheaper. Certainly, flat-rate boxes and envelopes are the most convenient for sellers, because there is no weighing and measuring. To find a shipping rate, go to www.usps.com and type in your package's weight and the zip code you're shipping it to. You can order free USPS shipping supplies online at http://shop.usps.com. There is also a special link for eBay sellers where you can order Priority Mail boxes with the eBay logo imprinted on them: http://ebaysupplies.usps.com.

A form of tracking or delivery confirmation is required by eBay to be eligible for many of the promotions, discounts, seller protections, and so on. Always use this. If you purchase your postage through eBay Labels (i.e., you initiate from My eBay and pay via PayPal) the USPS delivery confirmation number is automatically linked to your listing and uploaded to eBay for you.

Stealth Postage

One of the greatest features of paying for your postage online (either through eBay Labels or directly from the USPS) is *stealth postage*. With this tool, you can print a postage label that does not show the actual cost of the postage. It has a bar code that post office computers can recognize, but there is no postage amount printed on the label. So if your postage is $3.90 and you charge $4.90 for shipping and handling, your buyer will not be able to see this disparity when the package arrives.

EBAY LABELS

To receive an automatic five-star DSR for "Shipping Time," you must upload tracking information within one business day of receiving payment. This can be a pain if you have to manually enter delivery confirmation numbers for each of your items. It's easy to make mistakes too. However, if you use eBay Labels, your tracking information is automatically uploaded (and the buyer's address information is automatically entered into the label, so you have less risk of a clerical error). Be aware, though, that if you use eBay Labels, your buyer gets an automatic e-mail when you print the postage for their item. Many buyers misinterpret this to mean their item has been shipped. So don't print postage on Saturday if you're not going to ship the item until Monday. Remember, the upload requirement for the five-star DSR is within one *business* day, so weekends don't count.

The other advantage of eBay Labels is getting the online price. As well as free delivery confirmation, your actual postage rate is lower. This can add up significantly.

INSURANCE

You cannot charge a buyer for insurance separately. It has to be built into your shipping cost. You are responsible for the item getting to your buyer safely, so if it is lost in the mail, it is your responsibility. You are required to refund the buyer's payment or replace the item, and then you have to deal with claiming back from the carrier if you chose to purchase insurance.

The truth about insurance is that very few packages are ever lost. We have been selling on eBay for twelve years. In that time, we have lost only two packages out of the thousands we have shipped—and one of them eventually turned up.

I recommend the services of ShipSurance (www.shipsurance.com), formerly Discount Shipping Insurance (DSI). ShipSurance is a private discount insurer. Its rates are up to 90 percent less than those of the post office or of private carriers such as UPS or FedEx. Also, ShipSurance gives you a little card that you can drop in the package box to show the customer that his item was insured. Unlike the post office, you can claim losses much sooner and get paid in about five days instead of thirty to forty-five days.

BIZ BUILDER

If you will be shipping in large volumes—one hundred packages a month or more—consider calling ShipSurance and asking for a customized quote. The company's toll-free number is 866–852–9956.

Here is an example of how you can make a little extra money each year by using a discount insurance company. Consider the following costs:

USPS Priority Mail cost	$5.90	What you charge for S&H	$6.95
Insurance cost ($100 item)	$0.45	Your profit	$0.60
Your actual cost	$6.35		

This is not an unreasonable charge for shipping and handling. The key to getting this across to the buyer is to have a statement in your auction *and* in your end-of-auction e-mail that reads something like this:

> *Please note that our shipping and handling charge is designed to cover the cost of shipping the item, of insurance, and for materials to properly package your item so it arrives safely.*

If you ship 200 packages a month and make an average of $0.60 on each one, that is $120 extra income per month, or $1,440 per year.

PRIVATE CARRIERS

If you are going to be a high-volume seller of items weighing more than five pounds, then you should open an account with a private carrier, such as UPS, FedEx, or DHL. My current favorite service is UPS Ground. UPS has a discount for eBay sellers that brings their rates down by more than 30 percent, and you can get their rates and select services in the *Shipping Calculator* in the *Sell Your Item* form.

To receive available discounts, first go online to the carrier's Web site and open an account. Once you have an account, you will be given information on how to contact an account representative. Contact your rep by e-mail or phone and give her an estimate of your shipping volume. The representative will usually get back to you within a few days with a discount quote. Make sure you let her know that you are also getting quotes from her competition. For UPS, if you are printing your postage through eBay Labels and paying with PayPal, you will automatically get the reduced rate without having to open an account.

SHIPPING POLICY

Whether you use eBay's *Sell Your Item* form or a private auction management service, there is a place for you to spell out your shipping policy. This is an eBay requirement—you must specify your shipping charges and handling time (the time between receiving cleared payment and actually posting the item).

Buyers sometimes become confused when looking at and bidding on multiple auctions. If there is a misunderstanding during the payment process and you have specified a shipping policy in your auction, you can simply refer them back to the auction or copy and paste the specified shipping policy into an e-mail. Showing a buyer proof that he was informed of applicable costs usually circumvents any problem.

If you charge a handling fee in addition to shipping, this is the place to mention it. Remember: Don't just say, "We charge a handling fee on all sales." Instead, explain the reason for the extra cost: "I pack all our merchandise professionally in new packing materials. I add $1.25 to the actual shipping charge to cover the cost of shipping materials."

SHIPPING STATION

To pack and ship items efficiently, set up a clean, organized shipping area in your home or office, with all your supplies nearby. This station should include boxes and packing supplies, a tape gun, a label printer, and a postage scale. Remember that your time is valuable. Having a dedicated and orderly shipping area can save you hours each week.

BIZ BUILDER

Experienced PowerSellers and Top-Rated Sellers who manage large volumes of shipments often purchase cheap, secondhand computers for their shipping stations. To save time, you can connect such a computer to your postage scale and label printer. Also, because packaging items is so time-consuming, a lot of sellers hire neighborhood high school students to come over once a day and pack and ship their items. If the student has a car, she can even drop packages off at the post office or UPS store for you.

HOW TO PACK GOODS

How you package your items is a major factor in your customers' satisfaction. Poorly packaged goods can lead to all sorts of headaches, from additional costs incurred to refund a customer's money or replace the original shipment, to negative feedback. Remember, unpacking the item is the last impression your buyer has of you before leaving feedback.

Here are some packaging tips: For DVDs or CDs—whether they're movies, music, or software—use CD mailers. These are cardboard packages of just the right size for sending such items.

Tyvek mailers are ideal for shipping clothing and other soft goods. Wrap the clothing in blank newsprint or tissue paper and then place the merchandise in these water-resistant, tear-proof mailers. Because Tyvek is so lightweight, shipping in Tyvek mailers is cheaper than shipping in boxes, and you can get free Priority Mail-branded Tyvek envelopes from the post office.

Postcards, photographs, stamps, and sports cards are also simple to mail. You can place the item between two flat corrugated shipping blanks (sold at office supply stores) and then slide it into a bubble mailer, or you can purchase stay flat mailers. These mailers are difficult to bend and often come with self-adhesive strips on the flap.

For glass and other fragile items, I strongly recommend double boxing. This is your best protection against breakage. Here is the proper way to double-box: First, wrap your item in Bubble Wrap and then place it in a box, leaving approximately 2 inches (5 cm) of space on all sides of your piece. Fill this void with packing peanuts, balled-up blank newsprint, or kraft paper. You should then place this smaller box inside a slightly larger one and again fill the extra space with Styrofoam peanuts or Bubble Wrap.

Packing and shipping with care makes a big difference in your success as an eBay seller. When your box arrives at the buyer's house or office, his first impression is based on the condition of the package. If you send his treasure in an old shoebox stuffed with yesterday's newspaper, the impression will be less than flattering. He may not leave you negative feedback, but he won't be inclined to leave you positive feedback, either.

SHIPPING MATERIALS

Shipping materials such as boxes, tape, Bubble Wrap, Styrofoam peanuts, and so on can be very expensive. It turns out that one of the best places to shop for these materials is right on eBay itself. A number of dealers sell these materials at very competitive prices. Although shipping supplies are typically not heavy (with the exception of large shipments of cardboard boxes), they are bulky. Oftentimes, the shipping cost will have a large impact on your total cost.

The trick here is to shop locally. Look for eBay sellers that are located close by. I am close to Seattle. I once bought a large quantity of padded envelopes from a seller in Georgia and didn't bother to look at the shipping cost. By the time I received them, they ended up being more expensive than if I had just purchased them at my local office supply store at the regular retail price. I now purchase my shipping supplies exclusively from sellers located on the West Coast.

BIZ BUILDER

Your local gift shop is a treasure trove of free shipping and packing materials. These merchants receive daily shipments of fragile items requiring large amounts of Bubble Wrap, Styrofoam peanuts, and sturdy boxes.

Local laws may require these shops to recycle packing materials, rather than throw them away. This can be expensive. Believe me—store owners are usually happy to give these things away. Other stores that receive large quantities of shipping and packing materials include kitchen stores, gift shops, electronics stores (such as Radio Shack), and small neighborhood hardware stores.

You should add a small amount to your shipping cost for packaging and handling, but this fee should not be excessive. Bidders get upset when they are charged $5.00 for shipping and they receive a package showing that the postage cost a mere $1.25. While it's acceptable to cover the cost of the box and the shipping material, the costs you pass on to the customer should be reasonable. Remember, stealth postage is your friend if the postage cost is higher than the buyer paid. However, if you are offering free shipping or you are assuming some of the cost of shipping, then make sure the actual cost is on the label, so the buyers can see the value of what they got for free.

If something requires special packaging, such as an odd-sized box or large amounts of packing material, explain these circumstances in the auction description.

POWER MOVES

❑ Set up a shipping station with tape, a tape gun, a scale, and any additional supplies you will need.

❑ If you decide to use Priority Mail, go online and order your supplies.

❑ Visit the Web sites for the USPS, UPS, and FedEx Ground and compare the rates for the size and weight of the product you are shipping.

❑ If you decide to use a private courier service, visit the service's Web site or call their customer service and open an account. If you will be shipping large quantities of packages each month, consider calling the company to get a customized quote.

❑ Print postage online to receive reduced prices on postage and additional services.

CHAPTER 18

✦ BOOSTING YOUR PROFITS ✦ BY SELLING INTERNATIONALLY

THE ADVANTAGES OF SELLING internationally depend on the type of product you are selling and how easy or difficult it is to ship. Not all products appeal to international buyers, and some products are illegal or just too difficult to ship. For example, you cannot export tobacco, alcohol, or certain electronic devices containing encryption algorithms, and the USPS does not allow lithium-ion batteries to be shipped internationally. In general, you only want to ship products overseas that cost more than $50—otherwise, the shipping cost is too high relative to the cost of the item.

Despite the challenges, opening your listings to international buyers can greatly increase your profits. As we mentioned, eBay operates in twenty-seven countries across the globe. In addition, people from dozens of other countries surf the US eBay site. The first year I started selling internationally, overseas orders accounted for more than 19 percent of my business; today that percentage is even higher.

In this chapter, we'll discuss how to maximize your profits by selling internationally, and how to reduce costs so that your margins more than compensate for the additional effort and expense of selling overseas.

POWERFUL PROFITS

The main advantage of selling internationally is profit. International buyers, especially those from Europe and Japan, tend to pay more than American buyers do for the same products. And they don't seem to mind the high cost of shipping. Make sure you add the International Visibility listing upgrade on the Sell Your Item form during the listing process if you're speci- fically looking for international bidders. This way it will show up in their results on their home site (eBay U.K., eBay Australia, etc.) within the main results, as well as on the eBay US site.

FIND YOUR MARKET

There are three major issues to consider when you sell internationally. The first is your product—does it appeal to international buyers? The only way to find out is to list your products in overseas markets. You do this by adding the *International shipping* option into the Sell Your Item form and then specifying *Ship-to locations* (see Figure 18.1). Simply check off each country to which you will agree to ship.

BIZ BUILDER

The best items to sell internationally are those with high dollar values relative to their weight. These include collectibles like ephemera, coins and stamps, jewelry, small electronics such as personal digital assistants (PDAs), MP3 players, automotive accessories, and other lightweight, high-value items.

International shipping

Calculated: Cost varies by buyer location ▾

ⓘ If you offer international shipping, your item may be sold on another eBay site. If so, your listing will be subject to that site's eBay Buyer Protection and other policies.

Package type ⓘ
Package (or thick envelope) ▾
☐ Irregular package

Weight
Custom weight ▾ 0 lbs. 0 oz.

Ship to ⓘ
Choose custom location ▾

Services ⓘ ⓘ Research rates
USPS Priority Mail International ▾

☐ N. and S. America ☑ Europe ☑ Asia

☑ Canada ☑ United Kingdom ☑ Australia

☑ Mexico ☑ Germany ☐ Japan

Offer additional service

ⓘ Exclude countries you don't want to ship to by using the Exclude shipping locations option.
(If the option does not appear, click **Add or remove options**.)

Additional ship to locations - buyers contact for costs
Will ship to the United States and the following ▾

☐ N. and S. America ☐ Europe ☐ Asia

☐ Canada ☐ United Kingdom ☐ Australia

☐ Mexico ☐ Germany ☐ Japan

Combined shipping discounts ⓘ
No combined shipping discount rules have been created.
Create rules

International options ⓘ
• Handling cost: US $0.00
Change

Exclude shipping locations ⓘ

Figure 18.1 Ship-to Locations

I don't mind selecting regions (Europe, Asia, etc.), because you then look to the bottom of the section and create an exclusion list to exclude certain shipping locations. You can select specific countries within each region that you do not want to ship to, while allowing all other countries in that region to buy from you.

Provided you've set up your *Buyer Requirements* to block bidders in countries to which you don't ship, if someone tries to bid from a country on your exclusion list, even if her region is selected in the Ship-to locations, her bid will be automatically blocked by eBay. By listing internationally, you will be able to discern which parts of the world are viable markets for your product.

SHIPPING

The second consideration is shipping. Can you ship the product for a reasonable amount relative to its cost? As a rule of thumb, if the shipping cost would exceed 20 percent of the estimated final value, I would probably not offer the item internationally.

BIZ BUILDER

Outside the United States, I only sell to Western European countries, plus Japan, Singapore, Australia, Israel, and Canada, because credit card fraud is rampant in the other regions. These nations also have the largest overseas markets.

Calculated Shipping

When we discussed shipping previously, I stated that I prefer to use fixed shipping rates. The rates to overseas countries are so varied, however, that this is often impractical. Therefore, you'll most likely find yourself offering calculated shipping when selling inter-nationally. When you select this option, a shipping calculator will appear in your listing description. Overseas buyers can enter their country information, and the calculator will estimate shipping costs so they can see applicable rates before deciding to bid.

Your alternative is to use Priority Mail International Flat-Rate boxes. These are the same as the flat-rate boxes you use for domestic shipping. Each country has a flat-rate price, but the weight is restricted to 20 lbs (9.1 kg) for international flat-rate shipments otherwise you will need to pay the by-weight rate. The current Priority Mail Flat-Rate International rates are shown in Table 18.1.

TABLE 18.1 Current Priority Mail Flat-Rate International Rates

Item	To Canada & Mexico	To All Other Countries
Flat-Rate Letter-Size Envelope	$12.95	$16.95
Flat-Rate Padded Letter-Size Envelope	$12.95	$16.95
Legal Size Flat-Rate Envelope	$12.95	$16.95
Small Flat-Rate Boxes	$12.95	$16.95
Medium Flat-Rate Boxes	$32.95	$47.95
Large Flat-Rate Boxes	$39.95	$60.95

International Shipping and Customs There are essentially two ways to ship internationally: USPS Priority Mail International, and International carriers such as UPS, DHL, and FedEx.

USPS Priority Mail International Shipping via the US Post Office's Priority Mail International service has two distinct advantages: the costs are relatively low and you do not need a customs broker. On the downside, there's no signature required at the delivery end, making it difficult to prove delivery. In addition, the service may be quite slow. Local post offices in foreign countries can hold up items for weeks, awaiting customs clearance, before notifying the recipients that their shipment has arrived.

The good news is that PayPal offers their antifraud program (*Seller Protection Program*) on international parcels under $250, even if you don't have signature confirmation (which the USPS doesn't offer for Priority Mail International parcels). If you do need to file a claim, you will need proof of delivery, which you can obtain by entering the customs form number in the *Track and Confirm* box on the USPS Web site. If the item's cost is over $250, you will need to ship via USPS Express Mail International, because this provides tracking and proof of delivery, or via a courier service (UPS, DHL, FedEx).

One disadvantage of shipping overseas via USPS is that it's hard to collect on an insurance claim. It can take up to twice as long for the US Postal Service to investigate and pay an insurance claim for an overseas shipment as it does for a domestic shipment. However, DSI, the company we mentioned for insurance in the previous chapter, does a good job with international insurance. They are cheaper than USPS and they pay claims quicker.

International Carriers Such as UPS, DHL, and FedEx The advantages of shipping with private international carriers are threefold: reliability, the ability to insure the shipment (and collect on claims), and positive delivery confirmation with a signature. The primary disadvantage is the cost—these carriers are more expensive than USPS and, in most countries, your shipment must go through a customs broker. This incurs brokerage charges that start at $25 and can run as high as 1.5 percent of the value of the shipment, or as high as $250. The $25 minimum brokerage fee makes it impractical to ship items overseas that cost less than $100. So, what *is* the best way to ship? Whenever I sell an item under $100 overseas, I go with the USPS. Yes, every once in a while a package goes astray and I lose money on the order. However, this does not happen often, and the extra cost is easily offset by the increased profits I earn from overseas buyers who do receive their merchandise.

When I sell an item worth over $100, I usually use UPS's Calculated Shipping. In this scenario, I include a note in my auction that the buyer may have to pay a customs brokerage fee in addition to the shipping cost. I like to specify as many of the fees as possible in the item description. Be sure to be clear about the shipping method you'll be using, any risks associated with the item, the estimated delivery time, and if the buyer should expect any additional fees. eBay suggests that you advise potential buyers to research customs fees before placing a bid.

Feedback Related to Customs Delays

eBay understands that international parcels take longer to deliver and that expectations of buyers from other countries differ. So Detailed Seller Ratings from international buyers are *not* included in your seller performance standards. Also, if a buyer gives you a neutral or negative feedback referencing customs fees, customs delays, etc., eBay will remove that negative comment. However, you *must* have the following statement in your item description, and it must not be any smaller than the regular typesize of the rest of your listing:

> *International Buyers – Please Note:*
> *Import duties, taxes, and charges are not included in the item price or shipping cost. These charges are the buyer's responsibility. Please check with your country's customs office to determine what these additional costs will be prior to bidding or buying.*

Make sure this is part of every listing you make and your feedback rating is protected from a buyer with customs issues and a grudge.

.... BEST PRACTICES ....

A WORD OF ADVICE ON INTERNATIONAL SHIPPING

Whenever you ship overseas, you have to fill out a customs form that states the contents and the value of the item you are shipping. Buyers may ask you to mark the item as a gift or place a low value on the customs form so that they incur a lower duty. *Do not do this!* First of all, you would be breaking the law if you were using the US Postal Service. Second, if the item were lost or damaged, you could only claim the value stated on the form. Finally, eBay's policies state that you must obey the laws of *both* countries—the one you are selling from and the one you are shipping to. If you violate this policy, eBay will suspend you or, in repeated cases, cancel your account.

When shipping internationally, I always place an invoice in the box, specifying the item description and the price the buyer paid. This prevents the customs official from having to guess at the item's value.

PAYMENT

The third and final point to consider when it comes to selling internationally is getting paid. Fortunately, PayPal is set up to collect funds from forty-five countries (see the PayPal site for a complete list), as well as in several currencies, including the yen, the euro, and the British pound. eBay automatically converts the cost of a product to the user's default currency. So if a British bidder is viewing an item listed on the US site, she will see the cost in US dollars *and* in British pounds. To see what your product will cost in other currencies, visit eBay's currency converter at http://pages.ebay.com/services/buyandsell/currencyconverter.html.

If an overseas buyer pays via PayPal, you don't have to worry about the conversion rate. The buyer will pay PayPal in his home currency, and PayPal will pay you in US dollars (or the currency of your country). I would also not accept a credit card directly using your own merchant credit card account for any large overseas transaction, unless the buyer has an exceptionally high feedback rating (with excellent comments) and has been active on eBay for at least a year. Credit card fraud is much worse overseas than in the United States and Canada. The problem arises when someone pays with a credit card that clears, and then the credit card company discovers the card is invalid several weeks later—after you have shipped the product. If you used your own merchant account, you are out the money, whereas if you accepted the payment through PayPal, you are still eligible for the *Seller Protection Program*. This program protects you from fraudulent credit card transactions processed through PayPal. (You can learn more about this program at www.paypal.com.)

POWER MOVES

I would not suggest that you start shipping overseas until you have mastered domestic selling and shipping. But once you have successfully launched enough auctions that you know all the ins and outs of eBay selling, you should evaluate whether there is an international market for your product. You can do this in two ways:

❏ Search completed listings on eBay. Look for successful auctions where the items sold at very high prices. Often these winning bidders are international buyers. Use this information to determine if there is an international market for your item. Also, evaluate the shipping policies specified by the sellers.

❏ Go onto overseas eBay sites, such as eBay.co.uk (the United Kingdom eBay site) or eBay.com.au (eBay's site in Australia). Unless you speak German, French, or Chinese, I suggest that you limit yourself to the English-speaking sites. Search completed listings for the product you are selling and see if there is a market for it in these countries.

CHAPTER 19

✦ MONITORING AND REVISING ✦ YOUR AUCTIONS FOR SUCCESS

PROFESSIONAL EBAY SELLERS like to stay on top of their listings on a daily basis. They not only want to know how their auctions are doing, but they may wish to revise an ongoing auction if it is not performing well. Fortunately, eBay makes monitoring and updating auctions easy for sellers. This chapter will take you through the various tools eBay provides to help you monitor, manage, and revise your ongoing auctions.

THE MY EBAY DASHBOARD

eBay provides a convenient tool for monitoring your auction activity, called *My eBay* (see Figure 19.1). You can access My eBay from the top of any eBay page by hitting the *My eBay* button. The first page you come to is the *Activity* page. On the left sidebar you can see headings for Summary (including Buy, Lists) and Purchase History (including Sell). Within each of these are subpages for each of those headings.

As you can see in Figure 19.1, my landing page is set to *All Selling*. This is not the default, but it is probably the most useful for you as a professional seller. Look to the top right of the page and you will see The My eBay landing page is set to *All Selling* [Change] and the word *Change* is a link. On your page it will not say "All selling" until you click the word *Change* and select it.

The first section on the *All Selling* page is *Selling Reminders*. Here you will find recommendations for increasing your listing's exposure, reminders of questions from buyers on your current active listings, feedback reminders, information on open transaction dispute cases, and so on. This is a great quick-reference section, but it doesn't give you specifics about the performance of your listings.

The next section, *Scheduled*, shows the listings you have scheduled but have not yet started. In Figure 19.1 you can see I have no Scheduled Listings. All of mine are active. This brings me to the next section: *Active Selling.* This is the section you need to monitor to see how your listings are performing.

Figure 19.2 shows a selection of items in my Active Selling list. You can see the headings at the top right. The most important are the *Views/Watchers* and *Bids*. If you have a lot of views but no watchers, that can indicate that your product is priced too

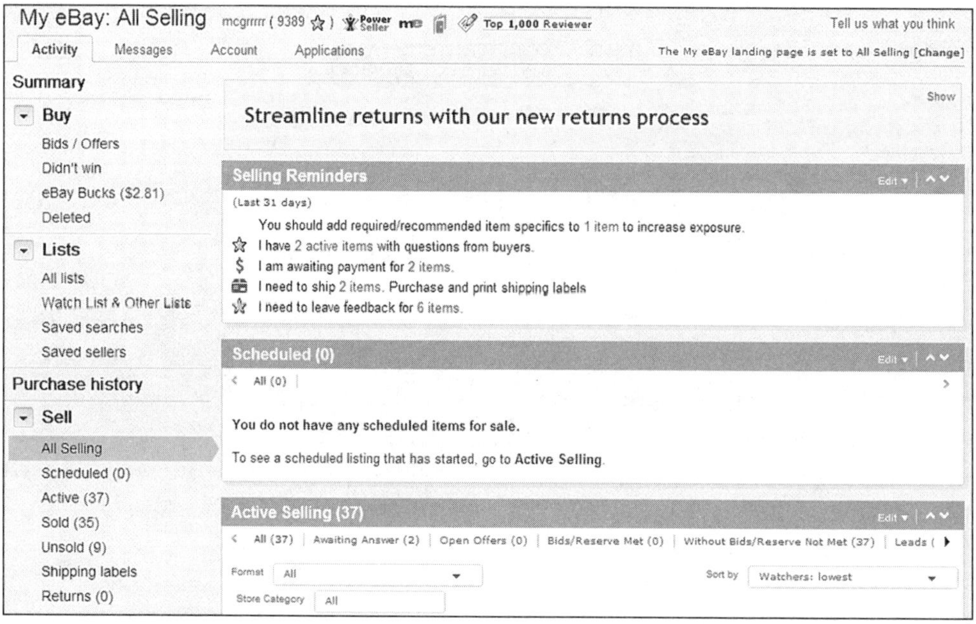

Figure 19.1 My eBay Page Summary

high, the photographs aren't good enough, or your item description needs work (or doesn't match the keywords used in your title).

All of the items I have in Figure 19.2 are fixed-price listings, so there are no bids. They show up in my *Sold* section each time an item from one of these listings sells. However, if I had auctions here you would see the number of bids too.

The *Actions* column has a drop-down menu (as shown in Figure 19.2) where you can select *Revise* to change details about your listing. If it is a fixed-price listing, you can make changes at any time. If it is an auction with bids, you can only add to the description.

This *More actions* menu is also where you can change the format from fixed-price to online auction or vice versa. You can also end the item here if you need to. Note, there is a fee for ending an auction that had bids on it, though (we'll talk about that in a moment).

When you monitor your auctions, you may notice some with numerous watchers and few (or even no) bids. Watchers are usually people who like to *snipe*—a term used for people who bid at the last second, or who use special software programs to do this for them. Oftentimes, an auction will run all week with few or no bids and then

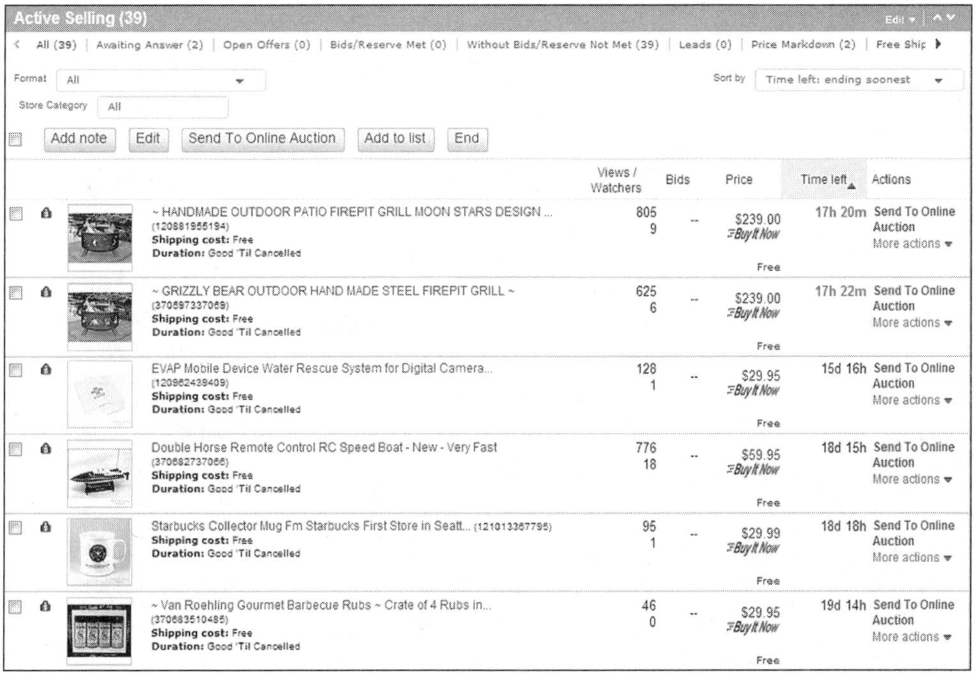

Figure 19.2 Active Selling

BIZ BUILDER

Every time I discover a competitor, I add him to My Favorite Sellers. When I
am about to launch a new auction, I go to My Favorite Sellers and see what
my competitors are selling the item for, if they have any clever new titles, how
many hits their auctions are getting, and so on. If someone has just launched an
auction with a starting price of $19.99, I might start mine, offering a similar item,
at $18.99 to attract more hits when our auctions run together.

will receive heavy bidding activity in the last few minutes. So don't despair if you look
at your auctions days before they end and they do not seem to be getting bids—this
is perfectly normal. Nevertheless, if you don't have any watchers, you might want to
check if it is getting any hits (you can find this information in My eBay or on the listing
page if you are using a hit counter). If not, you might consider revising your auction—
especially the title or the opening price. See below for details on how to do this.

SALES REPORTS

Subscriptions are special tools and reports for which eBay generally charges additional fees. One such tool offered by eBay is a monthly sales report. This particular report is free, but others incur charges.

eBay Sales Reports Plus presents a very detailed look at your sales. We spoke earlier about business metrics—how you measure your performance on eBay. You can determine most of your critical business metrics right from this report, and it's free so it's certainly worth using. From your My eBay page, click on the *Account* tab and then on *Subscriptions*. Then click on *Subscribe* next to Sales Reports Plus.

REVISING AN ONGOING AUCTION

Once an auction has been launched, you can revise almost any part of it, provided the item has not yet received any bids. If it *has* received bids, you can add comments and images to the auction, but you cannot remove anything listed in it.

The information that you can revise also depends on the time left before the auction ends. In most cases, you cannot change the listing format; that is, you cannot switch from an auction-style listing to a fixed-price listing.

If your listing has not received any bids and has at least twelve hours left to run, you may:

* Revise any information in the title or description
* Add or remove the following optional features: Buy It Now, eBay photos, reserve price, ten-day listing
* Add optional features to increase your item's visibility (e.g., bold)
* Change your gallery photo (the thumbnail image that shows on the search results page)

If your item *has* received bids, you cannot change copy, images, or words in the description; however, you can add special features, such as bold, and you can add additional images (although you cannot change or remove any of the existing images).

When you click on the link to revise your item from the *Active Selling* section of My eBay, a new page will come up, as illustrated in Figure 19.3—the Edit Your Listing page.

Simply modify any section that allows you to make changes. If you're not allowed to change something because of the restrictions I just mentioned, eBay will prevent you from doing so.

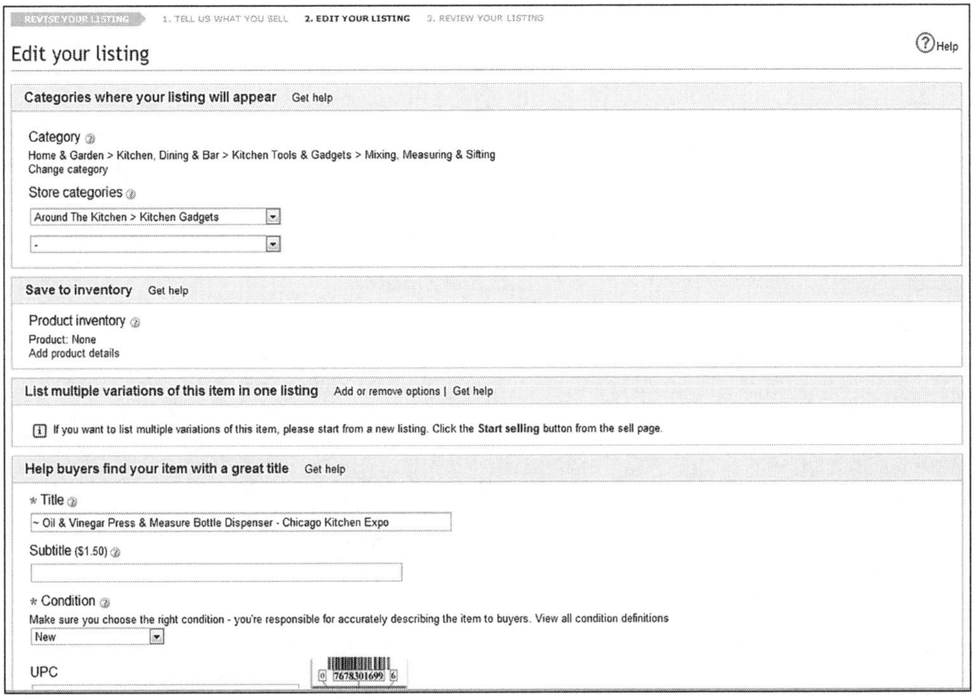

Figure 19.3 Edit Your Listing Page

ENDING AN AUCTION EARLY

If you inadvertently launch an auction for something you don't have, or if you find a critical mistake in your description and your item already has bids, you can still end your auction early.

If the auction has no bids, go to the eBay site map and select *End Your Listing* under the heading *Selling Activities*. If your auction has bids, select *Cancel Bids on Your Listing*. Remember that if you wish to end a listing early, you must first cancel any bids that have already been placed.

eBay does not want you canceling bids and canceling auctions. So if you do end a listing early, you are charged a fee that is equal to what the final value fee would be based on the current highest bid. Once per year you can cancel an auction that has bids and not be charged the fee. However, once you've used that up, you will be charged the fee every time, no matter why you ended the auction early. Note: If you end an auction without bids early, you are responsible only for the insertion fee and any optional upgrades you chose.

POWER MOVES

❏ Familiarize yourself with the layout on your My eBay Page and with all the links and tools available to you there.

❏ Click on the *Sales Reports* link through the *Subscriptions* link on your My eBay Account page to read and understand what kind of information this tool provides. Once you start selling on a regular basis, I recommend that you subscribe to this service.

CHAPTER 20

✦ GETTING PAID ✦

GETTING PAID IS WHAT IT'S all about on eBay. In the early days of eBay, there was no PayPal and very few eBay sellers were set up to take credit cards. I can still remember receiving checks, money orders, and envelopes stuffed with cash from customers. One buyer even sent me a box filled with rolls of dimes and quarters to pay for a rare naval history book I had sold him!

As we wrap up Week 2, we'll conclude by exploring the various payment methods available to you as an eBay seller and how to use them. In addition, we will show you how to deal with nonpaying bidders and we will expose some of the more common frauds and scams that unfortunately plague eBay from time to time—and we'll reveal how you can avoid them.

These days, all payments on eBay must be "paperless" (i.e., electronic). So checks, money orders, cash, etc. are no longer allowed. In fact, eBay restricts you to a very limited number of services you can use. These include PayPal (which eBay owns), ProPay, Skrill, Paymate, and credit cards that are accepted through the seller's own Internet merchant credit card account. A merchant account is a type of bank account that allows businesses to accept payment by credit or debit cards. It is an agreement between a retailer, a merchant bank, and payment processor for the settlement of credit card and/or debit card transactions. An Internet merchant account is a merchant account that is designed to handle online payment processing of credit cards. There are monthly and per-transaction fees associated with having an Internet merchant account and it's not really something I recommend for sellers starting out.

PAYPAL

Today the vast majority of eBay buyers pay with PayPal. It's easy to integrate PayPal into your auctions just by entering your PayPal e-mail address in the Payment section of the Sell Your Item form. The buyer will automatically receive an e-mail with a link to pay. When she clicks on the link, she will arrive at the eBay Checkout page like the one shown in Figure 20.1.

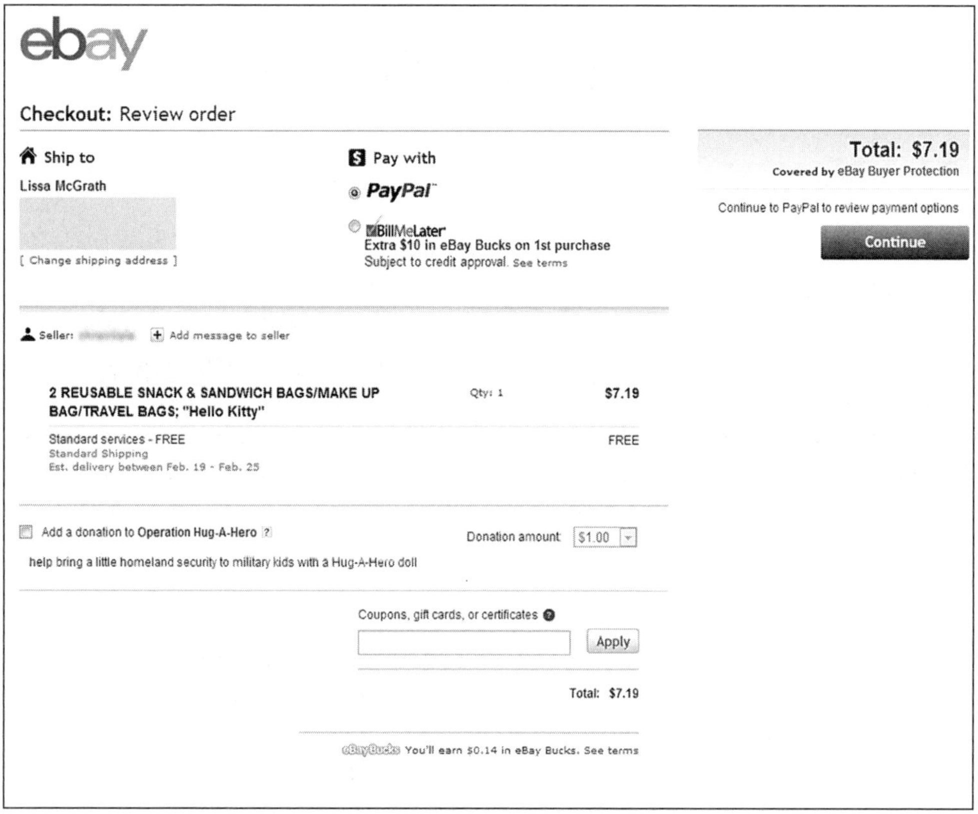

Figure 20.1 eBay Checkout Page

On this page the buyer can elect to pay with PayPal or with another method you've set up in your listing. If she selects PayPal, she will proceed to PayPal to log in and confirm the funding source (PayPal balance, instant bank transfer, credit card, e-check from bank account, etc.), as shown in Figure 20.2.

The buyer is then transferred back to eBay to confirm the payment (see Figure 20.3). Once the buyer confirms and pays, you will receive an e-mail from PayPal letting you know that you have a new payment. It will also provide the buyer's shipping information. If you, the seller, log into your PayPal account, you will see that the money has been deposited.

If you look at the PayPal checkout screen, you will also see several credit card logos. A buyer does not have to have a PayPal account to use PayPal, because PayPal will also process credit card transactions. If someone selects PayPal and does not have an account, he will be brought to a page where he can enter his credit card and

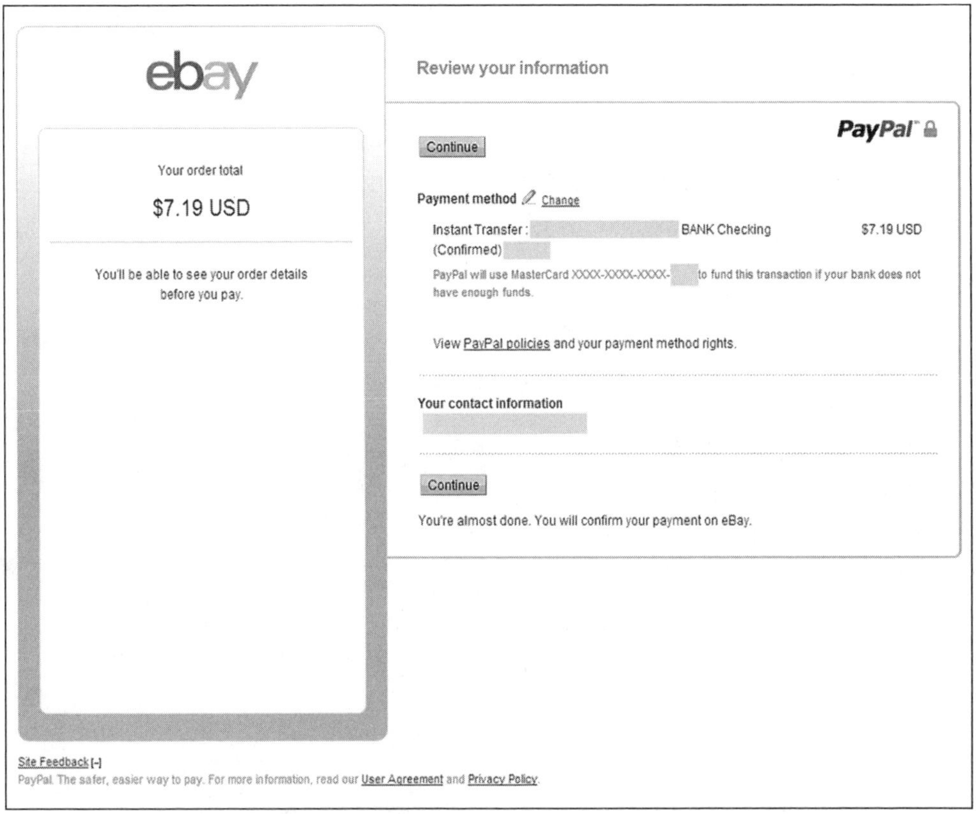

Figure 20.2 PayPal Checkout Page

shipping information. PayPal then processes the credit card transaction for you and you get paid right away, just as with any other PayPal transaction.

You're probably familiar with the popular AOL voice prompt "You've got mail." Well, if you have Microsoft Outlook, you can set up the program to always give you a voice or sound alert whenever an e-mail from PayPal arrives. One of my friends has his computer set up to sound "*Cha-ching*" every time an e-mail from PayPal arrives.

All kidding aside, it is a good idea to set up an alert like this. If you are near the computer, you can log on instantly and send the buyer an e-mail confirming that you have received her payment and that her shipment is on the way. People are amazed when they buy something on eBay and receive a shipping notice minutes later. This is a great way to boost your feedback rating. In chapter 23, I will show you how to automate this process so that buyers receive their confirmation e-mails instantly.

The vast majority of buyers have PayPal accounts, and their seller protection policy is pretty comprehensive, so in general I think that is the way to go. The other options are available if you really want them, but they tend to complicate the issue, so my advice is to just stick with PayPal.

Figure 20.3 Confirm and Pay

PayPal Seller Protection

Although there is some credit card fraud in the United States, it's much more prevalent overseas. If you have a merchant credit card account and it turns out that a credit card was stolen or invalid, you get a chargeback, which is a demand by the credit-card provider for a retailer to make good the loss on a fraudulent or disputed transaction. If you've already shipped the item, you're out of pocket with the funds *and* for the item.

You are more protected if you use PayPal, which is why I always require PayPal for overseas buyers, but it is worth understanding the PayPal Seller Protection policy for all sales too. The rest of this section will explain the PayPal Seller Protection policy. Essentially, you receive two protections from PayPal: 1) from a claim by the buyer that the item was not received and 2) from a chargeback for what the buyer says was an unauthorized transaction (i.e., the credit card was stolen). The basic requirements for all PayPal coverage is:

* You must have a Premier or Business PayPal account.

* You must ship to the address shown on the transaction details page (this is automatic if you're using eBay Labels).

* Your primary residence (as the seller) must be in the United States.

* The item must be a physical, tangible item that is shipped, not something digitally delivered or hand-delivered.

* You must respond to PayPal's requests for documents or information in a timely manner.

These are the basics. However, each type of protection also has additional requirements. For Item Not Received chargebacks:

* The payment must be marked "eligible" or "partially eligible" on the PayPal Transaction Details page for the item, which provides you the shipping address for your buyer and the payment information.

* You, the seller, must provide proof of delivery. This is defined as a document from the shipping company showing the item status as delivered, the date of delivery, the recipient's address that matches the address on the Transaction Details page, and signature confirmation proving receipt of the package if the total payment made to you was $250 or higher.

* It is recommended, but not required, that you get all parcels into the mail within seven days of receiving payment.

For Unauthorized Transaction chargebacks:

* The payment must be marked "eligible" on the Transaction Details page.

* You must provide proof of shipment or proof of delivery. Proof of delivery requirements are the same as for Item Not Received chargebacks. Proof of shipment is defined as a document from the shipping company that shows the date the item was shipped, the recipient's address matching the address on the transaction details page, the recipient's address showing at least city and state or city and country for international parcels, or zip/postal code.

PayPal also uses a Payment Review on occasion if a transaction raises a red flag. You will be notified that the funds are on hold and will be told not to ship the item yet. If you ship it anyway, you lose your Seller Protection. However, if the payment clears the review process but then turns out to be fraudulent, you are covered by PayPal Seller Protection.

With PayPal, you are also vulnerable to buyer disputes, because of PayPal's Buyer Protection. A buyer can claim that she didn't receive your item (in which case the Item Not Received protection also covers you) or that it was not as described. PayPal Seller Protection does not protect you from an Item Not As Described claim, but that will go through eBay's dispute resolution system.

Buyers are required to contact their seller via My Messages in all Item Not As Described disputes before actually opening a case; in fact, it will block the buyer from opening a case until he has sent the seller a message and three days have passed. This gives the seller the opportunity to work with the buyer. If you have not resolved the issue in those three days, the buyer can open a case for either Item Not Received or Item Not As Described. At that point, PayPal will put a hold on the amount originally paid to you by the buyer until the case is resolved.

Usually a forty-five-day period is allowed for the dispute resolution; if the issue is not resolved by then, the chargeback becomes permanent. Unfortunately, the burden of proof is on you, the seller. You need to prove that the item was received, or that the item was as described in the auction.

Lest you worry too much about this, let me reassure you that these kinds of problems are rare on eBay. Out of the millions of transactions that take place every day, only a tiny fraction result in disputes. During thirteen years of selling, I can count the number of disputed transactions I have had on one hand.

NONPAYING BIDDERS

Nonpaying bidders are another story—and they are much more of a problem than disputed transactions or fraud. Depending on the category of merchandise you sell, nonpaying bidders—or NPBs, as they are referred to by experienced eBayers—are fairly common. Sellers of low-cost merchandise, such as videos, CDs, DVDs, inexpensive jewelry, and the like, can often see NPB rates as high as 6 to 10 percent. For some reason, sellers of higher-priced merchandise experience lower NPB rates—usually closer to 1 to 2 percent. However, the eBay fees on higher-priced items are also much higher, so the dollar amounts at stake are often the same.

A WORD OF ADVICE ON THE SAVVY CAT AND THE FIRE PIT

Sometimes NPBs can come up with laugh-out-loud excuses. One day a bidder hit the *Buy It Now* button for one of my expensive ($250+) fire pits. Payment did not come through, so I sent her an invoice. Later that day, I received an e-mail back from the buyer claiming that she had been looking at the auction when her phone rang. While she was on the phone, her cat had walked across the keyboard and somehow "bought" my fire pit. Now, that is pretty funny when you consider that you must position your cursor directly over the *Buy It Now* button to activate it—and that once you activate the button, you are then taken to a *second* page with yet another button to confirm your purchase. I sent her a reply e-mail, congratulating her on having such a smart cat and asking if the cat would mind participating in the dispute resolution process so I could get my fees refunded. She fessed up and admitted that she needed to back out of the auction because her husband had gotten mad at her when he found out that she had purchased the pricey fire pit.

When a bidder doesn't pay, you can file an Unpaid Item Report with eBay through the resolution center. This will sometimes result in a payment; if not, eBay will credit your final value fees. The problem is that, in either case, the nonpaying bidder can and sometimes does leave you negative feedback. If the buyer refuses to participate in the process, eBay will neutralize any feedback he leaves. But if he does participate and pay up, he can still leave negative feedback. There is nothing you can do about it, even if you did nothing wrong.

First let's review how the dispute resolution process works. Then I will show you a shortcut that can save you time and aggravation, and almost eliminate the negative feedback risk.

Seller Opens an Unpaid Item Case

eBay has a Resolution Center for buyers and sellers where there is a transaction dispute. You can access this two ways—through the Customer Service tab at the top of every eBay page, or from the *Sold* section of My eBay (use the drop-down *actions* menu next to the listing you are having issues with). If you go directly to the Resolution

Center, you will have to enter the item number; however, if you link through from My eBay, the number will already be entered for you.

Sellers can report an unpaid item up to thirty-two days after the transaction date; the transaction date is the date when the buyer commits to buying the item and the seller commits to selling it. Usually the seller must wait four days after a listing closes to open an Unpaid Item Case (unless the buyer is no longer a registered eBay user).

eBay Contacts the Buyer

Once the seller opens an Unpaid Item Case, eBay sends the buyer an e-mail notification and displays a pop-up message if the buyer signs in to eBay within fourteen days of the filing with a friendly reminder to pay.

The e-mail and pop-up message will remind the buyer that payment has not yet been received, and it will provide simple instructions on how to respond or how to pay for the item. If the buyer does not respond to the e-mail or pop-up message within four days of the seller's opening the case, the seller may close the case and she will receive a final value fee credit. The seller also becomes eligible for a free relist credit. (Note: eBay does not refund the insertion fee; you must relist the item using the *Relist This Item* button on your My eBay page and pay the second insertion fee. If it sells again, eBay will credit your account with one insertion fee.)

When the buyer receives the e-mail or pop-up message, she is presented with several options for communicating with the seller:

* *I want to pay now:* The buyer can simply pay via PayPal, or by any of the other electronic payment methods accepted by the seller and approved by eBay, to close the dispute.

* *I already paid:* If payment has already been made, the buyer may provide details of the payment to the seller for review. The seller can then choose the appropriate option to close the dispute.

* *Communicate with the seller:* The buyer and seller can attempt to resolve the problem by communicating directly through the eBay Web site. The seller can close the dispute at any time after the case has been open for four days by choosing the appropriate closure option.

CANCEL TRANSACTION PROCESS

Another way to end an auction is using the *cancel transaction* option. In the Resolution Center, rather than selecting *I sold an item and haven't received my payment yet*, you can instead select *I sold an item and want to cancel the transaction*. You do not have to wait the four-day grace period if you are canceling a listing. This is the option to use if a buyer is returning an item for a refund, if the buyer changed her mind, if she requested a shipment to a country you don't ship to or to an address other than the one on the transaction details page, if you ran out of stock, etc. You can see the selections in Figure 20.4.

If you are canceling a transaction, you need to contact the buyer ahead of time and let her know that eBay will be contacting her to confirm the cancellation. You can initiate the process from the time immediately after the sale is made up to forty-five days after the transaction date. The buyer does not receive an unpaid item strike if you cancel the transaction—even if the reason is that the buyer hasn't paid. You do receive the final value fee credit either way, but if you cancel a transaction, your buyer is still eligible to leave feedback, whereas if the buyer receives an unpaid item strike and leaves you a negative comment, eBay will automatically remove it.

The buyer has seven days from when you initiate the cancel process to accept it. If the buyer doesn't do so within seven days, you can close the case and receive the final value fee credit.

Cancel a transaction

Item: NightBright LED Ultraviolet Light Dentist Approved Teeth Whitening System (120949767927) View purchased item

Transaction end: Jul-30-2012

Buyer: ▆▆▆▆▆▆▆

Case type: Cancel transaction

To send a request to cancel this transaction to the buyer, select a reason and click the **Send request** button.

Give the buyer a reason for wanting to cancel this transaction:

Buyer purchased item by mistake or changed mind ▾

-- Select One --
Buyer purchased item by mistake or changed mind
Buyer is returning item for a refund
Buyer and I disagreed over terms
Buyer is unresponsive
Buyer's payment hasn't been received or hasn't cleared
Buyer requested shipment to an unconfirmed address
Buyer requested shipment to a country I don't ship to
I ran out of stock
I sold item to another buyer
Other reason

Send request   Cancel

Figure 20.4 Options for Canceling a Transaction

A dispute case can be open for only sixty days after the transaction date. If the seller has not closed the dispute within sixty days, it will be closed automatically. When this automatic closure takes place, the seller does not receive a final value fee credit and the buyer does not receive an unpaid item strike, no matter what selections you chose to begin the process.

Streamlining the Process

eBay has an Unpaid Item Assistant program you can set up to automatically open unpaid item claims for you when a buyer hasn't paid within a certain period of time. It doesn't have to be four days—it could be seven, or however many days you stipulate in your listing. This is a huge time-saver if you have a lot of listings. You can still adjust an individual case if a buyer contacts you and requests more time or if you want to cancel a listing rather than file an unpaid item claim.

To turn on the Unpaid Item Assistant, go to the *Account* tab in My eBay and click *Site Preferences* from the left sidebar. Scroll down to the *Unpaid Item Assistant* and click the *Show* link to the right. Then to modify the settings for the Unpaid Item Assistant, click *Edit*. Now you can select how long you want the Unpaid Item Assistant to wait before opening a case (the shortest duration is four days and the longest is thirty-two). There are other options, including automatically relisting an item when the case is closed without payment (I prefer to do this manually, though).

As you can see in Figure 20.5, there is a box for entering user IDs that you want exempted from the Unpaid Item Assistant. If a buyer contacts you asking for extra time and you agree, then you can enter his user ID here and the Unpaid Item Assistant system will ignore any listings with that buyer.

FRAUD WATCH

As previously noted, fraud is relatively rare on eBay, but it does exist and there are several scams you should watch out for. Most fraud is actually perpetrated by sellers, not buyers. However, there are certain schemes aimed at buyers that you, as a seller, should still be aware of.

Stolen or Phony Credit Cards

As mentioned above, sometimes people attempt to buy items with bogus credit cards. You are protected by PayPal's Seller Protection Policy so long as you have a Premier or Business PayPal account and ship to the address provided by PayPal (automatically entered if you use eBay Labels to create your shipping label). Sometimes a buyer will ask you to ship to another address. If you do, you are no longer eligible for Seller

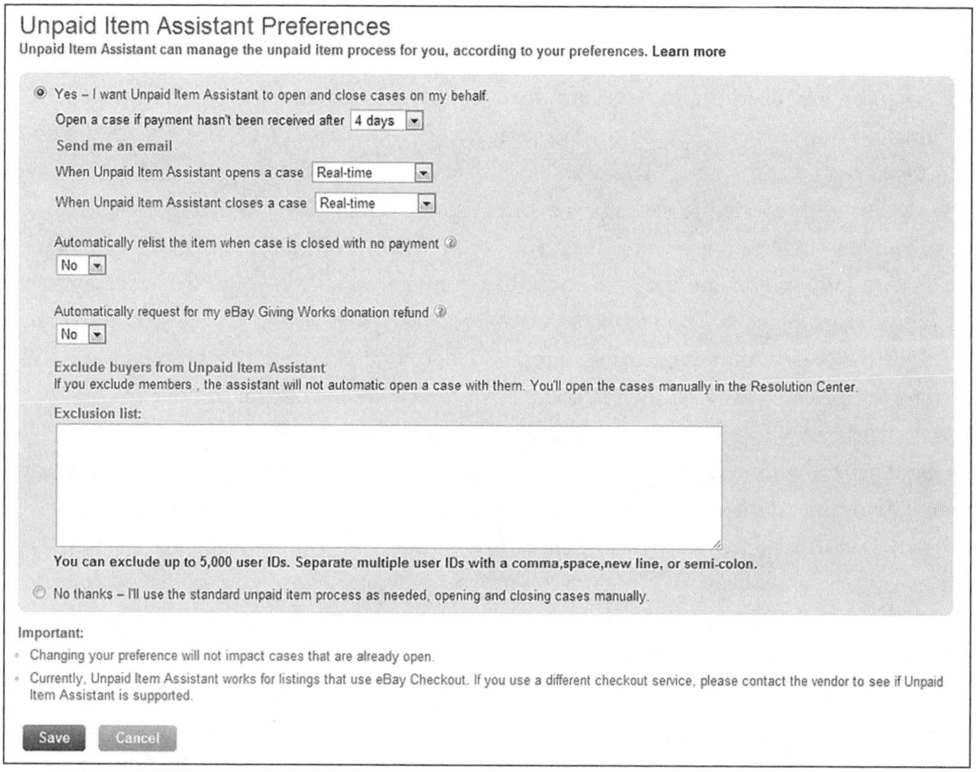

Unpaid Item Assistant Preferences
Unpaid Item Assistant can manage the unpaid item process for you, according to your preferences. **Learn more**

◉ Yes – I want Unpaid Item Assistant to open and close cases on my behalf.
Open a case if payment hasn't been received after [4 days ▼]
Send me an email
When Unpaid Item Assistant opens a case [Real-time ▼]
When Unpaid Item Assistant closes a case [Real-time ▼]

Automatically relist the item when case is closed with no payment ⊘
[No ▼]

Automatically request for my eBay Giving Works donation refund ⊘
[No ▼]

Exclude buyers from Unpaid Item Assistant
If you exclude members , the assistant will not automatic open a case with them. You'll open the cases manually in the Resolution Center.
Exclusion list:

You can exclude up to 5,000 user IDs. Separate multiple user IDs with a comma,space,new line, or semi-colon.
○ No thanks – I'll use the standard unpaid item process as needed, opening and closing cases manually.

Important:
• Changing your preference will not impact cases that are already open.
• Currently, Unpaid Item Assistant works for listings that use eBay Checkout. If you use a different checkout service, please contact the vendor to see if Unpaid Item Assistant is supported.

[Save] [Cancel]

Figure 20.5 Unpaid Item Assistant Options

Protection, so make sure you think about this before you agree.

eBay specifically restricts payments on eBay to electronic methods to prevent cashier's check fraud, money order fraud, etc. So if you have a buyer (particularly a foreign buyer) who specifically insists on paying with one of these methods, cancel the transaction. Remember, Western Union and MoneyGram are specifically forbidden too. Both companies actually have letters on eBay's Web site that inform their customers that their services are not appropriate for eBay transactions.

Account Takeover (aka Spoofing or Phishing)

This is still one of the most prevalent and insidious frauds on eBay (and on the rest of the Internet) today. You receive an official-looking e-mail from eBay (or PayPal) stating that there is some kind of problem with your account, that the credit card you have on file needs updating, or that your account has been compromised. The e-mail often threatens to suspend your account if you do not take immediate action. The e-mail contains a link you are requested to click to access your information so you can update it.

When you click on the link, you are taken to a page on "eBay" (or "PayPal") that asks you to enter your user ID and password, followed by your name, address, and credit card information—including the three-digit security code on the back. Well, this is kind of a pain, you think, *but what the heck?* The problem is that you are not on eBay or PayPal. You have been led to a spoof site, hosted on a server in Guatemala or Slovenia that looks just like eBay, but it's not. The thieves now have your eBay and/or PayPal password and all of your credit card information and they are about to empty any money in your PayPal account and go on a shopping spree. The first time you realize anything is wrong is when you get your credit card statement, perhaps weeks later, and learn that *you* have purchased a top-of-the-line Rolex watch at the duty-free shop in Santo Domingo or Kuala Lampur.

It's fairly easy to protect yourself from this type of scam. eBay and PayPal will never send you an e-mail directing you to click on an embedded link to enter either of their sites for account-specific information. Any legitimate account e-mail from eBay or PayPal will instruct you to go to the main Web site and log on in the normal way. Never click on any link in an e-mail directing you to a site where you are asked to enter security or credit card information.

Another scam involves My Messages. You receive an e-mail in your inbox with a question from a buyer. You click on the link, which would take you to My Messages to reply. Only the page you are taken to is not eBay. This way the scammer gets only your log-in information, but this can be used for a different type of fraud. This time the scammer takes advantage of your good feedback record and lists a number of high-ticket items. The buyers send the payment, but they never receive the items. This is called "account takeover" and it is a big concern. It's also a reason why you must never have the same eBay and PayPal passwords. If you do get caught in one of these scams, at least your PayPal account will not also be compromised. Usually in account-takeover situations, the scammer changes your password so you cannot get into your account to cancel the listings. If this happens to you, go to eBay's homepage and click the *Customer Support* tab at the top of the page, and then click the *Contact eBay* tab. Select *Account* and then *Unauthorized use of my account*. This will get you the contact information for the right department at eBay to help you.

Phony Escrow Web Sites

Typically, buyers are the victims of this fraud. I've included it here because if you sell high-priced items, your bidders could be at risk.

Fake escrow Web sites may be one of the most successful Internet scams of all time. They prey on big-ticket auction winners and rely on the consumer's trust of escrow Web sites—once considered the safest way to make an exchange when an online auction involves an item of higher-than-average value. Victims of phony escrow sites can lose tens of thousands of dollars at a time; total losses incurred by big-ticket auction winners quickly add up to millions of dollars.

If you're a buyer, the best way to protect yourself is to use the escrow service listed on eBay itself (www.escrow.com). Sellers should encourage buyers to do the same.

With all scams, your best defense is to be on the lookout for anything that appears too good to be true. It probably is. While you don't want to be paranoid about every e-mail you receive, it does pay to be a little cautious—especially when you're doing business outside the United States and Canada.

POWER MOVES

❑ If you haven't yet signed up for PayPal, open or upgrade to a Premier or Business account to be eligible for Seller Protection.

❑ Visit the Seller Protection page on eBay (via the site map or by clicking on Customer Service at the top of any eBay page and typing *seller protection* into the search box). Familiarize yourself with the eBay and PayPal protection plans for both buyers and sellers.

❑ Type the phrase *online security* into the eBay Help search box. This will bring up a series of links relating to fraud protection on eBay.

WEEK 3

RUNNING YOUR EBAY BUSINESS
TO MAXIMIZE INCOME

Now you've learned how to set up your business and get started, it's time to look at strategies to get better. How to improve your profits, how to take less time on mundane tasks, how to build your business, and ultimately how to expand your business outside of eBay.

CHAPTER 21

✦ COST CONTROL ✦

CONTROLLING YOUR COSTS is important in any business—selling on eBay is no different. There are two ways to increase your profits: launch more successful listings or cut your costs. So far we have dealt primarily with techniques to increase your sales. However, as your business grows, it is easy to lose sight of pesky little expenses that can eat into your earnings. eBay listing fees, for example, are small but can add up quickly. Packing and shipping supplies are another major cost for eBay sellers. Let's examine some of your typical costs and how you can get them under control and make more money on eBay.

FOR THE RECORD

The first step when you're trying to control your costs is to figure out what they are. While monitoring your costs, you can simultaneously track your sales and profits. If you are just starting out, create an Excel spreadsheet like the one in Table 21.1.

The first line indicates total sales for the month. Only factor in payments you have actually received, not payments from sales concluded that month that have not yet arrived. So, for example, don't add payments to this month's sales from a bidder who refuses to pay, or from an auction that closes on the last day of the month but for which you won't receive payment until the following month.

The next line, Cost of Goods Sold (COGS), represents the amount you paid for the merchandise you sold that month, including any shipping costs to bring the inventories to their present location and condition. When you subtract your COGS from your total sales, you end up with your gross margin (also called gross profit).

Next you want to list all expenses related to your eBay business. I have listed the most common expenses, but you may need to add a few more, such as computer payments, car mileage to pick up and deliver goods, and advertising. Be sure to include these items in your total expenses for the month.

Once you total your expenses, subtract them from your gross margin to arrive at your profit for the month. As long as your eBay business is fairly small, this system will work quite well. If your business starts to grow, however, consider investing in a program like QuickBooks, an automated accounting system that costs about $200. While there are several other accounting software programs on the market, QuickBooks is the one used by most bookkeeping and accounting firms. Here's another advantage of using QuickBooks: If your business is successful, you will need to retain a certified public account (CPA) or a tax service like H&R Block to help with your taxes. Most CPAs and tax services use QuickBooks; if you can deliver a QuickBooks file to them, they can prepare your taxes more efficiently—and usually for a lower fee. If you employ a part-time bookkeeper as I do, you'll discover that this program will easily pay for itself in money saved over having this person manage your books manually.

TABLE 21.1 Sales and Costs Worksheet, January through June

	JAN.	FEB.	MARCH	APRIL	MAY	JUNE
INCOME ITEMS						
Sales	$1,400	$2,155	$2,855	$3,366	$4,125	$5,241
Cost of Goods Sold (COGS)	616	948	1,256	1,481	1,815	2,306
Gross Margin (Sales minus COGS)	784	1,207	1,599	1,885	2,310	2,935
EXPENSE ITEMS						
eBay Fees	92	142	188	222	272	346
PayPal Fees	33	51	67	79	97	123
Cost of Shipping & Packing Materials	28	43	57	67	83	105
Shipping (UPS, USPS, etc.)	62	95	126	148	182	231
Monthly ISP/DSL Fees, etc.	22	22	22	22	22	22
Office Supplies & Expenses	25	29	36	42	55	63
Miscellaneous	10	15	20	25	30	35
Total Expenses	272	397	516	605	741	925
Profit (Gross Margin minus Expenses)	$512	$810	$1,083	$1,280	$1,569	$2,010

UNDERSTANDING YOUR EBAY FEES

If you look at Table 21.1, you can see that your eBay and PayPal fees represent a significant portion of your costs. There's not much you can do to reduce your PayPal fees; these fees are a fixed percentage of what you sell, plus a per-transaction fee. However, there are some steps you can take to reduce your eBay fees. Understanding how eBay calculates its fees is essential to learning how to control them, so first you must have a good grasp of eBay's fee structure and how the various costs relate to one another. eBay has several categories of fees:

* The insertion fees, or the cost to list an item for sale

* The final-value fee, or the cost eBay charges you for selling an item

* Fees for additional listing options

Now let's explore the specific fees for each type of listing. Table 21.2 summarizes this information. Note that the fees listed in this chapter were accurate when this edition went to press in 2013; however, eBay does change its fees occasionally. You can find the current eBay fees at http://pages.ebay.com/help/sell/fees.html.

TABLE 21.2 eBay Auction Insertion, Reserve, and Buy It Now Fees

EBAY AUCTION-STYLE LISTING INSERTION FEE

Item Starting Price	Fee
$0.01 to $0.99	$0.10
$1.00 to $9.99	$0.25
$10.00 to $24.99	$0.50
$25.00 to $49.99	$0.75
$50.00 to $199.00	$1.00
$200.00 or more	$2.00

RESERVE-PRICE FEES

Reserve Price	Fee
$0.01 to $199.99	$2.00
$200.00 and up	1% of reserve price (max.: $50)

BUY IT NOW FEES

Buy It Now Price	Fee
$0.99 to $9.99	$0.05
$10.00 to $24.99	$0.10
$25.00 to $49.99	$0.20
$50.00 or more	$0.25

There are two types of sellers on eBay: Standard Sellers and eBay Store Subscribers. We will talk about the store subscriber fees at the end of this chapter, and we will talk about the additional features you receive for the subscription in chapter 26. The fees we will talk about right now are the Standard Seller rates.

Insertion Fees

If you are a Standard Seller, you get to list fifty auction-style listings per month without paying an insertion fee. However, if you sell at fixed price or exceed those fifty listings (which include relists), you will have a per-listing fee to pay. The insertion fee for fixed-price listings is a flat-rate $0.50 no matter the price or the quantity of items. Remember, the first fifty free listings are for auction-style only. You will always pay for a fixed-price listing, and the minimum price for a fixed-price item is $0.99. Buy It Now listings are free for the first fifty auction-style listings per month, so the fee only applies after you exceed this number of auctions.

Final Value Fees

Once your item sells, you will be charged a final value fee by eBay. For auction-style listings it is 9 percent of the total amount of the sale, which includes your shipping charge, with a maximum fee amount of $250. For example, if you sell an item for $45 and charge $8 for shipping, your total sale amount is $53. The final value fee is calculated as 9 percent of $53 ($53 x .09), which is $4.77.

BIZ BUILDER

Final value fees are much higher than insertion fees. Therefore, it is very important that you keep track of any nonpaying bidders and file a claim in the eBay resolution center to get these fees refunded. Also, if a bidder doesn't pay, you are usually eligible for the Relist Credit, which means that if the item sells the second time it is listed, you get a credit back of one of the insertion fees you paid. Essentially, this is a "free relist," although you do pay the second insertion fee and it gets refunded only if the item sells the second time. Obviously, this only applies to single-item listings.

The final value fees for fixed-price listings vary, depending on your item's category. There are three category-specific final value fee tables (Electronics; Clothing, Shoes and Accessories; Books, DVDs and Movies, Music, Video Games) as well as one for

All Other Categories, so rather than show all of them, Table 21.3 shows the All Other Categories fees. Some of the category-specific final value fee percentages are lower than shown; some are higher. You can see all of the fixed-price final value fee tables at http://pages.ebay.com/help/sell/fees.html.

TABLE 21.3 eBay Fixed-Price Listings of Final Value Fees in "All Other Categories"

Selling Price	Final Value Fee
$0.99 to $50.00	11% of the closing value
$50.01 to $1,000.00	11% of the first $50.00, plus 6% of the balance
Over $1,000.01	11% of the initial $50.00, plus 6% of the value from $50.01 to $1,000, plus 2% of the remaining closing value

Here's an example of how the final value fee works. If an item sold for $1,450.00, you would pay 11 percent of the initial $50.00 ($5.50), plus 6 percent of the next $25.01 to $1,000.00 ($58.50), plus 2 percent of the remaining balance ($9.00). Add up all three amounts ($5.50 + $58.50 + $9.00), and you have your total final value fee of $73.00. That might sound like a lot, but consider that the total selling price was $1,450. That's not so bad.

Let's look at a lower-priced item, say $150. Your final value fee would be 11 percent of the initial $50 (still $5.50) and then 6 percent of the remaining $125 (or .06 x $125), which is $7.50. So the total final value fee for a $150 item is $13.00 ($5.50 + $7.50).

eBay charges you a final value fee only if your item sells. If an item fails to sell at an auction the first time, you are eligible for the Relist Credit if it sells the second time, but you get only one shot at this. If it fails to sell the second time, you do not get another chance at the Relist Credit. You still pay a final value fee if the item sells. There is no Relist Credit for fixed-price listings unless it is a single-item fixed price listing and ended with a sale but the buyer didn't end up paying.

Optional Feature Fees

As we noted earlier, eBay offers several optional listing upgrades designed to make your listing stand out and to attract the attention of potential bidders. Table 21.4 shows the fees for these upgrades. The first fee is for auctions and fixed-price listings running for 3, 5, 7, or 10 days. The second fee is for 30-day fixed-price listings only.

TABLE 21.4 Optional Listing Upgrade Fees	
Gallery Plus	$0.35/$1.00
Listing Designer	$0.10/$0.30
Item Subtitle	$0.50/$1.50
Bold	$2.00/$4.00
Scheduled Listing	$0.10/$0.10
10-Day Duration	$0.40/Free
List in Two Categories	Listing fee, doubled

Gallery Plus is free for all items in auction-style or fixed-price listing of any duration that are listed in the following four categories: Collectibles, Art, Pottery & Glass, and Antiques. Also, List in Two Categories doesn't double the optional Scheduled Listing fee, if you choose to use that. But the fees for all other upgrades (as well as the insertion fee) are doubled.

REDUCING YOUR EBAY FEES

Now that you understand how eBay charges for its services, let's take a look at how you can reduce your fees.

Insertion Fees

Right off the bat, you can see that eBay's insertion fees increase at various price points. If your starting price is on the cusp of one of these breaks, always go with the lower value. For example, if you started an auction listing at $200.00, the insertion fee would be $2.00. However, start the same item at $199.99—just one penny less—and your listing fee drops by half to $1.00—you save $1.00.

eBay Store Subscription

In chapter 26 we will talk about the benefits of having an eBay Store subscription. Essentially, the biggest advantage is lower fees. We will look at what you get for each subscription level (in addition to the fee reductions) in chapter 26, but for now Table 21.5 shows the fees for each type of listing and upgrade for eBay Store Subscribers.

TABLE 21.5 eBay Store Subscription Levels and Monthly Fees

Subscription Level	Monthly Fee
Basic	$15.95
Premium	$49.95
Anchor	$299.99

The insertion fee for auction-style listings is tiered exactly the same way for eBay Store Subscribers as for Standard Sellers, so I won't repeat it here (although remember that Store Subscribers do not get the free fifty auction-style listings per month). However, the fixed-price listing fee is significantly lower than the Standard Seller rate of $0.50 per item, as you can see in Table 21.6.

TABLE 21.6 eBay Store Subscriber Insertion Fee for Fixed-Price Listings

Subscription Level	Insertion Fee
Basic	$0.20
Premium	$0.05
Anchor	$0.03

To offset the cost of the Basic eBay Store subscription, you need to be listing fifty-four or more fixed-price listings per month. Fewer than that amount and you are financially better off sticking with the Standard Seller rate of $0.50 per item. Take a look at the math: The Standard Seller rate is 54 x $0.50 = $27. The basic eBay Store subscriber rate is 54 x $0.20 = $10.80, but then you also need to add the $15.95 subscription fee, which brings you to $26.75, which is as close to even as you will get.

The auction-style final value fee is different for eBay Store subscribers (as you can see in Table 21.7), and it is typically going to calculate out lower than the Standard Seller rate.

TABLE 21.7 eBay Store Subscriber Final Value Fees for Auction-Style Listings

Sale Price	Final Value Fee
$0.01 to $50.00	7.5% of the closing value
$50.01 to $1,000.00	7.5% of the first $50.00, plus 4% of the balance
Over $1,000.01	7.5% of the initial $50.00, plus 4% of the value from $50.01 to $1,000, plus 2% of the remaining closing value

Remember that the Standard rate final value fee is a flat-rate 9 percent. So let's look at an example. Let's say you sell a $100 item. At the Standard rate, the final value fee is $9 ($100 x .09). With the eBay Store subscriber rate, it is 7.5 percent of the first $50 ($3.50) plus 4 percent of the remaining balance ($50 x .04= $2). So the fee for the eBay Store subscriber is $5.50. That is a $3.50 lower fee than the Standard Seller rate for exactly the same item. This can really add up if you are selling a lot of items at auction.

The final value fees for fixed-price listings are the same for both Standard sellers and eBay Store subscribers, so I won't list them again here. The same is true for all the optional listing upgrades.

I'm sure you have seen how an eBay Store subscription can help reduce your fees, whether you are primarily an auction seller (because of the lower final-value fees) or a fixed-price seller (because of the lower insertion fees). Either way, it is volume that counts. After you have been selling for a couple of months, look back at your spreadsheet and work out what it would have cost you if you had had an eBay Store subscription. That is going to be your best indicator of whether it is worth subscribing yet.

Special Feature Fees

We discussed how to use eBay's special features in chapter 16. Each of these features can potentially increase the number of bidders and the final value of your auction. However, you have to calculate the potential return on investment (ROI) based on the expected value of the item you are selling. If you sell something for around $20, paying $2 for the bold feature might get you a 15 percent increase ($3) in the final value, so this would be a good investment. However, if it were a $10 item, paying $2 for bold would not be a good value.

eBay offers statistics on how well certain of these features perform, but these figures are averages for *all* auctions. A feature that gets an average 10 percent ROI for all auctions might not perform as well for your particular item. Also, this data is rarely new; it's sometimes six or more years old. The only way to know for sure is to run test auctions. Whenever I find a new product I want to sell on eBay, I run auctions both with and without special features to determine if the performance warrants the investment. This kind of ongoing product research is critical to success in most business ventures, and it's essential when you're building a business on eBay.

The other major cost factor for eBay sellers is inventory—the products you buy to resell on eBay. We will discuss controlling your inventory costs in the next chapter.

POWER MOVES

❏ Set up a simple spreadsheet in Microsoft Excel and list your expenses. Be sure to include things such as your ISP (Internet Service Provider) and cable or DSL fees, as well as charges for telephone, postage, and office supplies. Take a step back and analyze your costs. Which line items are costing you the most each month? What can you do to reduce your monthly expenses?

❏ In chapter 10, you bookmarked the eBay fee schedule at http://pages.ebay.com/help/sell/fees.html. Go to this page and print out the full schedule. Study the fee schedule until you are thoroughly familiar with how eBay charges fees. You don't have to memorize the fees, especially those for optional features, but you should have a good feel for what they are and when to use them.

❏ Now calculate the eBay fees for several items listed and sold at different prices. For example, calculate the fees for an item that listed at $9.99 and sold for $20.00. Now do the same thing for an item that started at $49.99 and sold for $75.00.

❏ Using this information, study the auctions you have launched thus far and evaluate your pricing. Have you been paying higher fees than necessary? What sort of ROI have you been realizing for the optional listing features you've used? List the steps you can take to lower your eBay fees and write them in the binder next to your computer.

CHAPTER 22

✦ INVENTORY MANAGEMENT ✦

INVENTORY CONSISTS OF all the products you purchase to sell on eBay. Unless you engage in drop-shipping (as detailed in chapter 7) or selling on consignment for others (see chapter 27), your inventory will represent your largest investment and potentially is your biggest financial risk. You incur this risk by purchasing inventory that either does not sell or cannot sell at a high enough price for you to make a profit. Business owners call this *nonperforming inventory.*

In chapter 4 we stressed how crucial it is to research a product before you purchase it so you can determine if it will sell on eBay. Product research is your best defense against being stuck with nonperforming inventory, but even excellent research is not foolproof. You can still end up with products that sell well at first and then fall in price as others begin selling them. In this chapter we'll examine how to manage your inventory so that you reduce costs and increase your monthly profits.

DEALING WITH NONPERFORMING INVENTORY

Purchasing large amounts of inventory at one time has its risks and rewards. Although you can get better prices by purchasing in large quantities, you need to consider how long it will take you to move the inventory.

eBay bidders pay close attention to an item's supply. When bidders see many identical items listed, they are reluctant to place high bids. They know that if they miss an item in one auction, they can just bid on another one. If you put too many similar items on eBay within a short period, you will drive down prices by increasing the supply. When you do this, you end up competing with yourself. eBay does not allow you to have duplicate listings for the same item active at the same time. Here are examples eBay gives of what they consider duplicates:

* Two auction-style listings for identical items, even if they have different ending times, start prices, or reserve prices.

* An auction-style listing with Buy It Now and an auction-style listing without Buy It Now for identical items.

* A fixed-price listing and an auction-style listing with Buy It Now for identical items.

These provisions ensure that a seller doesn't flood the search results page with multiple auctions for the same item, and they help keep you from competing with your own auctions.

Despite your best research, you might end up with a product that's just not selling at a price that's profitable. When this happens, the best thing you can do is sell it quickly for whatever you can get. When you are sitting on inventory that is not selling, you are tying up money that you could be spending on inventory that *will* sell.

Retail store owners understand the cost of nonperforming inventory and the value of inventory that makes them money. That is why every retail store has a sale table. If an item is not selling well, store owners mark the price down to move it out quickly and free up money and shelf space for inventory that will perform better. As an eBay seller, it is imperative that you do the same thing if you want to make a profit. When inventory isn't moving, you need to create a virtual sale table.

There are two strategies for getting rid of inventory quickly. One is simply to launch the items on eBay at a lower price. The problem with this approach is that listing a large number of similar items at one time could drive the price even lower than what you were hoping to get. A better way is to list the items in *Wholesale Lots*.

Almost every eBay category has a subcategory called Wholesale Lots. This is where people sell items in bulk. If, for example, you purchased a large lot of cell phone batteries from a supplier and were able to sell only a few of them before the price started dropping, you could take your remaining batteries and either break them up into small lots or sell them as one large lot. Small lots will usually realize a higher per-item price than large ones; there are many small eBay sellers who cannot afford to purchase a case of forty-eight batteries but who would be willing to buy a dozen at a time.

Another option is to use a fixed-price multiple-quantity listing. Fixed-price listings are much cheaper to list than auction-style and can run for thirty days. If you list a quantity over ten (say, fifty) of an item in a fixed-price multiple-quantity listing, the "quantity" that shows on the description page will just say *more than ten available*. If it's lower than ten, it will show the specific number that are unsold. If you list at a low price, you should be able to catch the impulse buyers and shift your inventory quickly.

TURN YOUR INVENTORY OVER OFTEN

Inventory turn refers to how often you replace your inventory in a given period. Keeping your inventory turning at a brisk pace is essential to making large amounts of money on eBay. Consider the following example:

You find a source for overstock designer blue jeans, and you can buy a pallet load of 100 pairs for $7 a pair. When you check the prices on eBay, you see that similar jeans are selling for between $18 and $29 a pair. The normal response is to list the jeans at the higher price. So you start launching auctions for the jeans at $29 a pair and find that you can sell about ten pairs a week. You are making a gross margin of $22 a pair before eBay and PayPal fees. Because you are selling ten pairs a week, you are realizing $220 a week. At this rate, it will take you ten weeks to sell all the jeans.

Now, let's say you lower the price of the jeans to $22 a pair, and you begin selling twenty-five pairs a week, as opposed to ten pairs. Your gross margin on each pair is now only $18, but you are realizing $450 a week because of increased volume. Plus, you will sell all the jeans in four weeks instead of ten. Your margin for the four-week period is $1,800. You can now turn around and invest that $1,800 into more jeans inventory, which you can sell again in another four-week period at the same price.

Compare the two scenarios: In the first one, you make $2,200 over a ten-week period at the higher price of $29. However, in the second scenario, you make $4,500 over the same ten-week period by selling the jeans at the lower price and reinvesting the profits. This is an example of using a lower pricing strategy to increase your inventory turn rate.

CONTROLLING YOUR INVENTORY

You can't control the flow of your inventory if you don't understand it. That's why it's important to keep good records. When you are just starting out, set up a simple Excel spreadsheet where you list your inventory (see Table 22.1). Create separate columns to list the item, the quantity you purchased, the quantity on hand, the date you acquired it, the cost per item, and the average selling price. (Every time you sell an item, you should update the quantity on hand.) Keep a record of each sale in a ledger so that you can determine the total final selling price for the entire lot.

If you are going to run test auctions for the same item at different price points, set up a separate line item for each test. This will allow you to compare the performance of the different price points over time.

There are two other ways to track and control your inventory. If you decide to make an investment in QuickBooks, this program has a built-in inventory function where you can enter inventory cost and performance data. The QuickBooks inventory function is fairly basic, although it's fine for most small businesses. If you sell a large number of different products, consider the more sophisticated inventory management program KwikInventory, made for Windows by Worth Data (www.barcodehq.com). Worth Data's system retails for around $300. You may also want to invest in a barcode printer and reader. These systems go for about $600, but there are plenty of used systems available on eBay for under $300.

TABLE 22.1 Sample Inventory Record

Item Description	Initial Quantity	Quantity on Hand	Date Acquired	Cost per Item	Average Selling Price (unit)
Men's Nautica Blue Jeans	44	17	8/12/2012	$19.00 pr.	$36.21
DKNY Silk Tops	12	8	10/11/2012	$24.00 ea.	$42.55
Nike Jordan Shoes	36	33	12/2/2012	$47.00 ea.	$68.77
Nautica Blue Bathrobes, Unisex	12	4	1/30/2013	$14.20 ea.	$22.00
Fila Men's Running Suit	12	4	2/22/2013	$39.00 ea.	$76.88
G. Vanderbilt Women's Jeans	40	22	3/15/2013	$19.22 ea	$29.56

The other way to manage your inventory is with an online system. In the next chapter, we'll return to auction management systems, which we touched on in chapter 15. Most of these services, including the ones I recommend, allow you to track your inventory, connect images and descriptions to each item, and even launch eBay auctions directly from your online system.

When you are first starting out, you will most likely be selling few product lines. Setting up an inventory control system might seem like overkill, but as your business grows, you will need to organize and track your products. Knowing how much inventory you have on hand, how much it costs, how long it is taking you to turn it over, and how much it is selling for are all integral to running a successful eBay business. If you get the process set up while your inventory level is low, it will be much easier to integrate higher quantities later, when you're obviously going to be busier, than it will be to try to set it up when you are also managing hundreds of auctions.

WEEK 3

POWER MOVES

❏ Set up a spreadsheet to list and control your inventory. Be sure to track the dates you acquire your inventory so you can assess how long it is taking you to move the inventory out.

❏ On this spreadsheet, track your average selling price (ASP) per item so that you can identify your most and least profitable products. Use this information in determining which products (and how many units of each) to reorder.

❏ Determine and implement strategies for dealing with nonperforming inventory. Consider listing items in a Wholesale Lots category or lowering your price to clear out slow-moving items.

CHAPTER 23

✦ AUTOMATING YOUR AUCTIONS ✦

IF YOU COULD HIRE A FULL-TIME employee for less than $50 a month, someone who would work with you in your eBay business—24 hours a day, 7 days a week—do you think that would be a good investment?

Uploading photos, writing descriptions, communicating with buyers, printing shipping labels, and posting feedback are just a few of the steps that you perform every time you launch or complete an auction. When you first start selling on eBay, you will be launching your auctions with the tools that eBay provides in the Sell Your Item form and you will be managing your information from your My eBay page. As you grow your business, you should consider adding services and software that can automate some or all of these functions. Automated services fall into three categories:

- ✱ eBay solutions (online and offline choices)
- ✱ Third-party offline software
- ✱ Online auction management services

Evaluating every product on the market to automate your auctions is beyond the scope of this book. Instead, let's look at the pros and cons of each type of service and then evaluate one service that is fast becoming the choice of many eBay sellers.

EBAY SOLUTIONS

eBay offers both auction management software and online systems. The three basic choices are Turbo Lister, Blackthorne, and Selling Manager. We now turn to these eBay solutions.

Turbo Lister

This is a free download from eBay that allows you to create listings offline and launch them onto eBay. Through Turbo Lister, you can list multiple items at once and save listings to reuse again and again. Convenient templates allow you to create listings easily with a WYSIWYG ("what you see is what you get") design editor (just like the HTML editor in the *Sell Your Item* form). Turbo Lister can also schedule your listings to launch at a later time.

Blackthorne

Formerly known as Seller's Assistant, Blackthorne is a software program that comes in two versions, basic and pro. These are eBay's all-in-one desktop listing and sales management tools, designed to automate the process of launching auctions. Blackthorne's tools help medium- to high-volume sellers launch auctions on eBay without requiring a constant Internet connection. Both versions offer several customizable features. The pro version includes sophisticated inventory control tools and detailed financial reporting. eBay charges $9.99 a month for the basic version and $24.99 a month for the pro version. Unlike Turbo Lister, which is primarily a launching and scheduling tool, Blackthorne has record-keeping and financial reporting capabilities. Blackthorne also allows you to automate the process of sending e-mails to winning bidders. You get a free thirty-day trial for either version, and if you download it before subscribing, you can spend as long as you like preparing the listings; then when you're ready to launch a bunch, you just sign up and the thirty-day trial starts at that point.

Selling Manager

This is eBay's online (i.e., Web-based as opposed to desktop-based) sales management tool. You access Selling Manager through your My eBay page, which makes this tool very convenient. Selling Manager also comes in a Pro version. Selling Manager is for low- to medium-volume listers, while Selling Manager Pro is better suited for high-volume listers.

Selling Manager provides additional automation for management of your ongoing listings as well as the postsale tasks. The basic level is free.

With Selling Manager Pro, you can relist multiple items at once; see a one-page snapshot of your business; track buying, selling, and account activities; create e-mails with custom templates; and print shipping labels and invoices. You also get bulk relisting capabilities and sophisticated inventory management and financial reporting tools. eBay charges $15.99 a month for Selling Manager Pro. But it also comes free with a Premium or Anchor eBay Store subscription (we will talk more about the benefits of these two levels in chapter 26).

The eBay Advantage?

With the various eBay solutions, all your auction management is integrated into your My eBay page. You can easily compare the features (and cost) of each of these options in the table at http://pages.ebay.com/selling_manager/comparison.html.

ONLINE AUCTION MANAGEMENT SERVICES

There are over a dozen companies offering Web-based automation solutions for eBay sellers. The leading companies are listed in Table 23.1.

TABLE 23.1 Leading Online Auction Management Services

Vendio	www.vendio.com
ChannelAdvisor	www.channeladvisor.com
Auctiva	www.auctiva.com

Both Vendio and ChannelAdvisor offer multiple marketplace integration (so if you also want to sell on Amazon you can manage all of your inventory through this one program). However, they are much more costly because of this. Auctiva is a great start-up for a newer eBay sellers. Here are some of the features of Auctiva:

* HTML templates to create your auctions.

* You can create item listings in inventory for launching later.

* Prewritten automated invoices, payment reminders, and shipping and feedback notices.

* One-page listing form (all the information is on one page so if you want to go back and revise something you can do it very easily).

* Free image hosting (up to twenty-four pictures per listing) with a free supersize feature.

* Auction scheduling without the per-listing fee charged by eBay.

* Listing templates (over 1,800 to choose from).

* Free scrolling gallery in all of your listings to cross-promote your other items.

Auctiva does have a free service, but it is very limited. If you are realistically going to be using this for more than just the scrolling gallery (which I personally believe every seller should have even if he is using the Sell Your Item form for every listing creation), then you should be looking at the Advanced Auctiva plan for $9.95 a month. This is peanuts when you consider the time-saving features and extra options available.

Personally, I favor the online systems over desktop-based programs. They save the most time and you don't have to worry about computer crashes and losing your data. Using such a system is like having a virtual employee—one who saves you time, helps you launch your auctions more efficiently, and keeps your costs under control.

You can see all of the tools (eBay and third-party) on the Selling Tools and Efficiency page of the eBay Seller Information Center. The direct link is http://pages.ebay.com/sellerinformation/sellingresources/sellingtools.html

POWER MOVES

❏ Visit eBay's Selling Resources pages and read the information about the eBay-based automation solutions: Turbo Lister, Blackthorne, and Selling Manager.

❏ Visit Auctiva.com (or any of the other sites listed in this chapter or in the Selling Tools and Efficiency page on eBay) and take a tour.

❏ Once you have selected an automation solution to try, either purchase a subscription or sign up for a free trial. Begin setting up your inventory and learning the system.

CHAPTER 24

✦ THIRD-PARTY PROMOTIONAL TOOLS ✦

YOU HAVE A GREAT PRODUCT that you can buy at a great price. You have mastered the art of title writing, using keywords, taking great photos, and all the basic steps you need for success. In addition, you've reduced your eBay fees and improved how you manage your inventory. So what else can you do to increase your sales and profits?

eBay is a very competitive sales venue, so anything you can do to either stand out from the crowd or convince the customer to do business with you instead of clicking away to another auction will put money in your pocket at the end of the month.

INCREASING AUCTION VIEWS

The single best way to boost the number of hits your auctions receive is by writing compelling, keyword-rich titles. If your auctions are getting very few views, the first thing you need to do is review the material in chapter 14 and make sure you are writing the best titles you can. The other factor that drives hits are the eBay promotional features covered in chapter 16, such as bold, subtitle, and so on.

Assuming that you've done the best job possible in these areas, what else can you do to increase hits?

Auctiva Scrolling Gallery

Even if you decide not to use Auctiva to launch your auctions and host your pictures, you can still use the Scrolling Gallery (see Figure 24.1) for free.

Just sign up for the free Auctiva account and select Scrolling Gallery from your list of options. You'll set up an *eBay Token* that allows Auctiva very limited access to your listings (just to link your auctions together using the Scrolling Gallery) and presto—all of your listings from now on will cross-promote your other listings.

This is particularly useful when you're selling similar items (such as clothes in the same size, or a range of items and their accessories), because buyers will look to your other items to combine shipping.

Web Site and e-Mail Promotion

Another way to promote your auctions is with an eBay button that you can post on your Web site (if you have one) or attach to all your outgoing e-mails. If you go to the eBay site

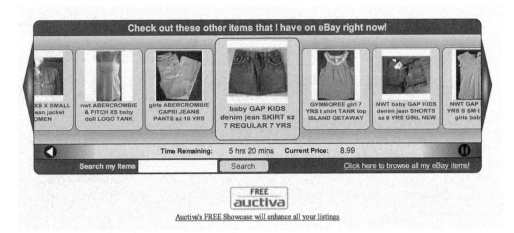

Figure 24.1 Auctiva Scrolling Gallery

map under the heading Selling Activities, look for the link that says *Promote your listing with link buttons*. This will take you to a page where you can copy a snippet of HTML code that you can paste into a Web page or insert as your e-mail signature. The code will create a little button that says "Right Now on eBay" superimposed over an eBay logo. When shoppers click on this button, it takes them to a list of your auctions on eBay.

Classified Ads

Here's another great way to promote your auctions that almost no one ever thinks of— classified advertising, both in newspapers and on the Web. This technique works best if you sell to a small, niche market. For example, let's say you collect and sell old fountain pens. You can take out small classified ads in newspapers that read something like this:

> *Old Fountain Pens for Sale on eBay. Just type 1234567890123*
> *into the search box at www.ebay.com.*

The number could be the item number of a pen currently at auction or listed in your eBay Store. This is the easiest way to lead someone directly to you, because the complete hyperlink to your auctions is too long and complex to put in a newspaper ad. If you have an eBay Store, you could direct them to http://stores.ebay.com/ yourstorename which isn't too long. If you are posting classified ads on the Web, you can use a simple HTML command to create a link to your list of auctions. Your online ad would read like this:

Old Fountain Pens for Sale on eBay.
<a href=your link to auctions goes here> Click Here </a> to see my auctions.

When you use the <a href=> code, the reader of an online classified sees this:

Old Fountain Pens for Sale on eBay.

Click Here to see my auctions.

You can find plenty of Web sites that offer free classified ads by just typing *free classified ad* into the Google, Yahoo!, or Bing search boxes.

WEEK
3

POWER MOVES

❏ Sign up for Auctiva (even if only the free version) to insert the Scrolling Gallery into your listings to enable easy cross-promotion of your items to the same buyers.

❏ Begin running online and newspaper classified ads for your auctions. Track the increase in sales to determine your ROI.

CHAPTER 25

✦ UPSELLING AND E-MAIL MARKETING ✦ TO YOUR CUSTOMERS

WE'VE ALREADY TALKED ABOUT using Auctiva's Scrolling Gallery to cross-sell your other items. If you use Vendio, they also have a version called a *scrolling marquee*, which is essentially the same thing. This is a great tool for cross-selling and upselling to buyers. If you have an eBay Store you can use the Cross-Promotions tool, which lets you display certain other listings on your item, bid confirmation, and purchase confirmation pages.

eBay has very strict rules regarding e-mail—especially when it comes to e-mail marketing to eBay members. In the early days of eBay, you could get any member's e-mail address right off the site. Now eBay hides or anonymizes all buyer e-mail addresses, even when you are directly involved in a transaction together. The only way to contact your buyer is using eBay's Messages system, and you better believe that is monitored and has flags for language related to buying items off eBay. You cannot send a link to a buyer in an eBay Message either (because you could be sending them to your retail Web site instead of selling through eBay). It will be automatically blocked by eBay, so don't bother trying.

So how do you upsell and market to your customers? Well, if you don't have an eBay Store, the only option is to include a note in your parcel to the buyer. Maybe a coupon for 10 percent off if they buy from your Web site. Maybe offer a free article about a relevant topic or download on your Web site, and print the link in your "thank you" letter that you include in the parcel.

NEWSLETTER AND WEB SITE MARKETING

Many specialty sellers—especially those selling collectibles—create monthly or bimonthly newsletters and invite buyers to sign up for a free subscription. Here's how this works: First, you create a Web site to sell products in the same category as those you're listing on eBay. Then you publish your newsletter right on the site. The navigation bar on your Web site homepage includes an internal link to your newsletter, and you might put a "teaser" box about the newsletter on the homepage to entice visitors to check it out. You then send out the newsletter's table of contents in an e-mail to your subscribers, with a link taking readers right to the applicable page on your site. This strategy is designed to drive prospective buyers to your Web site. Once they look around, you're counting on their purchasing something.

Don't worry if you can't write well enough to produce a newsletter. You can always produce a digest of news and articles about your topic. For instance, let's say you sell mineral specimens to rock collectors. Conduct a Google search on several terms related to rock collecting and use the News tab of the Google search feature. Whenever you find a relevant article, include the title and the first sentence or two in your newsletter with a link to the full article. It would look something like this:

GEM SHOW'S POOL OF TREASURES INCLUDES 96-YEAR-OLD'S AGATE

WHITTIER, CA -- Clarence Pool has been an avid rock hunter for more than half a century. He became a dedicated Rockhound in his 20s, at the urging of another collector . . . Read More

The words *Read More* would be a hyperlink to the article itself. You can include a series of these on your newsletter page. Consider writing your own comments below each article. You should make sure that the link opens a new window so your reader doesn't leave your Web site to go there.

You can also find free articles on hundreds of subjects at Web sites where authors post articles. You are free to post the article on your Web site, as long as you give author credit to the person who wrote it and include a link to the Web site it was posted on. Here are several Web sites from which you can copy or download articles:

* www.articlecity.com
* www.goarticles.com
* www.ezinearticles.com
* www.articleworld.net
* www.aracontent.com

Your goal is to build a content-rich Web site that makes your customers come back again and again.

The only way you can get buyers to subscribe to a newsletter on your Web site is to put a note in the parcel containing the item they bought from you inviting them to do so. You cannot include this in any e-mail communication or eBay will block it. However, if you offer an incentive—free shipping, 10 percent off the next order, etc. as well as the newsletter information, you are more likely to entice the buyer to visit your Web site.

THE EBAY E-MAIL MARKETING SYSTEM

eBay doesn't exactly promote this option, but you can request buyers to add you to their "Favorite Sellers" list. This can be part of your e-mail signature or something you encourage in your "thank you" letter in the parcel you send.

The advantage of having someone add you to their Favorite Sellers list is that they will then be periodically e-mailed by eBay to get them to check out your new items. Since the buyers will have had such a great experience with you (hopefully), the idea is that this will entice them to buy from you again.

In the Seller Information box on any listing page is a link to *Add seller*. If a buyer clicks this, she will be taken to a page like the one shown in Figure 25.1. If you have an eBay Store (see chapter 26), you can have a newsletter using the Off-eBay Marketing option. This program provides the following features:

❋ Buyers can sign up to receive your e-mail "newsletters" when they add you to their Favorite Sellers list.

Add to My Favorite Sellers and Stores

Save time by storing your favorite sellers and Stores in My eBay.

Seller: mcgrrrrr (9336 ☆)
Store: 🛒 The Auction Seller's Resource

Add a note to yourself

Your note will appear in My eBay, and be visible only to you.
250 characters left.

Email Subscriptions

Don't miss out! Subscribe to receive emails with featured items from this seller.

Favorite Sellers Top Picks - Email sent by eBay
You can set the frequency of this email on the Favorite Sellers page in My eBay.
☑ Subscribe here to receive an email summary of items available from mcgrrrrr

Example

Seller Newsletters - Email sent by mcgrrrrr
Subscribe and receive email newsletters directly from the seller with new listings, special promotions, and other information. Sellers choose when to send newsletters, but they can't send a newsletter more than once a week. You can unsubscribe to these emails at any time.
☐ Receive "General Interest" newsletters from mcgrrrrr   ☐ Receive "Interesting Kitchen Gadgets" newsletters from mcgrrrrr
☐ Receive "Starbucks Collectibles" newsletters from mcgrrrrr
☐ Receive "Learn To Sell on eBay" newsletters from mcgrrrrr

Example

Note: You can unsubscribe or manage your email subscriptions anytime on the Favorite Sellers page in My eBay

[Save] Cancel

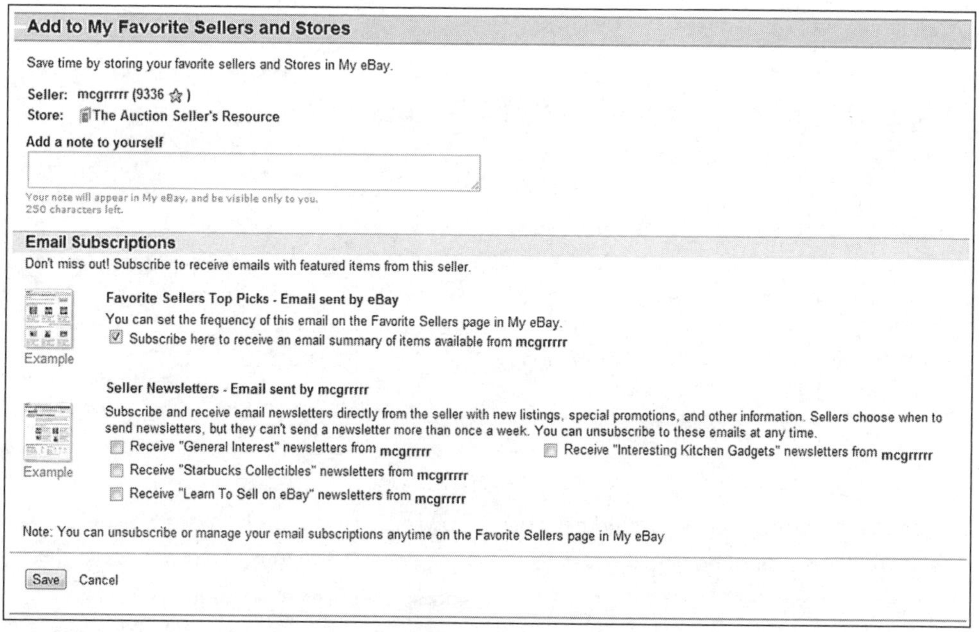

Figure 25.1 "Add to Favorite Sellers" Option

* Using a simple tool, you can create e-mails with links to your eBay Store and your listings and then send them to your subscribers. You can control which subscribers receive your e-mails, based on their interests, purchase history, and so forth.

* You can create up to five mailing lists that target different interests or types of promotions. For example, you could have a DVDs mailing list (alerting buyers to new DVDs you have in stock) and a Sale Notifications mailing list (alerting buyers to special discounts you are offering). Buyers choose which of your mailing lists to sign up for when they add you to their Favorite Sellers lists.

* You can measure the success of a targeted e-mail by viewing statistics, such as the number of bids and Buy It Now purchases it generated, and use this information to be reach out more effectively to customers.

Depending on your eBay Store subscription level (Basic, Premium, or Anchor; see chapter 26), eBay will allow you to send a certain number of free monthly e-mails to your subscribers. If you exceed your monthly allocation, you will be charged a per-recipient fee for additional e-mails. Monthly allocations and additional e-mail charges are outlined in Table 25.1.

TABLE 25.1 eBay Store e-Mail Allocation Breakdowns, by Store Type

Subscription Level	Monthly Free e-Mail Allocation	Additional Cost per Recipient (over allocation)
Basic Store	5,000 e-mails	$0.01 per e-mail
Premium Store	7,500 e-mails	$0.01 per e-mail
Anchor Store	10,000 e-mails	$0.01 per e-mail

For more on eBay Store fees, see chapter 26.

E-mail marketing, both on and off eBay, allows you to generate more business. And more sales mean more profits. If you can use your eBay auctions as a means of advertising for your eBay Store, where listing and selling fees are lower—or, even better, for your Web site, where there are no listing or selling fees at all—then your profits will increase exponentially.

POWER MOVES

❏ Evaluate the products you currently sell. See if you can come up with combinations that would lend themselves to upselling; in addition, write up a list of products you could buy or create for the purpose of cross-selling. Once you have identified these items and determined their pricing, start featuring them in your cross-selling promotions once you have an eBay Store, and make sure they are active at the same time for featuring in the Auctiva Scrolling Gallery on your listing pages.

❏ Learn about eBay's e-mail marketing program. (To find out more information about the program, click on the Customer Service tab at the top of any eBay page and enter *e-mail marketing* into the search box. The current direct link is http://pages.ebay.com/help/sell/e-mail-newsletter.html).

❏ Visit www.topica.com and read about Topica's programs for newsletter publishers. Consider how to create newsletters that would appeal to bidders and buyers of your specific product(s).

CHAPTER 26

✦ OPENING AN EBAY STORE ✦

YOUR EBAY STORE SUBSCRIPTION gives you cheaper insertion fees for fixed-price listings and cheaper final value fees for auction-style listings than if you didn't have an eBay Store. However, the trade-off is that you do not get the fifty free auction-style listing insertion fees per month. If you look at the difference between the insertion fee and final value fees, though, you still do better with an eBay Store subscription if you sell in volume (either in fixed-price or auction-style listings).

In addition to the reduced fees, you also get other benefits for having an eBay Store subscription. You get a page specifically for your listings (auction and fixed-price), which you can organize into subcategories, as shown on the left sidebar of Figure 26.1.

Figure 26.1 eBay Store Page, as Viewed by a Buyer

eBay provides a dedicated *Store search* box within your eBay Store, enabling buyers to search through your items and find exactly what they want.

You control the look and feel of your store. A professional-looking store gives you credibility as an online retailer—and makes shopping easier for your buyers. Since an eBay Store is essentially a Web site, it has its own URL that you can use to drive buyers directly there, from both on and off eBay. You can even optimize your Web address so that it shows up in search engine results. (You can find complete instructions for doing this through the *Manage your store* link once your eBay Store is set up.)

An eBay Store also allows you to cross-promote your products to prospective auction bidders. If you're already using the scrolling gallery you might not be concerned about this, but it does let you pick specific items that complement the one the buyer is already looking at, which can be helpful if you have a large amount of inventory.

TYPES OF STORES AND FEES

There are three kinds of fees for eBay Stores:

* Monthly subscription fees
* Listing and final value fees
* Special promotional fees

Let's look at each type, and what you get for your money.

Subscription Fees

eBay charges all sellers monthly subscription fees for their eBay Stores. There are three subscription levels for eBay Stores, each of which comes with additional features and benefits:

* Basic: $15.95/month
* Premium: $49.95/month
* Anchor: $299.95/month

Basic Store Subscription With a Basic Store subscription, you can showcase all your auction and fixed-price listings in a custom "storefront" that you design, and you can use the cross-promotion tool to cross-sell your inventory on all your Item, Bid Confirmation, and Purchase Confirmation pages. The Basic subscription level also gives you a free subscription to Selling Manager and phone customer service between 5 a.m. and 10 p.m. Pacific Standard Time (PST).

Premium Store Subscription With a Premium Store subscription, you get all the Basic Store benefits plus additional exposure, including:

* Featured placement on the eBay Stores main page (http://stores.ebay.com)
* Prime positioning in the Stores Directory pages
* Free subscription to Selling Manager Pro (usually $15.99 a month)
* Marketplace data and sophisticated traffic statistics, allowing you to see where your traffic is coming from

At $49.95 per month, a Premium Store may seem expensive, but when you deduct the $15.99 subscription fee to Selling Manager Pro (which you would probably need at this level anyway), the monthly store subscription fee drops to $33.96.

All levels of eBay Store allow you to choose up to 300 categories and subcategories of merchandise to sell. This is helpful if you are selling different types of products and you want to direct customers to the right place in your store. For example, if you were selling men's, women's, and children's apparel, you could have a separate category for each one, and then size or type of item subcategories within the main categories (just as eBay's auctions have). This would spare a woman visiting your store to get clothing for herself from having to page through dozens of men's and children's items. Similarly, if you were selling after-market car accessories, you could have separate categories for all the popular car companies—Nissan, GM, Toyota, Chrysler, Honda, Ford, Mazda, and so on.

Anchor Store

The Anchor Store is quite expensive at first glance. The benefits are almost identical to the Premium Store level, so unless you need the extra allowance for e-mail marketing (2,500 more for Anchor over Premium subscribers) or you are extremely high volume, you can probably stick with a Basic or Premium store. You can see a very clear comparison of all three subscription levels and what they include at http://pages.ebay.com/storefronts/subscriptions.html.

Account Limits

It is important to note that new eBay sellers have selling limits. You may be restricted to a certain number of items in a particular category, a total number of listings, etc. Limits may apply if you:

* Have been registered on eBay for under ninety days
* Haven't sold multiple items in that category before
* Haven't sold in that category for over a year
* Have had eBay Buyer Protection cases on over 3 percent of your total sales over the previous year

Not every category has limits. They are particularly used for electronics and items known to be targeted for fraud, through fakes or otherwise. You can see a full list of categories with limits and learn more about general account limits at http://pages.ebay.com/help/sell/sellinglimits.html.

To see if you have limits, go to My eBay, select *All Selling*, and then look for the *Monthly Selling Limits* section. If there is no section, you don't have limits. If you do, they will be stated clearly here.

I strongly advise that you do not open an eBay Store until you have any selling limits removed. You can build up your inventory and get your listings organized and prepared, but wait until you don't have limits; otherwise, you won't be able to utilize the full benefits of having an eBay Store.

Listing Fees and Final Value Fees

I covered the fees for eBay Stores in chapter 21 so I won't repeat them here. However, essentially remember that you need to be a high-volume auction-style seller (because of the lower final value fees for this format) or a high-volume fixed-price seller (because of the lower insertion fees) to make it worthwhile to have an eBay Store. Typically, you need to be listing approximately fifty items in either format per month for it to be worthwhile.

SETTING UP SHOP

No matter which subscription level you opt for, setting up and branding your eBay Store is fairly simple and takes only a few minutes. Best of all, you have complete control over the look and feel of your store. eBay allows you to:

* Customize your store's homepage

* Select a color scheme for your header and left navigation bar

* Insert your own custom graphics into your header

* Choose the default option of how you want your items displayed

* Create up to 300 custom categories within your store

* Provide additional information to your buyers, including descriptions about your store, yourself, and your store's policies

Creating custom graphics for your store is important for branding purposes. If you don't have any experience in the field of online graphics, there are plenty of people on eBay who can do this for you. Simply type *eBay Store graphics* into the eBay search engine and you will find dozens of auction listings for people who offer this service. Most sellers charge between $50 and $150 for this service, but some may charge higher fees for more sophisticated graphics.

Promoting Your eBay Store

There are two ways that eBay lets bidders know you have a store: by placing a small store icon after your user ID, and by including a link in all your listings to *See other items,* and beneath that, including a link to your store. Unfortunately, very few buyers actually click on these links. Your challenge is to change that—to encourage buyers to click through to your store so you can cross-sell other items.

Having an eBay Store allows you to set up separate categories, like departments in a department store. The goal is to drive people viewing one of your listings to a specific category in your store. Here's how it might work: Let's say you sell bird feeders and other bird-related products. In every listing, right under your product description, you include a paragraph that describes all the other bird-related items you sell. The paragraph would contain both an invitation and a clickable link to a specific category in your eBay Store, like the one below:

> If you love songbirds, please visit my eBay Store,
> *<ahref=http://www.your_store_link_goes_here>BirdsForAll</a>,*
> where you will find a large selection of bird feeders, bird baths,
> birdhouses, and books on birds and birding.

The HTML code is the clickable link right to the appropriate category in your eBay Store. The name *BirdsForAll* will appear in light blue and underlined, indicating to prospective buyers that they can just click on the link to visit your store. Bidders will read it as follows: "If you love songbirds, please visit my eBay Store, Birds For All, where you will find a large selection . . ."

Another way to attract visitors to your eBay Store is to offer free shipping on combined shipments, or offer free shipping in an auction to drive bidders to the fixed-price listing. I often do this by adding a statement to my auctions like this:

FREE SHIPPING FOR MY EBAY STORE CUSTOMERS

> You do not have to wait for the auction to end to buy this Garmin GPS unit. They are available in my eBay Store for immediate shipment. If you buy this item now from my eBay Store, I will ship it for FREE anywhere in the US. If you are in Canada or overseas, I will give you a $5.00 credit toward the shipping cost. I also have several other Garmin models in my Store in different price ranges. Click here to buy now or to see all the items in my store.

While you'll have to pick up the cost of shipping, you'll be generating sales you would not have made otherwise. Many store sellers deliberately set the prices in their stores a bit higher to cover the cost of this giveaway. Once you get the bidders to check out your store, be sure to make it as easy as possible for them to buy. As we mentioned above, you need to direct the buyer to the correct category, because this saves him time and, hopefully, prompts him to buy other items of interest.

BIZ BUILDER

I make it a point to prominently feature the search box that allows buyers to search my store. Once a potential bidder is in your store, anything you can do to get her to the product she is looking for as quickly as possible will produce the best results. If you were selling apparel, for instance, you could invite buyers to search by size. If you sold different brands of cameras, you could place a message next to your search box, inviting customers to search by brand, such as Nikon, Sony, or Kodak.

It is imperative that you categorize your items. You're really shooting yourself in the foot if you just have one "general" or "other" category. The point of an eBay Store (as well as the fee reduction) is cross-selling. For example, if you sell children's clothes and have 300 active listings but just have one "general" category, the buyer has to either search for the size or browse through all of those listings. They're not going to do it. However, if you have category links on the sidebar showing categories by gender and size, you are much more likely to get the buyer to click through on a whim and check out what else you have in that size. It also lets you separate your product lines. You may be active in three or four different niches. Potential buyers in one may not be interested at all in another of your product lines. So by categorizing you make it easy for the buyer to find what they are interested in without cluttering their results with items they are not interested in.

You can also promote your eBay Store from outside eBay. eBay automatically submits your store's URL to several search engines, such as Google and Yahoo! Be sure to use keywords in your store description and in each item title, to increase your chances of getting hits from search engines.

Markdown Manager

Another feature of an eBay Store is the ability to put your items on sale via Markdown Manager. When you do this, eBay shows buyers who have the item in their watch list that it is on sale. They also show it prominently on the listing page, as you can see in Figure 26.2.

Figure 26.2 Item on Sale with Markdown Manager

To get to the Markdown Manager, go to My eBay and select *Marketing Tools* from the *Account* drop-down menu. Under *Item Promotion* on the left sidebar you will see *Markdown Manager*. Incidentally, this is where you will also see the *Cross-Promotions* settings.

If you decide to lower the price on any of your fixed-price items, using Markdown Manager is far better than just changing the price. You can also put items on sale for a fixed period of time; that way the buyer has a sense of urgency to buy them now, rather than waiting any longer.

Vacation Hold

If you have hundreds of active listings and you decide to take a week's vacation, it can be a huge chore to pull listings down and then put them back up. A better option for eBay Store subscribers is the *Vacation Hold*. You can choose to put a note at the top of your listings that explains that you are on vacation and items will not ship until whatever date you specify. Alternatively, you can just let your auction-style listings expire before your vacation (and not list more) and then set your fixed-price listings to "hidden" until you return. Yes, you will continue to pay fees for listings that are hidden, but you don't have the hassle of relisting hundreds of listings when you return. It is worth it, believe me.

To put your store on vacation, go to the *Messages* tab in My eBay and select *Change settings* from the top right of the page (see Figure 26.3).

Here you can turn on your store vacation settings, and also an out-of-office reply to your messages, so potential buyers won't think you are ignoring them.

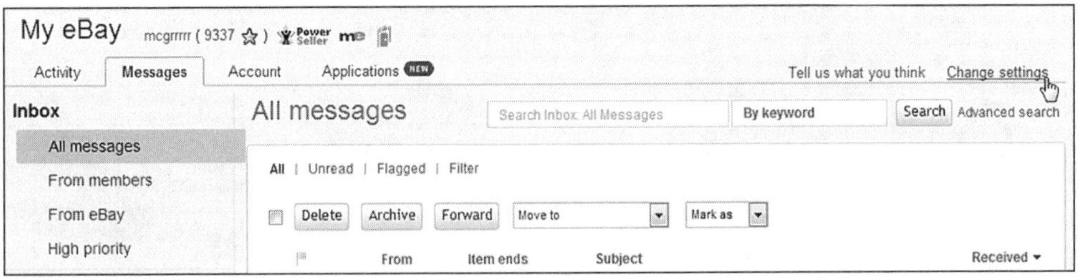

Figure 26.3 Setting Your eBay Store to Vacation Mode

POWER MOVES

❏ Visit the eBay Stores hub page (http://stores.eBay.com). Click on several of the store listings and become familiar with how stores are listed and how other sellers promote their stores.

❏ Make sure you do not have selling limits on your account and that your sales volume is high enough to cover the basic subscription fee with the change in fee structure.

❏ Sign up for a Basic Store (the signup link is on the eBay Stores hub page).

❏ Start linking all of your listings to your store and be sure they are in categories that make sense and lend themselves to cross-selling.

CHAPTER 27

✦ EBAY CONSIGNMENT SELLING ✦

I LIKE TO CALL SELLING goods on consignment for others "the perfect eBay business." Oftentimes, the biggest problem eBay sellers face is finding products that they can resell at a profit. Luckily, there's an alternative. If you're finding it difficult to locate products of your own, you may be able to make money selling items for others.

For every successful eBay seller, there are others who can't figure out how to sell effectively or profitably on eBay. Also, believe it or not, there are still people who are not convinced that eBay really works, who are afraid to try it, and/or who are computer illiterate. There are also plenty of people who just don't have the time to learn the skills needed to sell successfully on eBay. That's where you come in.

In 2002, eBay launched the Trading Assistant program. It has been revised quite a few times since then; however, the basic premise has remained the same. A trading assistant is an eBay seller who sells products for eBay members who either don't know how to or don't want to sell their goods themselves. If you go to the eBay site map and look under the Selling Resources heading, you will see a link to the *Trading Assistant program*. Although meeting the requirements to become an eBay Trading Assistant will take you more than three weeks, you can start selling on consignment at any time after you qualify for the program—and it's useful to understand how the Trading Assistant program works, so that, if you choose, you can incorporate this program into your long-term success plan.

THE TRADING ASSISTANT PROGRAM

When you join the Trading Assistant program, you tell the world that you are willing to sell for others. Trading Assistants charge fees or commissions for their services. Selling as a trading assistant allows you to leverage your selling expertise without having to find products yourself—clients provide the products and you are compensated for your efforts on mutually agreed-upon terms. Many sellers already do this as a way of making money on eBay; profit margins can be significant, especially for higher-priced items.

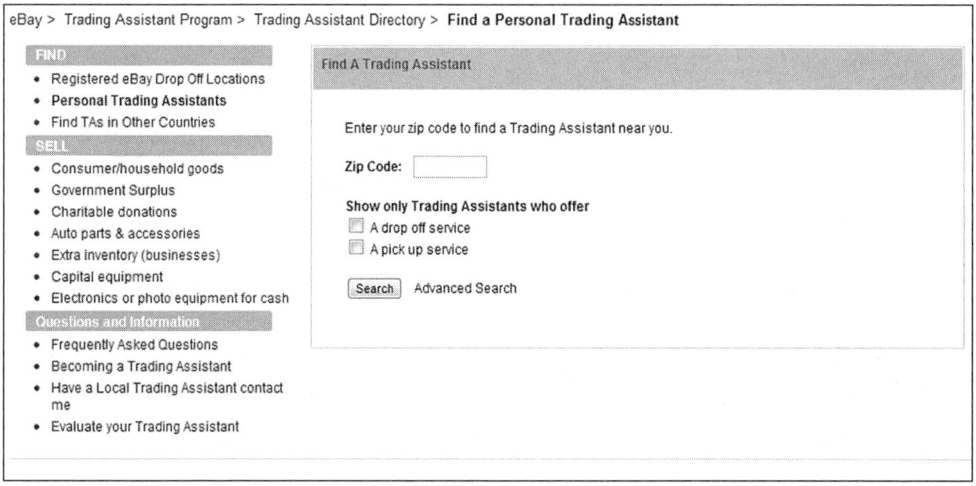

Figure 27.1 The eBay Trading Assistant Directory

Do You Qualify?

To join the Trading Assistant Directory (see Figure 27.1), you must have sold at least ten items in the last three months and must maintain a ten sales per three months average. You must have (and maintain) a Feedback score of one hundred or higher, and at least 98 percent of your feedback must be positive. You also must be in good standing with eBay and abide by the Trading Assistant Style Guide (go to http://ebaytradingassistant.com/index.php?page=home and then select "Style Guide" from the Trading Assistant box). Joining the directory is free.

eBay does not endorse the assistants listed in the directory. As eBay states in its description of the program:

> Including yourself in our Trading Assistant program directory is a lot like running a classified ad for your services. Trading Assistants are not employees or independent contractors of eBay. Nor do we endorse or approve them. Each Trading Assistant runs his or her own independent business free from any involvement by eBay.

How It Works

Through the Trading Assistant program, eBay gives any eBay seller who qualifies an opportunity to start a consignment business. When an eBay member is looking for a Trading Assistant, she goes to the directory, where she can type in her zip code and search for an assistant in her area. Once the seller performs a search, she receives a list of Trading Assistants within twenty-five miles and their contact information. If your name comes up in the list, the seller (in this case the *consignor*, or the person who supplies your products) can either e-mail or call you to work out a deal directly.

eBay also provides Trading Assistants with promotional material. There is a *Toolkit* link on the Trading Assistant page. From here you can download posters and flyers in Microsoft Word format that you can personalize, print out, and use in your marketing efforts. There are also business card templates and Trading Assistant images that you can use online.

Signing up to be an eBay Trading Assistant should be your first step in starting a consignment business.

THE TRADING ASSISTANT BUSINESS

There are thousands of eBay sellers running consignment businesses. These range from regular sellers who sell on consignment as a side business to full-time, large commercial businesses operating out of retail storefronts. eBay has extra regulations for retail storefronts (called a Registered eBay Drop-Off Location, or REDOL), which are set up to provide consignors with a convenient place to drop off merchandise for consignment sellers to list on eBay. In addition to the standard Trading Assistant requirements, REDOLs must also carry a $1,000,000 general liability insurance policy (in addition to any other state requirements), have a $25,000 bond, be open five days a week with business hours posted, have outside signage, and adhere to a number of other standards as set out in the REDOL user agreement.

A woman in my hometown used to own a consignment shop right in the heart of the retail district. She sold good-quality antiques and collectibles on consignment and had a very nice business for several years. Three years ago she tried selling some of the goods in her shop on eBay. After some trial and error, she began doing very well. Earlier this year, she closed the shop; she now sells exclusively on eBay.

Like many consignment sellers, she finds people with goods to sell by placing ads in the local paper and on free community bulletin boards, by approaching previous customers who know her, and by word of mouth.

Consignment selling on eBay is not a new idea. There was a huge boom of franchise consignment stores a few years back, but that model was largely unsuccessful for the actual sellers (because of the high franchise costs) and it fizzled out within about a year. eBay's REDOL requirements came into effect in 2008, and that reduced the number of storefront consignment sellers. But there are still thousands of Trading Assistants who are full-time consignment sellers, with or without a retail storefront.

How big can an eBay consignment business grow? That really depends on several factors: how big you want your business to grow, what resources you have, and how much you can invest. I watched a large REDOL's auctions on eBay and I estimated they closed about $50,000 worth of auctions a week. Most consignment stores' basic commission schedule is 40 percent, so that works out to a gross margin of $20,000 a week. Now, you aren't going to take in this much without a sizable investment, several full-time employees, a hefty advertising budget, and so on. But I firmly believe that anyone who is well skilled at selling on eBay can develop a small business that can realize a gross margin of $1,000 to $3,000 a week. This would require you to launch an average of twenty to fifty listings a week. Many PowerSellers and Top-Rated Sellers today routinely launch over a hundred listings a week, so twenty to fifty a week is certainly doable. In chapter 23, we discussed automating some of the common tasks that allow you to do this.

MARKETING YOUR EBAY CONSIGNMENT BUSINESS

Once you have honed your eBay selling skills, it's not hard to market your services. If you want to find consignors, you have to go looking for them. The eBay Trading Assistant Directory may bring you some business, but probably not enough to live on.

Finding consignors takes little time and money. Here's how I market my eBay consignment services:

* *Classified ads:* I run small newspaper classified ads that read something like this: "I will sell your treasures on eBay. Call Skip 360-555-1111" or "Raise cash by selling your unwanted merchandise on eBay. Professional eBay seller does all the work for you. Call Skip at 212-555-2222." Many newspapers offer deals on multiple placements of classified ads. Speak to your newspaper's classified ad rep about working out a volume discount.

* *Networking:* I like to use what I call the "3-foot (0.9 m) rule." Everyone who comes within 3 feet (0.9 m) of me learns what I do for a living. I always carry business cards or even a small flyer that explains what I do. Whenever I meet people, I tell them that I am a professional eBay seller and that if they have something they would like to sell, I would be glad to help them.

* *Free bulletin boards:* This works the same way as classified ads. Just create short ads on 3-by-5-inch (7.6 x 12.7 cm) cards and place them on community bulletin boards in supermarkets and laundromats. I always carry push pins or thumbtacks, so I'm ready whenever I come across one of these corkboards.

* *Direct mail to attorneys:* Create a short letter that explains the services you offer and mail it to all the estate and bankruptcy attorneys in your county. When an attorney has to settle an estate or sell off the proceeds of a bankrupt individual or company, he often works with a local auctioneer. If you explain to an attorney that you can raise far more money for the estate or the creditors by exposing the merchandise in question to over eighty million prospective eBay buyers—rather than relying on the couple of hundred people who show up for a local auction—he will most likely be all ears.

There are many other ways to market your eBay consignment service, but these four techniques should net you enough business to keep you busy—and profitable—for quite a while.

POWER MOVES

❏ If you would like to try consignment selling, visit the eBay Trading Assistant page (on the site map, click on *Trading Assistant program*, under Selling Resources) and read the requirements to see if you qualify.

❏ Create some small classified ads and 3-by-5-inch (7.6 x 12.7 cm) cards advertising your services as a consignment seller, and start placing the ads in local papers and placing the cards on community bulletin boards in supermarkets, laundromats, and the like.

❏ Once you have some experience as a consignment seller, if you decide to pursue this business more aggressively, visit my Web site, www.skipmcgrath.com, where you'll find my book on this subject, *How to Start and Run an eBay Consignment Business.*

CHAPTER 28

✦ BEYOND EBAY ✦

EBAY IS A GREAT PLACE to start an online business. It has a low barrier to entry and you can learn while you're making money. But there *is* life beyond eBay. My wife and I started selling on eBay in 1999. Today we still sell on eBay every day—but now we also sell on Amazon and Buy.com, and we maintain two different Web sites offering a variety of products.

While eBay is certainly the largest online auction site, there are a number of other successful sites. Buy.com is very similar to Amazon except that they only sell new products. If you sell used, vintage, or handmade arts and crafts, the fastest growing site is Etsy.com. The format is fixed-price, but Etsy has become one of the most successful alternatives to eBay.

AMAZON

Once you master eBay, you might want to explore selling your goods on Amazon. Karen and I have been selling on Amazon since 2006. We did okay, but still sold more on eBay. That changed in 2010. That is the year we moved into a program Amazon runs called Fulfillment By Amazon (FBA). FBA is a program whereby you ship all of your merchandise to Amazon and they store it in their warehouse. When something sells, Amazon collects the money, ships the item, and basically handles all the customer service. As you can imagine, all of that service comes at a cost, so Amazon FBA fees are higher than eBay fees. Yet we still make more money today on Amazon than we do on eBay, because the sales are so much higher.

If you sell used goods or vintage goods, then eBay (or Etsy) is still the best place. The exception to that are books, CDs, or DVD. Used items in those categories are huge sellers on Amazon. But if you sell new merchandise, you should definitely give Amazon a try once you have mastered your eBay business. If you go to my Web site, www. SkipMcGrath.com, I offer an eBook called *eBay to Amazon* that explains how to make the transition.

In addition to Amazon, there are all sorts of targeted selling sites. AbeBooks.com is a high-traffic site for selling books. Craigslist (www.craigslist.com) is a well-known classified ad site that allows you to sell goods regionally. (We use Craigslist to sell large items that we do not want to ship.)

YOUR OWN WEB SITE

In the past, setting up your own Web site was a daunting challenge. If you didn't know how to write HTML code and upload pages, you would have to hire a Web designer to do it for you. This could cost anywhere from five hundred to several thousand dollars and, once the site was designed and launched, you needed help to maintain it. Over the past few years, an array of new Web services have come on the market, allowing anyone with minimal computer skills to design and maintain an e-commerce Web site. If you can click, point, and type, and have the skills to launch an eBay auction, then you can build a Web site.

These new Web service companies use a system of predesigned templates and shopping carts. All you have to do is point and click to select colors and designs and to upload photos, and then just type text into an HTML editor that looks like a Microsoft Word document to create the headlines and text for your Web site.

There are literally hundreds of companies that offer Web site building services. Simply Google the term *build a Web site* and you will get a ton of results. Having said that, let me give you my two favorites. If you are a complete novice and want a lot of handholding, check out Site Build It at www.buildit.sitesell.com. The only downside to Site Build It is that you have to pay a separate fee for each site you build, but the system is simple, they have excellent support, and you end up with a full-featured, very professional-looking Web site complete with a fully functioning shopping cart. And they help you with SEO (Search Engine Optimization), which is how you get found by search engines such as Google, Yahoo!, and Bing.

If you have fairly good computer skills but still want a simple system to build a Web site, take a look at XSitePro at www.xsitepro.com. The advantage of XSitePro is that you can build an unlimited number of Web sites with purchase of the software. (You can work from a PC only—it will not work with Mac unless you have a program like Boot Camp, which allows your Mac to run Windows.) XSitePro is very easy to learn. Typically it will take you three or four hours to build your first site, but after that you can build a fully functioning Web site in about an hour. I know people who have mastered XSitePro and who make up to $500 each by building Web sites for local businesses.

ONWARD AND UPWARD

I hope by now you are well into your third week of activity and closing auctions successfully. The most important advice I can give you at this point is this: Don't give up!

Things will go wrong—they always do. As with any new venture, you will certainly make mistakes, and they can frustrate and demoralize you. Whenever you make a mistake, go back to the basics and analyze what you did and what you can do differently the next time. Take risks and experiment—but remember to stay within eBay's guidelines when you do. When you take risks, such as selling a new product, remember to take lots of small risks instead of one large one. Don't commit to buying a large amount of inventory until you have thoroughly tested the market.

Finally, remember that eBay is a community. eBay members love to help each other. If you are having problems, go on the eBay message boards and ask for help. There are also a number of eBay help groups on Facebook. You'll be amazed at how many people will reach out to assist you with terrific advice.

Besides being profitable, selling on eBay is supposed to be fun. If you always try to view your business in this context, you will enjoy yourself, your mistakes will be less frustrating, and you will probably make more money in the end.

Good luck on eBay—and beyond!

APPENDIX A

Here is a short checklist you should consult before launching your auctions:

- ❏ Have I checked my listing for any spelling or grammatical errors?
- ❏ Is my type readable? Is it too large or too small?
- ❏ Did I use short paragraphs with breaks between them?
- ❏ Are my photos clear and high resolution?
- ❏ Have I checked all my fees and options?
- ❏ Did I use the correct listing format and duration (number of days)?
- ❏ Does my auction end at a good time and on a good day?
- ❏ Did I include clear shipping information, costs, return policy, and other terms?
- ❏ Is my item description accurate, clear, and complete?
- ❏ Did I include information as to the product's size, weight, and so forth?
- ❏ Did I mention any flaws or discrepancies?
- ❏ Did I clearly spell out the payment terms?
- ❏ Does my title communicate what I am selling?
- ❏ Does my title contain the appropriate keywords for item searches?
- ❏ Did I invite bidders to e-mail me with questions?
- ❏ Did I include active links to my eBay Store and About Me page?
- ❏ Is my About Me page up to date?
- ❏ Did I include a Buy It Now price?

APPENDIX B

POPULAR WHOLESALE SOURCES

Here is a listing of some of the popular wholesale sources used by eBay PowerSellers. Some of these sources will require a state resale license (sales tax ID). All of these sources are listed on the special Web page set up for readers of this book at www. skipmcgrath.com/3_weeks. (Don't forget the underscore.)

LIQUIDITY SERVICES at www.Liquidation.com is one of the largest closeout and surplus dealers on the web. They act as the surplus dealer for major department stores such as Macy's and chain stores like Target and BJ's Wholesale.

Liquidation.com has hundreds of bulk auctions to bid on at any given time. You get access to a variety of lot sizes, including pallets, box lots, and trailer loads. They are an auction-style site that links buyers and sellers (just like eBay does, but only for wholesale items). Through Liquidation.com you can find a variety of surplus products: overstocks, closeouts, shelf pulls, refurbished products, and more.

Liquidation.com uses an auction format similar to eBay. A typical pallet will vary in price anywhere from $200 to $2,000. Recently I saw a pallet of game machines, including several of each Nintendo DS, XBox360, and PlayStation3 game consoles, that went for an average price of $40 each. Another pallet had a thousand pairs of new name-brand blue jeans (Polo, Lee, Boss, etc.) selling for less than $1.70 each.

Warning #1: Before you bid on an item at Liquidation.com, be sure to check the shipping cost. The dealers who sell on Liquidation.com are located all over the country. It can be very expensive to ship a pallet load of goods, so try to buy from suppliers who are close to you. For example, if you live on the East Coast, it could be very expensive to ship a pallet from California. Before placing a bid, either get a shipping estimate or limit your bids to sellers who are less than 1,000 miles from your location.

Warning #2: Make sure you know what you are buying. Be careful of buying Returns—these are items returned to the stores by customers, and some of them could be defective. If you are not sure, e-mail the seller and ask if the goods you are thinking of bidding on contain product returns or warranty returns.

The merchandise changes every day, and you can sign up for e-mail alerts to make sure you don't miss any specials. Liquidation.com also owns and operates Government

Liquidation (www.govliquidation.com), which is the official Web-based auction site for the Department of Defense.

VIA TRADING, at www.viatrading.com, is another large closeout dealer that deals only in the pallet load—however, many of their pallets sell for as little as $250. They deal in surplus, overstock, and returns from major department store chains. One thing I have found when dealing with Via Trading is that they are very honest in describing the merchandise. In short, you will get what you pay for. But once again, whenever you buy pallet loads of merchandise, always check the shipping charges first.

LUXURY MAGAZZINO, at www.luxurymagazzino.com, is the most well-known supplier of famous-name designer goods among eBay PowerSellers. They sell all the famous brands—and best of all, you can get small quantities. I recently bought a lot of six Prada Tussoto handbags for just over $450 total. They all sold for between $150 and $175 each.

Not all Luxury Magazzino products sell well on eBay, however. Once again, *before committing to a large purchase, research the items on eBay to make sure they are selling well.* Hint: Always search "completed listings" so you can find out what something actually sold for, instead of what the current bidding is.

MADISON AVENUE CLOSEOUTS, at www.madisonavenuecloseouts.com, is a great source of good-quality clothing for men, women, and children. They also carry men's big and tall and women's plus sizes, which are great sellers on eBay.

The pricing is excellent, and they run many specials. In addition, they are very honest about describing the quality and make-up of the goods—although you do have to e-mail a request for that info, as it is not posted on the Web site.

T-SHIRT WHOLESALER, at www.t-shirtwholesaler.com, sells a lot more than T-shirts. This is a great source for name-brand men's and women's tops of all kinds.

THE SILVER SOURCE, at www.silversource.com, is one of the largest and most reliable sources of silver jewelry on the Web. They have been supplying flea market dealers and jewelry stores for over twenty years and supplying eBay sellers since 1998. They literally have thousands of styles of almost any type of jewelry—rings, pendants, necklaces, toe rings and more. Sterling silver rings start at under $2.00 each. The minimum order is $100.

TEEDA, at www.teeda.com, is another jewelry company; they specialize in cubic zirconium, marcasite, and sterling silver jewelry at excellent wholesale prices.

DRAGON DISTRIBUTING, at www.dragondistributing.com, is a leading, wholesale distributor that specializes in the distribution of automotive and consumer electronics to independent dealers. You will need a tax resale number and a commercial checking account to do business with them. They carry all the hot brands of car-audio amps, speakers, cable, and accessories.

TELEBRANDS WHOLESALE, at www.telebrandswholesale.com, is probably the leading supplier of "As Seen on TV" goods to eBay sellers. There are several companies in this industry, but this one is the best, in my opinion. They sell most products in one-case lots and the prices are typically 50 to 60 percent below the price advertised on television. The other big "As Seen on TV" supplier is **SALCO,** which runs a drop-shipping operation for eBay sellers at http://ezdropshipper.com.

BOONE'S ANTIQUES, at www.boonesantiques.com. Yes, you can buy antiques wholesale. Boone's Antiques supplies antique dealers and decorators all over the country. Their main store is in Wilson, North Carolina. Actually, "store" is an understatement, considering it is four acres in size.

APPENDIX C

eBay has spawned an entire industry of companies that create resources for eBay sellers. I have listed some of the most popular ones here. Once again, you don't have to type in the hyperlinks; all of these are listed at www.skipmcgrath.com/3_weeks as clickable hyperlinks.

AUCTION MANAGEMENT SERVICES

✳ Auctiva: www.auctiva.com

✳ AuctionHawk: www.auctionhawk.com

✳ ChannelAdvisor: www.channeladvisor.com

✳ InkFrog: www.inkfrog.com

✳ Vendio: www.vendio.com

AUCTION MANAGEMENT SOFTWARE

✳ AuctionSubmit: www.auctionsubmit.com

✳ eLister: www.blackmagik.com/elister.html

PRODUCT RESEARCH SERVICES
HammerTap (www.hammertap.com)
HammerTap sifts through the masses of auctions to help you pinpoint the hottest-selling items up for bid in your particular niche. This helps you determine how likely specific products are to sell. The tool gives you the ability to drill down and narrow your search to find the most successful brand or product feature within a given list of products.

HammerTap uncovers the market trends that lead to higher auction-success rates. Discover which day of the week to end your auction listing, find out whether or not to use a reserve, choose starting prices that attract more bids, and much more. HammerTap provides a wealth of data to discover how to maximize your auction listings and final values.

Terapeak Research Service (www.terapeak.com)

Terapeak is one of the newer research services for eBay sellers. They offer all the features of HammerTap plus a keyword analysis tool. Terapeak information includes:

* Average sales price

* Total sales for your item

* Total listings

* Success rate

* Total bids received

* Demand for your item

* Prices realized on eBay

* Time of day to sell

* Top-ranked sellers

* Total bids they receive

* Total sales market share

* Sell-through rate

Terapeak also allows you to download the data to Excel for further offline analysis.

AUCTION NEWS AND INFORMATION

EcommerceBytes (www.ecommercebytes.com)

EcommerceBytes (formally AuctionBytes), run by David and Ina Steiner, is the authoritative independent news source for eBay and the online auction community. They publish a daily newsletter for the online auction community and a weekly wrap-up with longer stories, advice, and articles from online auction experts. The site also contains several free resources and links to hundreds of Internet services.

AUCTION PROMOTION TOOLS

Google Ad Words (https://adwords.google.com)

Google Ad Words is a pay-per-click service that you can use to drive business to your eBay store.

Yahoo Search Marketing (www.content.overture.com)

Yahoo Search Marketing is essentially the same as Google Ad Words except for the Yahoo search browser instead of Google.

✦ GLOSSARY OF TERMS AND ✦ ABBREVIATIONS

Active user: An eBay member who has bought or sold at least once in the prior twelve months.

ADDY: *E-mail address.*

Ad Words: Google's term for pay-per-click advertising.

aka: *Also known as.*

A/O: *All original*; auction term used to describe the condition of an item—usually used in the auction title to save space.

As is: Condition of items that are sold at auction without warranties as to the condition of the property. Item may be damaged or have missing parts. See *Caveat emptor,* below.

ASAP: *As soon as possible.*

ASP: *Average selling price.*

ATM: *At the moment.*

Auction-style listing: A traditional auction, in which there is a fixed duration and bids are made incrementally. The winner is the bidder who has made the highest bid when the auction time period ends.

Best match: The default search results order, which uses an eBay algorithm designed to match the buyers with the best sellers of the most closely matching items they are looking for.

Best offer: An option for sellers of fixed-price items to allow a buyer to submit an offer below the stated price for the seller's consideration. This is essentially a way to haggle about the price.

Bid increment: This is the amount by which you must increase your bid over the current high bid. The bid increment is established by the former bid price.

Bid rigging: The unlawful practice whereby two or more people agree not to bid against one another to deflate value.

BIN: *Buy It Now;* eBay's BIN option allows a seller to set a purchase price that, when selected by a bidder, ends an auction immediately and sells the item on the spot.

BIN rate: The percentage of your items sold that were sold with BIN or with any fixed-price format.

B&W: *Black-and-white.*

BC: *Back cover.*

BRB: *Be right back.*

BTW: *By the way.*

Blocked bidders: eBay feature that allows sellers to create a list of specific eBay members who are not allowed to bid on or buy items they sell. A person on the list will be blocked from participating in all of a seller's auctions.

Caveat emptor: A Latin term meaning "Let the buyer beware!" A legal maxim stating that the buyer takes all the risk in a transaction.

Chargeback: A demand by the credit-card provider for a retailer to make good on the loss on a fraudulent or disputed transaction.

COA: *Certificate of Authenticity;* auction term used to describe an item as genuine (usually certified by an expert).

Consignment selling: The owner of an item pays an experienced seller to list the item for sale. The seller receives a commission from the owner of the item once the item sells.

CONUS: *Continental United States,* not including Alaska and Hawaii.

CR: *Conversion rate;* the percentage of auctions closed successfully (i.e., sold) versus the number listed.

DBA: *Doing business as.*

DBB: *Deadbeat bidder;* one who bids and fails to complete a transaction.

DOA: *Dead on arrival;* a term used to describe an item you bought that does not function properly upon receipt.

DSL: *Digital subscriber line;* a high-speed Internet connection through a dedicated phone line.

DSR: *Detailed seller ratings;* part of eBay's feedback system, in which the buyer can rate the seller from one to five stars based on four aspects of the transaction: Item As Described, Communication, Shipping Time, and Shipping and Handling Charges.

eBay Checkout: The electronic process buyers must use to pay for items.

Emoticon: A specific group of characters used to form a facial expression in e-mails. For example, :-) is a smiley face (turned sideways).

Escrow: A buyer's deposit or fund entrusted to a third-party company that holds the payment in trust until the seller makes delivery of the merchandise to the buyer.

FAQ: A list of *frequently asked questions* and their answers.

FedEx: The shipper Federal Express.

Feedback: A comment about the transaction experience that is accompanied by a rating of positive, negative, or neutral from the buyer, or a comment accompanied by a positive rating from a seller. (On eBay, sellers are not allowed to give neutral or negative feedback to buyers.)

Fixed-Price Listing: An online listing in which there is only one price and there is no bidding. Either the buyer chooses to pay the price listed or she moves on to another listing.

Flame: (n.) An angry e-mail message or post to a message board; negative feedback sent many times. Or (v.) to insult someone, electronically or otherwise.

Flameout (aka crash and burn): Slang for what happens when you don't follow the advice in this book and your eBay business fails. To have a spectacular failure or fall from grace. Believed to have originated from losing an aerial dogfight.

FOB: A trading term meaning *free on board* (also known as *freight on board*). This is a term that means the seller will pay for the delivery of the freight to its FOB location. The buyer will pay the shipping for an imported item *from* its FOB location. For example: If I quote you a price for a pallet of goods, FOB Trenton, NJ, that means that I, the seller, pay for the freight to its delivery location in Trenton (which is included in my total price). The buyer is responsible for picking up the freight from its FOB location.

FTP: *File Transfer Protocol*; method of sharing files on the Internet.

FV: *Final value*; the price something sells for on eBay, not including shipping.

FVF: *Final value fee*; the fee eBay charges for making a successful sale; it is based on the total cost of the item, including shipping.

GMS: *Gross Merchandise Sales*; the total dollar value of your sales over a specified period of time.

Gently used: Description of item that is used but shows little wear.

Good 'Til Canceled: A fixed-price listing that auto-renews every thirty days until canceled by the seller or the quantity available listed reaches zero.

HTML: *Hyper Text Markup Language*; the code that computer programmers use to create what you see when you view a Web page.

Hyperlink: A clickable photo or text on a Web page that takes you to another page on the Internet (also known as a *link*).

IMHO: *In my humble opinion.*

IMO: *In my opinion.*

ISP: *Internet service provider.*

JPEG: *Joint Photographic Experts Group;* the most commonly used file format for pictures on eBay (pronounced JAY-PEG).

Link (hyperlink): A clickable photo or line of text on a Web page that takes you to another page on the Internet.

LOL: *Laughing out loud.*

Lot or Lots: Similar items sold in bulk quantities. Lots are normally sold at discount or wholesale prices.

LTD: *Limited edition.*

Mint: An item that has never been used and is in perfect condition.

MIB: *Mint in box.*

MIMB: *Mint in mint box.*

MIMP: *Mint in mint package.*

MIP: *Mint in package.*

MNB: *Mint, no box.*

MOC: *Mint on card.*

My eBay: A page that displays your ongoing listings, status, and sales history.

Multiple-Variations Listing: A fixed-price listing where the items offered are not identical. The buyer chooses options from drop-down menus to select the item she wants (the options may be size, style, color, etc.).

NARU: *Not a registered user* (i.e., a suspended user or a user who has closed his eBay account).

NBW: *Never been worn.*

Newbie: Someone recently new to eBay.

NC: *No cover;* referring to books that have lost their jacket or paperbacks that have lost their cover.

NM: *Near mint;* a very subjective term. See *mint.*

NPB: *Nonpaying bidder.* See also *deadbeat bidder.*

NR: *No reserve* price on auction; indicates that there is no reserve price on the item being auctioned.

NRFB: *Never removed from box.*

NWT: *New with Tag.*

OEM: *Original equipment manufacturer.*

OOP: *Out of print.*

PayPal: eBay's own electronic payment processor. Used by over 90 percent of buyers.

PayPal Seller Protection: Protects sellers from chargebacks from claims from buyers of Item Not Received or Unauthorized Transactions.

PayPal Verified Buyer: A buyer who confirmed his or her address and account information through PayPal.

Phishing: A spoofed Web site is typically made to look like a well-known, branded site (such as eBay, PayPal, or Amazon) with a subtly different URL. A spoofed e-mail looks like it came from eBay, PayPal, or your bank. However, the link leads you to the fake Web site. It is used to deceive online shoppers into disclosing their credit card numbers, bank account information, Social Security numbers, passwords, and other personal information.

PPC: *Pay per click.*

PM: *Priority Mail.*

PowerSeller: An experienced eBay seller with at least $3,000 in sales on eBay over the previous twelve months.

Private Auction: An auction in which the buyer's identity is not disclosed to anyone except the seller.

Proxy Bidding: A bidder enters the maximum amount he is willing to spend on an item. eBay will then automatically continue incremental bidding until either he is the highest bidder or his maximum bid is reached.

REDOL: *Registered eBay Drop-Off Location.*

Relisting: Process of listing again an item that did not sell.

Reserve Auction: An auction in which the seller reserves a minimum acceptable price. Sellers sometimes disclose the reserve price to prospective bidders.

Reserve Not Met: An auction term that means no bid is currently high enough to match the minimum price that the seller will accept.

Reserve Price: The hidden minimum price that a seller is willing to accept for an item to be sold at auction.

Retaliatory Feedback: When a nonpaying bidder posts negative feedback because the seller complained about him or her to eBay.

ROI: *Return on investment.*

RMA: *Return Merchandise Authorization.*

ROFL: *Rolling on floor laughing; see also* LOL.

SCO: *Second-chance offer;* an option for sellers to offer an identical item to a nonwinning bidder, after an auction ends, for that bidder's highest bid in the auction.

Seller Dashboard: A database that eBay provides in which the seller can check his or her performance standards, fee discounts, Top-Rated Seller status, etc.

Shilling: Fraudulent bidding by an associate of the seller; done in order to artificially inflate the price of an item. Also known as *bid rigging* or *collusion.*

SKU: *Stock keeping unit;* a numerical identifier used to distinguish individual items in an inventory.

Snail mail: A slang term for ordinary mail delivered by the US Postal Service.

Spoof Web site: see *Phishing.*

Sniping: Bidding at the last possible moment.

Spam: Unwanted e-mail; eBay will discipline you for sending e-mail to bidders in auctions you are not involved in.

TRS: *Top-Rated Seller;* a seller with $1,000 in sales and one hundred transactions over the previous twelve months. A TRS must maintain the highest level of feedback and Detailed Seller Ratings.

Top-Rated Plus: A status that includes a seal displayed on the listing page for items from Top-Rated Sellers; these are sellers who have specified a fourteen-day or longer money-back returns policy and a one-business-day handling time between the time the bidder's payment is received and the shipping of the item.

TM: *Trademark.*

Trading Assistant (TA): Experienced eBay sellers who meet eBay requirements and will sell another person's items on eBay for a fee or commission. Also known as an eBay consignment seller.

Unwanted bid: A bid that does not meet the seller's terms, as stated in the auction. For example, seller states in the auction that item is only shipped to US locations and the bidder is located overseas.

UPS: *United Parcel Service.*

Upselling or Cross-Selling: The art of enticing a buyer who is already either considering or committed to purchasing one item from you to purchase a more expensive item or buy an additional item that complements the one they are already committed to.

URL: The address that identifies a Web site on the Internet. It stands for *uniform resource locator.*

USPS: *United States Postal Service.*

VERO: eBay's *Verified Rights Owner* program, which enforces copyright and trademark laws within the eBay marketplace. If you sell counterfeit goods on eBay, the rights owner can file a VERO complaint against you and eBay will shut down your auctions.

VHTF: *Very hard to find.*

Winning Bidder Notification: The email sent by eBay to the buyer notifying them of their purchase through a Fixed Price or Auction listing. This also includes a link to eBay Checkout to arrange for payment.

WYSIWYG: *What you see is what you get;* quality of a program that displays what your final HTML page will look like while you are creating it. eBay and other auction management services provide WYSIWYG HTML editors to help sellers create their auction listings easily.

✦ INDEX ✦